Global Visions & Missions
For
Leaders in Higher & Technical Education

Global Visions & Missions

For

Leaders in Higher & Technical Education

B M Naik

GenNext Publication

Published by

GenNext Publication
5, Ansari Road
Daryaganj, New Delhi-110002
Phone: 011-47034999, 9811692060
E-mail: gennextpublication@hotmail.com

Distribution Network
gyanbooks.com
India, USA, Canada, UK, Australia, France

ISBN: 978-93-5663-435-0 (HB)
First Published, 2025
Printed at: Gyan Press, Delhi.

Global Visions & Missions For
Leaders in Higher & Technical Education
Author: B M NAIK

Contents

Preface

It Is a proven theory that nations where there are global visions & missions people flourish, and where there are no global visions & missions people perish.

Why Higher & Technical education In India urgently need modernization? The world is changing fast. Technology is advancing by leaps and bounds, Hi-tech in every sector is coming. Job contents are changing, old jobs are becoming obsolete. Skill set of the people ought to change with time. Skill set at entry level is continuously changing. When the whole world is changing, Can Higher & technical education remain stationary? It must also change. It is changing but at snail's pace. Many graduates have degrees in hand but no jobs. NEP-2020 is being implemented to overcome short comings all over the country. Yet thousands of students in increasing numbers are going abroad for higher education. They are paying huge amounts of fees in foreign universities. Many do not return after studies are completed. It is a big brain drain & money drain. Is it because they are not happy with the higher education in India? Are they rejecting Indian universities and colleges although available at much less fees? They are going to developed countries because their universities offer far better job-oriented and relevant education. Globalization and Internationalization has set in, collaborations and partnerships national and international has become the order of the day. Should Indian universities & colleges not jump at global opportunities, foreign collaborations & partnerships? Should India not modernise education to cope with changing times?

Indian political and administrative leaders who oversee governance and management of universities & colleges ought to become familiar with winds of change in world. Their present visions & missions are old outdated, primitive. So, the universities & colleges are behind time. How can they give world class education? Hence the students are leaving the shores for higher education. Our students and professors are brilliant, as brilliant as their counterparts abroad, but they do not get opportunities to grow professionally in globalised world because of lack of latest job relevant hi-tech education, lack of research and innovation culture and necessary infrastructure. Only a few students who can afford to go abroad to study there, some of them become CMD/CEO of big companies like Microsoft, IBM. There are many jewels and diamond like students who remain in India but because of improper education they get frustrated and result in far inferior career. India remains a poor developing country, with many people living below poverty line.

Can India become a developed country without well-educated human force?

India is aspiring to be a developed country in 2047. It has undoubtedly high potential. How this potential is unfolded matters. Without proper, globally competent quality education India may not realise its dream. Do the leaders in Government, leaders in universities & colleges realise this? To make Indian leaders familiar with global visions & missions of world ranking institutions this book is giving the strategies they must adopt. Dr Babasaheb Ambedkar gave the need & importance of advance education to India way back through the Indian constitution. Government and political parties are using his name to win votes but unfortunately neglecting his suggestions on education

Where does Higher & technical educations fall behind?

Professors in universities & colleges are not familiar with the latest in their subjects, because of lack of research & innovation facilities. Mostly they teach that knowledge which is stale coming to them from foreign. Universities & colleges so also government has no ambition to enable professors to be equal to their counterparts in advanced countries like USA., Not many Professors have opportunities to go abroad and take part in research with their counterparts. They are far too behind the winds of change in developed countries. So, ranking of Indian universities in the world is not high. Investment in infrastructure for research & innovation is too low. Government is investing heavily in highways, rails, industry, housing etc. This is necessary but equally it is necessary to invest in higher education. Government must invest in universities & colleges with higher priority. Modernising higher & technical education is in fact far more important. It is the competency of human capital that matters in development of a nation. Government ought to invest heavily, on massive scale in universities & colleges to make them as good as in foreign. Government of India in 1991 had thought of raising the budget for education to 6% of GDP. But till today it has not done so. Planners have to realise that education is a driving force for development. Only around 3% of GDP is spent on education. When other countries like USA can provide 1even more than 10% of budget for education, why India cannot? Higher and technical education in effort of development is a weak link. World over, education is undergoing rapid changes, collaborations are necessary for becoming job oriented at local & global levels. The job contents and job skills are changing fast with change in technology. In India it is however, more bookish, rote learning, not matching with job entry requirements. No wonder if many graduates remain jobless.

Short comings in systems.

Triple Helix organization structure which is practised in developed countries is not followed in India, faculty upgradation schemes are not available to many, alumni associations which bring strength and vigour in education are not fully activated. Strategic Planning is not well practised, Total Quality Management technique is not well utilised, Board of Governors of universities & colleges are not well formulated, Chancellor of universities is the Governor of the state, who is mostly not qualified in academics but is authorised responsibilities like selection of VCs, curricula of courses are outdated, professors do not teach the latest in their subjects, these and many other things fall short of requirements. They are outlined in various chapters of the book. They are very useful for leaders in the implementation of NEP-2020, and modernization of higher & technical education.

The book is addressed primarily to leaders in universities & colleges who matter most in bringing about transformation in quality and quantity of education.

Who are the leaders?

The leaders include principals, vice-chancellors, and professors in universities & colleges. Leaders also include administrators in Government, central and state, so also administrators in universities & colleges. Leaders include all the members of academic, senate, governing body members who shape the higher & technical education, the book is also useful to politicians who are passionate to shape and improve education, and who seek election to parliament and Assembly.

It is hoped that leaders will find the book useful and, will adopt global visions and missions in their respective universities & colleges to make India a developed nation in the year 2047.

The author thanks all my colleagues for their valuable suggestions.

B M Naik

Author

If you charge higher & technical education with the spirit of innovation, creativity, and discovery then you do not have to do anything else, but if you do not do this and instead do everything else that is not going to matter much.

Chapter - 1

Is the Role of Universities and Colleges Vital in Employment Generation? Can Indian Universities Afford to Ignore? At What Cost? Who Pays?

– B M NAIK

Abstract

This paper presents the need and importance of productive employment, which is a significant issue in India. The government is currently considering sustained scientific efforts such as technological innovation, creativity, and start-ups in hi-tech through higher education to generate jobs. The education offered by universities follows traditional methods and does not align with the changing world. Governments are now exploring opportunities and scopes to generate productive employment through innovation, incubation, and research parks, among others. It is observed that a strong, innovative university system is a prerequisite for increasing the employability of graduates and for employment generation and development. It is recommended to urgently take steps to create entrepreneurs, new knowledge, new technology, patents, and intellectual property rights, and establish technology-based firms in partnership with the industry. This paper presents the new role and responsibility of universities and colleges in imparting education in an innovative way, fostering synergy with industry, and keeping up with fast-advancing technology. This has become essential in these changing times, especially under globalization pressures. Case studies from developed countries are presented in support of this. It is recommended that funding agencies such as the World Bank, UNESCO, the Asian Development Bank, and developed countries prioritize reforms in higher education and guide

India in increasing employability for productive jobs. This paper briefly presents problems in the adoption and implementation of innovation methods. Policy implications in this effort to generate jobs are identified and presented to facilitate the government's adoption of new approaches to fulfill the growing aspirations of the people. Conclusions are drawn to enhance the employability of graduates by making them creative and innovative for job generation.

Keywords: Employment Generation, Indian Universities, Productive Employment, Fast-Advancing Technology, Case Studies, Innovation Methods.

Introduction

India is facing a serious problem of unemployment and underemployment among the educated and uneducated population. The answer to this problem can be found through innovative education in universities and colleges. Developing the capacity to modernize universities in line with changing world needs is a significant challenge for developing countries.

This paper has objectives related to SDGs

Member of:

The main factor behind unemployment is an insufficient focus on research, innovation, and entrepreneurship. The roots of unemployment lie in the lack of high-end research and innovation in universities and colleges. Consequently, education in countries like India is not aligned with job demands, leading to thousands of youth migrating to developed countries in search of employment. The number of Indian students going abroad has increased by 19% in the years 2021–2022 (Naik, 2018).

On the one hand, there is a noticeable level of unemployment and underemployment among the population. On the other hand, there is a shortage of entrepreneurs to develop innovative enterprises. India possesses abundant natural resources, yet there is a shortage of finished goods and services. The Indian market is flooded with goods and services from East and West countries, thereby snatching up employment opportunities in India. Indian industries and SMEs lag significantly behind the rest of the world, ranking as low as 48th globally. The human resources in India are severely underdeveloped, ranking 127th development index.

Innovation is a strong stimulant for job growth. Individuals with innovation skills in India are in short supply. This is the major barrier to job creation and development. The paper suggests that research skills, innovation skills, and entrepreneurship skills must be integrated into the teaching curriculum of each subject in universities and colleges. Enabling students to learn innovation in colleges and universities is the only way, at this juncture, to enhance employability. It is found that students who learn innovation at a young age practice it throughout their lives. Universities have become key players in innovation systems. The ability of countries to grow and prosper now depends critically on the ability of universities and university systems to adjust to this new role of innovation. This new role of universities, as it has evolved the world over, is to provide training to employees to keep pace with fast-advancing technology, avoid obsolescence, and keep the workforce competent in the global market. Developing countries like India should understand and adopt this new role of innovation. Universities should not be confined to national boundaries. They ought to go far and wide. This is what is needed in a globalized world to ensure productive employment and economic growth.

Innovative professors and their students make value additions in business supply chains, increase their competitiveness, and also increase the placement of students, making the colleges preferred nationally and internationally. Professors are not only knowledgeable but also skilled at applying knowledge to problems in the industry and solving them. But the lack of synergy with the industry does not permit them to work with it. India needs to act fast to realize that university education can provide an innovative solution to the problem of unemployment.

It is observed that innovative individuals never remain idle or jobless. They are always in demand. Professors in developing countries have a high level of knowledge and capacity to teach innovation, but they need to be oriented and trained. Syllabi need to be revised to remove the deficiency in innovativeness. Universities have to depart from the traditional methods and contents of teaching.

The mindset of professors and university administration today is not fit for purpose. Because of the fast obsolescence of technologies and the fast changes in job contents in vocations and professions all over the world, university education ought to cope with these changes. This is essential to promoting employment.

The jobs of today will not be the jobs of the future. Jobless growth seems to be the prevailing trend at present. This necessitates continuous training for employees throughout their lives to retain them in jobs and avoid joblessness. Individuals must make efforts to transition from low-productivity jobs to higher-productivity jobs. Immediate challenges in countries, under the pressures of globalization, are to make college education job- oriented and offer lifelong continuing education courses for in-service personnel. This is exacerbated in the era of globalization due to the rapid obsolescence of knowledge and technology (Bowden, 2004). The competency of individuals depends on their learning and relearning rates. The challenge for universities is to make learning joyful, job-oriented, competitive, and innovative.

During election times, governments make promises to provide jobs to everyone, which is commendable. However, they have not adequately addressed the new vision of modernizing universities and colleges and providing skill-oriented education. The necessar y financial resources are not allocated in the national budget. The methods used to provide employment are improper and deviate from the use of emerging technology, which is the need of the hour. It is encouraging that higher education is growing, but there is a lag in innovation and the acquisition of skills for the commercial exploitation of new technologies, which is the demand of the time. The real challenge for higher education is how to provide new visions, missions, policies, and practices to cope with the changes in the global job market.

The main vision and mission of universities and colleges should now focus on producing more entrepreneurs and continuously improving the skill set of the workforce. India has taken some initial steps in this direction with the emergence of a greater number of startups, which is a positive contribution from the government. However, most of these startups are in the area of established technologies, and there are too few in the field of emerging technologies, such as New Technology-Based Firms (NTBF). This is due to inadequate research and innovation in universities and colleges, which form the foundation for employment.

The synergy between universities and business supply chains needs to be strengthened to ensure employment for all. India still has a long way to go in addressing employment with inclusive growth. The problem is significant, and reforms are currently insufficient. If research skills, innovation skills, and entrepreneurship skills are taught in universities and colleges, it can undoubtedly provide a sustainable and long-lasting solution.

The questions that are often asked are, What is the cost of not adequately educating students in innovation and entrepreneurship? Who bears the burden? The cost is significant, so significant that the entire country remains impoverished, with 20% of the population living below the poverty line and many youths struggling with unemployment and low wages. Additionally, there is an increase in crime rates, corruption, poverty, robbery, political misconduct, and various other undesirable consequences.

Developing countries must prioritize the reformation of universities and allocate increased funding in their national budgets. International aid organizations such as the World Bank, UNESCO, and the Asian Development Bank should provide greater financial assistance to universities in developing countries to foster a new culture of innovation.

Government initiatives such as Atmanirbhar Bharat Abhiyan, Smart Cities, Make in India, Digital India, Startups, and Incubation Centers have great potential for employment promotion. However, they require strong synergy between industry and universities to maximize their effectiveness. It is crucial to avoid mismatches in higher education, generate more productive jobs, and enhance the employability of youths (National Knowledge Commission, 2007).

1. Changing Role of Universities and Colleges in Developing Countries under the Pressures of Globalization

The conventional wisdom of universities and colleges as "Teaching shops" falls short of their purpose in the present stormy weather of globalization. Teaching without a research base and without innovation is ineffective, outdated, irrelevant, and obsolete. Based on experiences elsewhere in the world, it is recommended that developing countries like India tap into the untapped innovation potential of professors and students in universities and colleges. Brilliant students and professors are eagerly waiting for this opportunity. The new role has the potential to convert brain drain into brain gain. A strong, innovative university system is a prerequisite for development, without which India cannot hope to provide employment. Urgent steps for strategic changes to create entrepreneurs, new knowledge, new technology, patents, intellectual property rights, and the establishment of new technology-based firms are recommended. This is essential for creating a knowledge- based economy and integrating it with the global market. UNESCO and the World Bank are calling for a prominent shift in education from basic literacy to lifelong professional education.

The lack of the latest and most relevant knowledge and technology is the main cause of unemployment. It is observed worldwide that current job growth occurs in new knowledge and technology. Even if there is abundance in natural resources like land and minerals, employment opportunities in them are significantly lower compared to employment in new technologies, as noted by Nobel Laureate Robert Solow. Developing countries like India need to focus more on research, innovation, and start- ups in universities. Research is a wealth-creating agency. Increasing the state budget for research and innovation has been strongly recommended by many commissions and committees in the past, but it has not yet been put into practice. Research funding is significantly low, around 0.8% of GDP, while in developed countries, it is around 5%. Insufficient investment in innovation in universities and colleges leads to slow job growth, low productivity, unemployment, and poverty. It has been observed in India that many high-tech jobs remain unfilled due to a lack of skilled individuals, such as in the field of artificial intelligence. Education in universities and colleges is not aligned with the needs of employment, resulting in a mismatch. Consequently, thousands of dissatisfied students are going abroad, paying substantial sums of money, resulting in a significant brain and money drain. Indian universities, in the absence of innovation infrastructure, have become mediocre and are not recognized globally. The cost to the nation is very high, and it is the young generation of students who pay the price by missing out on opportunities in life. India must make conscious efforts to avoid such an undesirable situation. Roles for universities in developing countries have been identified.

1.1 Think Globally and Act Locally

Think globally and act locally - the first and foremost role of universities and colleges in eradicating unemployment. Universities should not think in a routine manner like in the past. Globalization presents new opportunities and serves as a strong catalyst for change. Universities need to adopt a different approach. They need to go beyond classroom instruction and become enterprising, fostering synergies with the industry to generate new knowledge, new technology, and patents, as well as intellectual property rights.

Indian universities and colleges should possess global visions and missions to generate new knowledge and technology. Vision is in short supply, but not resources. The potential of students and professors in Indian universities is high, yet it remains unexplored and wasted. It is observed that many of the CEOs of world-famous companies like Microsoft and IBM are Indians. Many Indians have gone abroad for studies, pursued masters and doctorates there, served for many years, and then risen to the position of CEO. India has many brilliant youths. However, not all of them get the opportunity to go abroad. Indian universities need to acquire new visions from world-class institutions to adapt to the new world. Therefore, the role of universities is to dream big and establish technology clusters attached to university campuses, utilizing youthful talent for research and innovation. These clusters have been observed as major contributors to employment generation. Incubators and technology parks act as spark plugs for employment. Universities should now aim to produce not only graduates but also entrepreneurs who can leverage new technology.

1.2 Special Drive for Advanced Education

The second role is to embark on a special drive for advanced education, synergizing with the industry, to teach research skills, innovation skills, and entrepreneurship skills to address the problem of unemployment. The urgent need in developing countries is to teach research skills, innovation skills, new technology generation skills, knowledge discovery skills, patents, and intellectual property rights to students. If this is not addressed, institutes in India will remain lagging behind, and unemployment and underemployment will persist. Learning skills that align with industry needs is becoming increasingly crucial for individuals and industries alike. Universities must reconsider their approach and adopt skill-oriented education on a large scale. The existing policies in Indian universities and colleges for higher education require a reset. This is an urgent necessity. A significant gap is observed between Indian education and the talent requirements of employers, resulting in a mismatch. There is unemployment on the one hand and a shortage of individuals with skills in emerging areas on the other. Universities must engage in strategic thinking that aligns with global market needs and bridge these gaps. Job- oriented courses are the pressing need of the time.

1.3 Bridge the Gap with Respect to the Counterparts

The third role of universities in developing countries is to bridge the gap with their counterparts in developed countries. Unless this gap is bridged, unemployment will persist, and brain drain will continue.

Indian universities possess knowledge but lack innovation. Students have to spend significant amounts of money to secure admission to foreign universities. Foreign universities are innovative, creative, and research- oriented. Their graduates become leaders and entrepreneurs on a global scale, while Indian graduates become employees and servants in companies owned by foreigners. Indian labs conduct experiments to test outdated concepts, while foreign labs conduct experiments to discover new knowledge, new technology, patents, and intellectual property rights. The challenge for universities in developing countries like India is to bridge this gap. The cost of brain drain is significant, estimated to be equivalent to the cost of establishing five IITs.

1.4 Infrastructure for Innovation

The next important role is to provide infrastructure for innovation, which in turn generates employment. Indian universities should focus on providing research and innovation infrastructure. These countries lack a long- range vision for creating infrastructure and conducting experiments to develop new, emerging technologies. They lack a global vision regarding the changing landscape of education. They adhere to the old ways instead of embracing the new. As a result, they continue to import, while foreign countries continue to sell their innovations. Universities in developing countries are disconnected from the needs of businesses. They lack insights into business supply chains, the talent requirements of employers, and the regional needs of industries. Incubation, innovation, and intellectual property rights infrastructure are still not provided in universities. As long as they do not provide this infrastructure, there will be unemployment among graduates, and the problem of joblessness in developing countries will persist. The challenge lies in equipping universities with the necessar y infrastructure for innovation, research, and start-ups.

1.5. Innovative Graduates

The next role is to produce innovative graduates who can play a vital role in employment. It is observed that innovative individuals are never jobless. They are always in demand. Students who acquire innovation skills become lifelong innovators. In developing countries, there is a shortage of such individuals. Developed countries have achieved their status because they have a large number of innovative and creative individuals. They have corporate education centers to update the skills of employees and foster a lifelong learning society. They have a learning culture consisting of learning organizations and individuals. The proportion of mid- career students in US universities is much higher. The developing countries need guidance from external agencies, particularly international aid organizations, to play these roles.

1.6. Visionary *Leaders*

Money is a passive resource. It is not active like people. Money is necessary, but visionary men and women are essential for generating employment. Human capability and leadership matter the most. Efforts are being made in developing countries to educate and enhance capabilities, but they are far from sufficient. Education is not given priority. Inadequate budget allocations are provided for higher education in the national budget. Joblessness is a significant issue in almost all developing countries. Political figures make promises to the people during elections, but once the elections are over, these promises are forgotten. Real solutions that effectively increase people's capabilities through education in universities and colleges are not implemented. While the availability of physical natural resources is desirable to accelerate industrial growth and employment, people's innovation can compensate for this deficiency. For example, Japan is weak in natural resources like minerals and raw materials such as iron ore, but it imports them from India and exports finished steel goods to India.

India's Human Development Index and the technological capabilities of its people are quite low, with India ranking 127th in the world. The challenge lies in making governments wiser and more globally competent.

1.7. Innovators and Job Generators

The next role is to produce innovators and job generators. Product innovation and process innovation are common types of innovation. Innovative individuals like Mahatma Phule and Dr. Ambedkar in India were social reformers. They had a passion for innovation and tirelessly worked day and night with boundless energy to reform societal systems. These are common characteristics of innovators. Universities should strive to produce leaders who are innovators, and then joblessness will diminish.

1.8. Facilitate Professors to Grow Professionally

The next role is to facilitate professors to grow professionally, become innovative, and generate employment. The real capital needed is the capital of innovative professors with new ideas. If universities acquire an innovative character, they will produce graduates capable of generating breakthrough and disruptive ideas. These individuals are crucial in addressing joblessness. These ideas generate employment and job opportunities. Ideas are the true capital. New ideas are necessary for success. They emerge from innovation. An idea generated is an opportunity generated, leading to the creation of many more jobs. Institutions serve as legitimate places, crucibles for experimentation, and factories of ideas. In a knowledge economy, institutions have no reason to exist if they do not generate new knowledge and ideas. Institutions are where dreams are created and where capacity and imagination are instilled in young people to implement those dreams. This new role is evolving in universities worldwide.

The need and importance of innovation for a country's economic future are being realized by universities and colleges in India, and infrastructure is being created to address the shortage of innovative individuals for innovation and entrepreneurship. Today, the competency of the workforce is understood in terms of its ability to innovate. People need to be innovative to foresee upcoming opportunities. The Government of India understands that this is the key to increasing competitiveness. However, the process is rather slow.

India possesses the largest pool of youthful workforce and high-quality human capital, which is its competitive advantage. India is striving to prepare these individuals to be globally competitive and entrepreneurial according to global standards and needs. Then, India will not only produce CEOs but also many globally recognized companies.

1.9 New Technology Based Firms (NTBF)

The role of universities is to produce New Technology Based Firm (NTBF) start-ups, which are crucial for employment generation.

Universities and colleges are the appropriate institutions where new knowledge and technologies can be generated and simultaneously disseminated to the younger generation for commercial exploitation. Through NTBFs, universities foster a culture of innovation and play a key role in developing innovation systems and promoting the necessary investment for skill development. By spinning off NTBFs, universities can contribute to solving the employment problem in India. Universities are significant contributors to research and development (R&D) due to their youthful scholars. However, this long- term vision is lacking in developing countries, resulting in a weak R&D base. International experience confirms that university research drives job growth. The role of universities, in partnership with industry, is evolving in favor of research, innovation, and entrepreneurship.

Invention, when commercially exploited, is known as innovation. Innovation transforms invention into monetary value. Unfortunately, research conducted at Indian universities rarely leads to commercial exploitation. Most theses written by scholars today are irrelevant and of limited use to business and industry. Libraries are filled with theses that lack industry relevance, and universities make no efforts to derive economic value from them. In the absence of innovation centers, students struggle to convert their research into usable products and processes. This diminishes the chances of conducting relevant research and innovation, resulting in minimal returns from research efforts.

Despite the increasing student population in universities, the focus on innovation is lacking. This presents a serious gap and challenge in India.

Universities lack innovation infrastructure, including incubators, IPR centers, and research parks. The academic environment in universities tends to prioritize examinations and rote learning of theories rather than fostering an enterprising mindset. National wealth generation stems from harnessing new knowledge and technology. Developed countries have reaped significant benefits from new technology, enabling their students to become highly competitive within a shorter timeframe. They tap into the global market, including developing countries. India, through the New Education Policy-2020, is orienting universities toward research, innovation, and entrepreneurship. However, the mindset of people, including professors, is still in the process of aligning with this policy. Identifying and removing the roadblocks is a necessary step forward.

1.10 Train Students to Use Sunrise Technologies

The next role is to train students to use sunrise technologies instead of sunset technologies. This is essential for youth employment. Currently, in India, time, effort, and money are spent on teaching irrelevant subjects, focusing on outdated knowledge. Professors do not impart the knowledge and skills needed for today and tomorrow because they are lagging behind. They do not engage in research. They simply teach without researching. In the 21st century, traditional working methods from years past are becoming outdated. Technological obsolescence occurs at a faster rate (Duderstadt, 2009). Jobs in old technologies and outdated knowledge are rapidly disappearing. Technology is advancing swiftly, and so are job skills. People have to continuously learn and upskill to stay employed. It has been observed that individuals need to upskill every seven years. This was not the case in the past, when once a person learned a job, they could perform it for a lifetime. Men, along with machines, are becoming obsolete. If people do not continue learning, they become jobless. Employees and employers in developing countries must allocate a budget for lifelong learning. They must strive to build a learning society comprising individuals committed to continuous learning. Universities and colleges must drive the creation of a learning nation. By redesigning courses to align with industry demands, unemployment is likely to decrease. Students need to be taught skills in robotics, artificial intelligence, and other critical areas.

Research and innovation skills are of utmost importance for students to learn. They should also acquire entrepreneurial skills. Continuous innovation and the lifelong training and retraining of individuals necessitate advanced research infrastructure and professors who possess knowledge of the changing world. A Continuing Education Center in the field of project management at Boston University was visited. Similar centers should be established in Indian universities.

1.11 New Ideas to Industry Leaders

The next role is to provide new ideas to industry leaders to help them succeed in the global economy. If they become beacons for industries, they will generate new jobs.

Entrepreneurs who start enterprises in the NTBF with the support of universities tend to be more successful. They exhibit greater competitiveness in the global market and generate high-tech, well-paid employment. Additionally, they create numerous downstream jobs. Evaluation reports of Research Parks conducted in the USA clearly demonstrate that this is an effective approach to fostering innovation. Universities in developing countries should not overlook such innovative infrastructure and should promptly adopt it. The investment in these centers is highly productive.

Almost all universities in the USA, Europe, and other developed countries like Japan and Korea have Research Parks on their campuses. Several Research Parks in the USA and Europe have been visited. Finland has the renowned Oulu Park, while Toronto University has the well- known Medical and Related Sciences Park (MaRS). This system has been successfully implemented in developed countries. China has also established many Research Parks, which have resulted in job creation and increased industrial output. An evaluation of Research Parks in the USA was conducted by Battelle and the Association of University Research Parks (AURP), and their findings were published in a report in 2012. It revealed significant employment growth through these parks. AURP offers courses for university professors on how to initiate parks, and it is advisable for key individuals from developing countries to participate (AURP, 2013). This would give a boost to the movement in developing countries like India (National Academy of Sciences et al., 2007).

Universities in developed countries are actively spinning off companies in the NTBF. Research entrepreneurs are benefiting from this and establishing offices on campuses. They gather around researchers, professors, and young scholars to tap into new ideas. As a result, universities have become birthplaces for NTBF companies. Developing countries like India greatly require such initiatives.

2. Case Studies

Countries like the USA, Canada, and Europe have innovative universities. They are leaders in research, innovation, and start-ups. They have greatly benefited from innovation infrastructure and have achieved growth through employment. Developing countries can also benefit. Case studies from developed countries are presented as examples for emulation.

2.1 Stanford University

Stanford University in the USA has given birth to as many as 3000 hi-tech start-ups, or New Technology Based Firms [NTBFs], employing millions of educated men and women worldwide, each earning a high income. The university receives millions of dollars in royalty payments from these companies each year, which are reinvested in research to create even more companies and jobs. Universities in other developed countries like Europe, Australia, China, Singapore, and New Zealand are also focused on Research, Innovation, and Start-ups. They earn significant royalties on the patents they sell to the industry. For example, in the mobile industry, the material cost of a mobile is hardly Rs 500, while the rest, in thousands, is the royalty paid for patents used in mobiles. Additionally, research-based companies are often found flocking around universities to obtain brand new ideas and provide high-tech, high-paying jobs, among other downstream benefits.

Universities in developing countries like India do not pay attention to the developments taking place in developed countries. It is due to the advanced research and innovation atmosphere that these countries have almost no employment problems. They face a shortage of man-power. Indians have high capabilities, but due to shortcomings in universities, their potential remains untapped. These countries lack a long-range vision, are inward-looking, and do not benchmark against others. As a result, the employability of graduates is low, at only 17%, and unemployment is high. Consequently, these countries remain in the developing stage with low incomes and poverty in society. The people are talented, but the systems do not nurture them properly (Rhodes, 2001).

2.2 MIT Boston

MIT is an innovative and enterprising world-ranking university. It has so far spun off thousands of entrepreneurs, similar to Stanford. It has an Entrepreneurship Department with ten full professors dedicated to teaching, promoting, and researching entrepreneurship. It also has a technology licensing office that sells patents and intellectual property rights to industries. Furthermore, it has a center donated by Dr. Gururaj Deshpande. Every month, MIT organizes face-to-face meetings for innovators to showcase their innovations, patents, and intellectual property rights, while entrepreneurs can explore and acquire the latest technologies. One of these meetings was attended, and it was highly productive. The discussions at MIT and those at other universities are broadcast on TV daily. Entrepreneurs share their viewpoints and market needs with innovators, fostering a continuous upgrading of technology in New Technology Based Firms (NTBFs). MIT even has its own venture capital firm to provide financial support to its start-ups. When these start-ups grow and become profitable, they pay royalties to MIT, which are reinvested in research and innovation, further boosting employment opportunities.

2.3. Chinese and Australian Universities

Chinese universities are now giving birth to 100 New Technology Based Firms (NTBFs) every year. Australian universities are giving birth to 50 start-ups, or NTBFs (Zhao, 2004). Developing countries ought to adopt this model for their universities to create innovative regions and cities and generate employment. Universities need to adopt a vision of corporate development and contribute to the success of industries.

2.4. Toronto University

The unique feature of the Medical and Related Sciences Research Park at Toronto University, Canada, is that it is housed in 17 tall buildings in downtown Toronto. This park is home to many research-based companies that employ over 6,000 PhD degree holders. MaRS, started by Prof. Evans long ago, initially occupied one building and later expanded to 17 buildings. To accommodate the expansion, MaRS purchased properties in downtown at market prices and constructed buildings according to their requirements. Researchers in this park deliver lectures to students at the university, and they utilize research ideas and experiences from the university to further their work in the company. MaRS provides an innovative infrastructure for research and learning. It also offers extension services to institutions and universities in many foreign countries, such as India. Canada has 17 research parks like this across its universities. Due to such innovative structural reforms, Canada has a very low unemployment rate. It faces a shortage of people and thus imports a large number of individuals every year. Developing countries should emulate this model in their own countries and undoubtedly achieve success.

2.5. Universities in Singapore and New Zealand

Universities in small countries that are half the size of Mumbai, like Singapore and New Zealand, rank high on the world list. They continuously innovate and strive for innovation.

If universities lack innovation centers, they are deemed ineffective. By providing innovation infrastructure, they can produce graduates who can create job opportunities for others. First-mover entrepreneurs may emerge, eliminating joblessness. Graduates have ambitious dreams and think big when they are exposed to innovation. Through innovation, they learn and develop their creativity and imagination. They contribute to the economic surplus, making the nation wealthier. Students no longer remain confined to the bookish learning of outdated knowledge. Instead, they become job creators rather than job seekers.

Innovation is largely absent in most universities in developing countries like India. Students study for examinations and quickly forget what they have learned afterward. They fail to meet global standards of capability and fall behind the times. Joblessness is a consequence of this situation.

3. Government of India Initiatives

The Government of India has recently launched initiatives such as Atma Nirbhar Bharat, Start-ups, Skill India, Technology Incubation,

Research Park, Make in India, and more. These initiatives are highly welcomed as they are in their initial stages and have already started creating jobs and fostering the emergence of entrepreneurs. Innovation systems are being developed, and technology incubators in collaboration with industry are being established in universities and engineering colleges. Furthermore, top foreign universities are invited to establish their campuses in India. Prime Minister Mr. Modi has taken a strong initiative to boost innovation in universities and colleges. The industry is also responding positively by competing in the global market based on innovation. The government has established a national innovation board to provide funding to universities and colleges. The challenge lies in effectively implementing these schemes.

It is important to make universities innovative and enterprising to address joblessness. Lack of innovation is a significant factor contributing to joblessness in India. The insufficient focus on innovation skills in universities and colleges has resulted in underperformance, low productivity, and unemployment. India has now recognized the full potential of the innovation phenomenon, leading to the formation of innovation councils in various states.

The Modi government has taken initiatives to revamp working systems in various sectors such as defense, agriculture, industry, construction, roads, railways, and more. The challenge lies in effectively implementing these schemes to bring about meaningful change.

4. Problems in Adoption and Implementation of Innovative Methods

Presently, universities and colleges teach the acquisition of knowledge. Students learn from professors, through books, and through practicals in labs. All the knowledge they acquire is good, but they do not learn how and where to apply that knowledge in real-life professional situations. As a result, problems continue to remain unattended in professions and vocations, even though the knowledge to solve them is available. The application of knowledge to live problems in today's education is missing. Students do not acquire the attitude and skill to apply that knowledge to make people's and professionals problems easier. Innovations are needed to identify and evolve solutions. For example, in many cities like Aurangabad, water leakage problems have been noticed on roads for many years, despite a water shortage and people not having access to drinking water. No one tries to solve these problems, They need to be perceived, defined in scientific language, and efforts made to solve them. This highlights the need for innovative universities.

A deviation in the vector direction of studies in universities and colleges is needed, moving from the mere acquisition of knowledge to its application. Students are examined on their acquisition of knowledge but not on their application, innovation, and creativity. That reformation angle is lacking among professors and students.

Universities and colleges in developed countries have had technology innovation centers, technology incubation centers, patent and IPR centers, and research parks for over a hundred years. Some of the problems are,

- *Lack of Research in Universities and Colleges:* Research is the mother of innovation. The absence of research has led to a lack of innovation. The mindset of university administration and professors is not oriented towards research and innovation. The focus is primarily on learning known knowledge and known technology in the syllabus. There is a lack of focus on innovation. Examinations only test the knowledge acquired by students and do not assess their innovative ability and creativity.
- *Lack of Expertise in Research, Innovation, and Entrepreneurship:* Universities and colleges need to abandon the traditional approach and embrace an innovative and creative approach. The mindset of professors should now favor creativity and innovation. They should engage in discussions and debates on this aspect of innovation in their universities.
- *Lack of Connections between Indian Universities and Innovative Universities Abroad:* India has neglected global changes in higher education. The higher education landscape in the world is evolving, but it is sticking to old traditional practices. There is a need for entrepreneurship and a risk-taking approach.

5. Policy Implications

Effective licensing of intellectual property rights (IPR) is needed to promote innovation, which is a basic requirement for increasing innovation and generating jobs. There is a strong relationship between effective licensing of IPR and the diffusion of innovative technology, job creation, and economic growth. To expedite the diffusion of innovative technology from incubators, research parks, and centers of excellence, effective licensing of IPR is advocated. Only then can high-quality jobs, characterized by high-tech and high income, be generated. Without such jobs, India is at risk of being stuck in low-growth, low-income, low-wage-driven economies rather than becoming an innovative developed economy. The national IPR policy holds the key to the growth of innovative and creative industries and research-based disruptive industries, which are essential for generating high-end jobs. The generation of low-end jobs often relies on the creation of high-end jobs. Strong IP standards alone can fuel the growth of domestic research-based industries, attract foreign direct investment (FDI), and enhance India's prosperity. Hence, effective licensing of IPR is strongly advocated for accelerating innovation, employment generation, and economic growth in all developing countries.

Innovative professors are needed to create a culture of innovation and, in turn, eradicate unemployment. India aims to develop world-class universities because it has been observed that universities with high rankings produce globally competent professionals and political leaders, along with capable human capital essential for managing national and international affairs. Countries can only become developed when they have world- class universities, even if they possess abundant natural resources. In today's knowledge-based economy, employment is driven by research, innovation, and entrepreneurship, which thrive best in world-class universities. If developing countries aspire to become developed nations, they must focus on making their universities world-class and eliminating unemployment. By creating research-based, world-class universities, developing countries like India are more likely to eradicate unemployment. The challenge lies in effectively implementing this goal.

The liberal import of technology is the main cause of unemployment. An OECD study observed that those nations that lead in innovation tend to snatch jobs from those that lag. Invention, when exploited commercially, is known as innovation. In India, no conscious effort is made to convert research into innovation because vision in this direction is lacking.

Joblessness and industrial slowdowns are common phenomena in India due to a lack of innovation. The government has now launched programs like the Technical Education Quality Improvement Program. However, this is only for a few selected institutes and not for all.

Universities ought to become fountainheads of new knowledge and technology and lighthouses for industry. The universities in developing countries should dream big, think great, and jump at technology generation and diffusion, which are achieving high significance, to wipe off unemployment. They should deserve the status of lighthouses for the industry. They ought to become the birthplaces and maternity homes of NTBFs.

Budget should be increased for universities at the national level. Today, in most developing countries, the budget is too meager to provide good-quality education. It is true that these countries do not have much money. However, they must mobilize money from international sources for the cause of universities. Investment in higher education is an asset, not a liability.

The university and industry should set up a forum where they can meet regularly at intervals, provide structural connections between universities and industry, and set up Corporate Education Centers. In isolation, they both cannot achieve peak performance. The university and industry are like two wings of a nation. They must synergize and function in harmony with each other to produce jobs and skilled people to do the jobs. Many universities in developed countries have corporate education centers, like Boston University in the USA.

Traditional regulations of universities and governments in today's globalization do not suffice. They must remove constraints and introduce flexibility and autonomy. If universities are not revitalized, opportunities for employment will slip out of hand, and economic stagnation may prevail.

Conclusion

Universities in developing countries ought to take research and innovation seriously, as these factors alone can solve the problem of unemployment. They must align immediately with business supply chains, meet the talent needs of employers, and address regional needs. Universities and colleges are expected to produce innovative leaders for the industry and leaders with imagination for all other areas of life in order to generate employment and facilitate growth. Synergy between universities, business supply chains, the talent needs of employers, and regional needs must be established. The role played by Indian universities and professors in the present government is showing signs of improvement. The number of such firms they can produce is a pertinent question that should be directed to universities and professors. The speed at which Indian universities acquire an innovative character will determine the future of employment. India is at risk due to a lack of innovative and creative universities.

Universities should aim to nurture professors who can produce the latest kinds of innovations, including product innovation, process innovation, financial innovation, and organizational innovation. Universities should have the ambition to develop systems that enable professors to become innovators rather than just teachers. Universities and colleges in India should adopt and accelerate a new vector of promoting startups rather than merely focusing on bookish teaching. Laboratories in colleges should always strive for innovation, conducting experiments to discover new knowledge, theories, and technological applications instead of just testing known theories and technologies. Every professor should be groomed to become an innovator. They must realize that universities are crucial for innovation and employment promotion. Education charged with the spirit of research, innovation, entrepreneurship, and discovery is not a luxury. It is a basic need to make education job-oriented and promote employment. Resources are not lacking, but visionary individuals are needed to design and evolve university systems. India has implemented the NEP-2020 to boost startups, which is a welcome step. The government and international agencies should prioritize increased funding for innovation. Creating innovative universities should be given top priority. Television programs for young aspiring entrepreneurs should be initiated, similar to those in the USA. Each university should organize weekly discussions on innovation conducted by the university and make them accessible to entrepreneurs in society. Research, innovation, and startups are today's mantras for employment promotion.

References

1. AURP. (2013). *Driving Regional Innovation and Growth.* Retrieved from https://aurp.memberclicks.net/assets/ documents/aurp_batelllereportv2.pdf
2. Bowden, R. (2004). *Globalization, Impact on Our Lives.* Rain Tree Publications.
3. Duderstadt, J. J. (2009). *A University for the 21st Century.* University of Michigan Press.
4. Naik, B. M. (2018). *Education and Leadership: Role of Indian Universities and Colleges in Nurturing Future Leaders.* Atlantic Publishers & Distributors (P) Limited.
5. National Academy of Sciences, National Academy of Engineering, & Institute of Medicine. (2007). *Rising Above the Gathering Storm: Energizing and Employing America for a Brighter Economic Future.* The National Academies Press, Washington. https://doi.org/10.17226/ 11463
6. National Knowledge Commission. (2007). Retrieved from https://epsiindia.org/wp-content/uploads/2019/02/ Knowledge-Commission-Report-20071.pdf
7. Rhodes, F. H. T. (2001). *The Creation of the Future: The Role of the American University.* Cornell University Press.
8. Zhao, F. (2004). Academic entrepreneurship: case study of Australian universities. *The International Journal of Entrepreneurship and Innovation,* 5(2), 91-97. https://doi. org/10.5367/000000004773863246

Chapter - 2

Changing Role of Universities & Colleges Under Globalization Pressures Focus Ought to be on Innovation & Entrepreneurship

"The power of research is demonstrated not only by the single isolated innovation but by the ability to create new technology based industries, some of them becoming the most economic power drivers."

Synopsis

Universities & colleges, the world over, have now been playing new Roles namely, Creating Hi-Tech startups, generation of New Knowledge, New Technology, Patents & IPR, New Technology Based Firms. This has become essential so as to meet Market Demand. The paper outlines in brief, the need and importance of building a **knowledge based economy** in India, in the context of globalization. This is with a view to enable people to be more competitive to make most of global opportunities. Strong higher education system is however, a pre-requisite for development, without which India in spite of potential can not hope to become a strong economy. Urgent steps for strategic changes in creating entrepreneurs, new knowledge, new technology, patents, IPR, establishment of new technology based firms etc are recommended.

Conventional wisdom, of institutes as "teaching shops" in present stormy weather of globalization falls too short of purpose, and does not suffice. Teaching with out research base and with out innovation is found to be ineffective, outdated, irrelevant and obsolete. From experience in the world it is recommended that India should harvest its untapped research, innovation and entrepreneurship potential lying idle in higher education institutes. Brilliant students and faculty are eagerly waiting. The new roles have a potential to convert, brain drain in to brain gain.

Introduction

Pressures are mounting on higher education institutes like colleges, polytechnics and universities to play a key role in creating knowledge based economy and bringing about integration of the Indian economy with global. Corporations, governments, and international organizations like UNESCO, World Bank are calling for a more prominent role for education from basic literacy to life long professional education.

OECD defines **"Knowledge based economy that is to say knowledge driven economy is one in which the production, use and distribution of knowledge and information are critical to the process of economic growth".**

Not surprisingly the role of university is central to the emerging knowledge based economy. World experience tells us that those regions/ nations whose institutes can quickly adapt to the rapidly changing economic, political, technological and social climate will have much greater prospect of success. They are identified as major drivers of change to achieve economic growth. A region where more enrolment takes place in institutes, and liberal, broader, quality education is offered, globalization at faster pace takes place. Higher education has considerable potential to reduce adverse effects, and increase impact of globalization in stimulating economic growth. Knowledge inculcated by institutes can enable people to derive maximum benefits from entry in global market. India has the potential to leap frog the educational infrastructures and effectiveness of developed countries. Raw talent of Indians is good and anxiously waiting to be nursed well.

Colleges and universities in India after independence have made a laudable progress, yet they are observed to be poorly equipped and woefully unsuited to the demands of globalization. They are far too behind their counterparts in developed world. Thousands of students every year are going abroad for higher education. Institutes emphasize memorization that is "rote learning," and do not offer innovation, entrepreneurship and leadership skills needed in world market. Institutes, in globalization have to play a key role in developing knowledge society. They need to be repositioned, and restructured in terms of their relationship with people, government, industry, private sector and the world. Our true wealth resides in educated citizenry.

Most profitable investment lies in education. People who are willing to learn, rich as well as poor, need to be educated to fit them in today's complex globalize world. They need to be allowed to grow to the level they are capable for. Otherwise they tend to become a liability and threat to the national as well as world peace. It is being realized that lack of education is closely linked with unemployment and in turn to crime. India should have now to invest with priority in colleges or else it will have to spend more on building prisons for those who do not get education, and wind up in committing crimes. If investment in colleges by choice does not take place government will be forced to invest more on prisons? Should the government therefore not be investing adequately in building institutes? Public Investment in education will have to increase for it is the best use of tax payer's money

Need and Importance of building a knowledge society

In globalization, knowledge and intellectual capital has become more important than physical resources like land, buildings, equipment etc. Intellectual skills of people in modern job market have achieved more significance than hand skills. Colleges, Polytechnics, universities have come to be known as power houses producing new ideas. They increase brain power and enable the nation to win in brain race. They generate and disseminate new knowledge needed to keep the people competitive. Universities & colleges have moved from periphery of development to the center.

Institutes produce National Leaders and captains for industry

Development to take place fast and remain sustainable requires educated people and visionary leaders. More educated people are observed to choose better leaders. Institutes are now called upon to produce leaders for industry, and leaders for economy, society and every walk of life. They could produce world class leaders for which essentially institutes would have to be world class by themselves, which is so essential to win in world economy. We know that today's leaders in politics, industry, economy etc were yesterday's students. We must look at today's students as tomorrow's leaders, and institutes as generators of visionary and creative leaders.

Each one is affected by globalization and each one is impacting globalization. We are now the citizens of one world. We have to be competent by world standards. The boundary lines between the nations are becoming thinner. Students and people in globalization would have to develop international perspectives, tolerance and negotiation skills needed in world market. This is essential so as to keep pace with the world development. World over, this is found to be a winning strategy. We should not delay in its adoption. Else, expert leadership, critical skills, professional services, and new knowledge on which its future in globalize world depends would remain subdued.

More students entering the pipeline

More students entering the education pipe line in India is a welcome sign. This is the critical input for development. As the world due to globalization, is getting more and more interconnected, the higher education which is meant to drive knowledge, creativity, and innovation, in human society is becoming more crucial. Colleges, polytechnics and universities all over the world have always been the creators of new knowledge and its keepers. They have sought to prepare new generations with the skills, cultural and scientific literacy, flexibility and capacity for critical inquiry and to make their contributions to society.

Development of a nation today is said to depend on its capacity to educate people in relevant knowledge and state of the art technology.

No society, region or nation will prosper without good institutes of higher and technical education.

They form the core of development and hence need to be reformed with priority. It is the well educated people, people with capability and competency, who make the investment and efforts in development projects fruitful. It is this interaction between education and development that shapes our collective future as global citizens. World Bank in its report of 2002 has underlined the importance of higher education for creating able leaders for development of nations. A close coupling exists between 'education and competitiveness of human force 'which needs to be kept in view, in today's stormy weather of globalization.

In India proportion of students entering the pipe line of higher education of the age 17 to 23 is around only 17%. This proportion in USA is 65 %. World average is around 40.4 %. It is observed that countries with higher levels of education will be least affected due to shift taking place in employment. In globalization people are found to change jobs 3 to 7 times in service career. The proportion of older students for upgrading skills world over is therefore increasing. U K has declared recently skills revolution, and urgent action taken to up grade people's competitiveness. Most successful nations shall be those who invest in life long learning, and create a learning society. Getting educated only once is not enough. Higher education has become critical to win in business. India would have to work and match with its competitors. Are our students and faculty aware of importance of education for economic development? What our institutes are doing to promote life long education?

Institutes build Knowledge society

A central theme is emerging in which significant social, economic transformations are taking place on global level. They are challenging the traditional role and traditional position of universities in society. It is argued that these institutions now are a "think Tank ". They need to find ways of addressing these important complex challenges facing the nations with imagination. India has many hidden jewel professors. It is necessary to explore, reward and felicitate them Professors are expected to be equal to their counterparts in developed world. How are they enabled in India to be so? They should be enabled to establish alliances with world best institutes, political system, social system, and world economic system. They should not be merely teaching but influencing public policies and society.

They should be researching themselves and guiding students for research. There is tremendous positive impact on the transfer of science and technology from institutes to private sector and then to economy, thereby creating marvelous number of jobs with high pay off. Institutes now stand for creating a learning society and a learning economy. Institutes in globalization can and should bring about a cultural revolution, and contribute to collective wisdom, so essential for bright future of our children and grand children. Questions are being asked, are we educating students to understand global systems? Do the students understand that they have to have tolerance for the culture of others? Knowledge society will give kick start to Cultural Revolution.

Protect civil and political rights for knowledge society to thrive

Protection of civil and political rights is a prerequisite for establishment of knowledge based economy. There is a close and inseparable relationship between the quality of higher learning on one hand and the quality of effective and democratic governance on the other. Economic development depends on level of education of the people and level of education depends on quality of governance of the nation. Just as it is very hard to imagine sustainable and democratic development without higher education, it is futile to promote higher education in a society where civil and political rights are systematically suppressed and denied. Experience shows that countries that thrive best in global economies are those which are truly open. Openness means open trade, open investment, open borders. It also refers to open societies that invite new ideas, show a high tolerance and open descent and criticism and rethinking, reworking of their own governance. True development occurs when knowledge is owned and operated by communities, and by women and men who form those communities. Higher education is not a luxury for the rich it is a necessity especially for the poor. E-governance is said to provide solutions. Openness and transparency is consciously promoted by state government through, Right to Information Act. What kind of e-governance? What are the limits? Who will out line the strategies? It is the well educated who can show the way

Privatization accelerates arrival of Knowledge Based Economy

While the importance of higher education world over is increasing, state budget allocated to higher education per student is observed to be decreasing. In countries like USA, UK per capita public investment on education is reported to be falling. Tuition fees are therefore rising. Private and public investment taken together is however observed to be rising. In India the situation is not different

Increase in tuition fees is resented by students. They are however paying, because higher education is bringing to them benefits like higher salaries, and an opportunity for better jobs which weigh far more. Private investment by philanthropic organizations, industry, and fees paid by students are found to make education responsive to market needs. This is a great advantage.

Privatization leads to stimulate competition to get good students, good faculty thus improving relevance and quality of education. Privatization leads to quick response of education to market forces, which the students and economy needs.

The internal rigid structure of government, universities and colleges is a major obstacle to quick changes needed in education. Private institutes have flexible structure Privatization has an edge over government regulated institutes in this respect. As such there is no substitute for privatization. But privatization may not protect students coming from low income families. Government would have to cover them by scholarships, bursaries etc. There is no substitute for public funding. Almost 70% of the students in USA are taking education in government funded institutions. In Germany all institutions are Government funded, and education from KG to PG is free of cost.

Funding alone by government even if it can leads however to mismatch and waste of resources. Therefore both public and private funding must simultaneously go on. Funding by government for poor and deserving is essential. Can we afford to lose students because of high fees? This has to be viewed as an investment in creating leadership from weaker sections of society. All needs of education however can not be visualized by government. It is the inherent weakness of the government regulated systems.

Many times advanced education of superior quality by government is neglected, Privatization makes up the gap. Public funding alone leads to over centralization, and increase in overheads without commensurate gains. These weaknesses are overcome in privatization. Where lays the golden mean of public and private funding? Who will find? This requires well educated people.

The model of private and public funding is found to be more rewarding.

Globalization brought Opportunities

Some view economic globalization as inevitable, and therefore advocate to focus on necessity of institutional reforms to harvest benefits arising out of globalization. Others view economic globalization as unnecessary evil where economic interests have displaced broader social, human and democratic concerns. The later argue in favor of resistance while the former says resistance is futile. Globalization can benefit human civilization as a whole. However some may benefit more while others less. People in India to benefit more will have to upscale the skills and knowledge of its people. India is a developing country. It remained less developed so far, by world comparison because its economy was localized and less globalized. The region can be richer if the digital divide between the region and developed world is reduced. We must wake up to this reality and act fast with our full strength to accelerate international trade and commerce, which demands more knowledge of the world. Do we share the same planet, same environment? Then we must nurse globalization.

Opportunities are not risk free

There is however more uncertainties and more risks involved in harnessing global opportunities. So as to harvest them demands new knowledge new skills, and positive human attitude to go round the world. Survival of fittest is the law.

There is an impact of new technology on jobs and business. Are our institutes preparing youths to cope with? Are they providing skills required in global market? Globalization means mixing of cultures, shrinking of time and space. Globalization means business at the speed of thought, instant communication and instant decisions. Globalization means abandoning traditional methods, systems and procedures in favor of modern, which requires education. Keeping the risks to a minimum and harvesting opportunity requires education. Who provides the scientific approach to harvesting opportunities? Higher and technical education will.

Institutes as Drivers of change

Student's and entrepreneurs in search of new knowledge tend to migrate else where because good institutes are very few in number. Good institutes are found to function like magnates to attract intellectuals. Institutions in India except IITs are observed to be far too behind their counterparts in US, UK. Thousands of students are seen migrating for admissions elsewhere. After studies many of them do not return. India to that extent looses talent. USA has gained lot of intellectual manpower from foreign countries like India, China by creating world class universities. If India creates world class institutes it can reduce brain drain if not eliminate, and attract brains from other developing and developed countries.

Wealth of a region now depends upon knowledge possessed by the people. He who possesses knowledge becomes well to do, hence is its importance. Is it the local people who posses technological knowledge? We must ensure this. Development is said to primarily aim at generation of knowledge, acquisition of the intellectual capital. It is not merely construction of roads, bridges, factories etc. Institutes in the state will have to grow to the level of their counterparts in rest of world. Winners are not those who manufacture goods, but those who develop talent.

New role of higher education:

To produce captains for industry, to commercialize new knowledge, generate new technology, patents & IPR, Starting New technology Based Firms, research parks? It is high Time for institutes to become enterprising and to give kick start

Institutes can and should derive financial advantage of innovation capacity of students. Institutes ought to be autonomous to do that.

Indian higher education institutes are late starters but now after independence, observed to have made lot of progress. The number of universities, colleges has substantially gone up. They are found to be doing a good job. A revolution is noticed in every state and in the whole country Students are coming to institutes in larger numbers. People are giving high priority to education. Even if they do not have money enough, they are found borrowing from banks, selling land and houses. The job opportunities in globalization are large enough that they get more than they spend on education. Many are taking jobs abroad in countries like USA, UK, and Japan etc.

Universities abroad are now highly enterprising in creating knowledge based society. There is a world wide wave in this respect. There is however, a serious deficiency in the institutes in India. They are observed to be too weak in research, innovation, patenting & IPR, and spinning off of new technology based firms. If we make bench marking of our institutes with their counterparts in developed countries a big gap is noticed. For example USA universities are spinning off new technology based firms very large in number. MIT Boston is obtaining more than 150 patents every year. The royalty earned from patents is 20 % of the yearly budget of the institution. It is spinning off around 50 companies every year. A study conducted in the year 1994 found that 4000 companies owe their origin to MIT. They employ 1.1 million people, and generated 232 billion dollars in world trade. In the United States companies employed 733000 people or one out of every 170 jobs in the country. Indian institutes have not taken any financial advantage from creating innovations.

Higher education can not grow where R & D is absent.

The universities in Australia are also quite active in this respect. Each university is spinning of as many as 50 new technology based companies. Chinese universities are also not behind. Each university in China has set up technology incubator, business incubator and they are pumping new technologies and innovations in industry. Countries like Germany, UK, and France are far too ahead. From 1980 universities in Germany have set up technology transfer and patent centers. The author was given a fellowship by the ministry of education government of India, in the year 1996 to visit patent and technology transfer centers in universities of Germany. He has personally visited six universities and observed that students acquire innovation, patent skills. They sow the seeds of entrepreneurship while studying.

How many of the universities in India have obtained patent & IPR? How many companies have been born in universities? Do the students learn innovation skills? How much commercial exploitation is done of the PhD thesis? Are they just lying on library cupboard? They are being exploited by foreign companies, for obtaining patents. Many Indian traditional researches like of turmeric [Haldi], Wheat, Basmati, Ayurvedic medicines etc are being exploited by foreigners. It is because our institutes have so far ignored patenting. There is vast untapped potential available for exploitation. Shall we not hurry up in this regard?

Prof Terman of Stanford University in the year 1950, gave the principle for establishment of research parks, that "University professors need access to industry to make application of the findings of research, so also industry need access to University research to keep industry globally competitive." Based on above Silicon Valley was born, with the backing of Stanford and California university, research Triangle Park at North Carolina is set up with the lead of Duke University, 128 street in Boston with the initiation of MIT and a large number of university related parks have come up in Japan, Germany, and UK, with a view to induct new knowledge and new technology to make industry globally competitive.

Department of Science and Technology Government of India have started a similar scheme of Science and Technology Entrepreneurs Park [STEP]. Twelve such parks are operating in universities in India. University of Pune, Cochin University, IIT Kharagpur etc parks reports are encouraging. IIT Mumbai has started a technology Incubator. TIFAC is set up to give fillip to patenting. The schemes need to be driven further with greater strength and vigor.

Transnational Linkages essential to build knowledge society

Securing the connections between the developing and developed institutes to build capabilities of knowledge generation is essential. We can not afford to ignore good policies and practices developed else where in the world. IITs were developed in collaboration with foreign. So they are found to shine in world.

Rests of higher education institutes were disconnected and although they spent more they lagged behind. Now we can not afford to ignore the global scene in education. Why our institutes do not stand in the world list? Why thousands of students are going abroad? Strategic international partnerships have a great potential to bring new knowledge and relate knowledge to local conditions. Who will give directions in this respect? Who will caution the government of fatal consequences of not adequately interacting with world? It is the educated galvanized people who can.

Examine hold ups

Higher education institutes world over are declared as primary engines of economic and social development. Our industry has under nourished the relationship with applied research, innovation, in engineering colleges and universities. Synergies in their relationship like in foreign are yet to be achieved. Inventors, discoverers, creators in colleges and polytechnics must have to be respected, honored and rewarded if these activities are to flourish. We must examine why such activities are not being conducted satisfactorily? Not many professors do research. What are the factors holding up? Policies and practices, visions and missions need reconsideration. Who will do it? There are thousands of eligible students who desire to take admission in higher education institutes, but due to various reasons they can not. The factors need to be identified and solutions evolved, to make accessibility easy.

What can we conclude?

Demand for higher education in decades ahead will grow exponentially. Advanced education will become even more pressing both for individuals and society. Education will change in profound ways; much of the change will be driven by market forces. We have to develop capacity in institutions to change. This is a big challenge before the nation. Universities must remove constraints. We can not afford to waste talent.

"Think globally, Act locally", is the first and fore most new role and responsibility of higher education institutes in the present stormy weather of global changes. They should not think routine way like bygone days. Globalization offers new opportunities and is a strong driver of change. Institutes have to perform differently. What is the new role institutes have to play? They have to look beyond instruction in class rooms become enterprising to generate new knowledge, new technology, patents & IPR so as to make knowledge society effective. Institutes should have to volunteer to show leadership in this noble cause.

Another new role is to **"Dream Big "Jump start technology clusters** attached to institutes using youthful talent for research and innovation. They are found to act as major contributors to regional development. Incubators, technology parks act as spark plugs for development. Institutes now should *have to produce not only graduates but produce entrepreneurs using New Technology.*

Thirdly, higher education in global circumstances has to aim at "**corporate development**." They must produce captains of world class industry. Building synergy between the education and business for national growth is essential. New technology is driving business to greater heights, requiring more skilled and flexible graduates. *Universities and corporate presidents should establish a new forum of partnership to achieve synergy.*

Fourth role is to take a special drive for advanced education. It is becoming ever more pressing both for individuals and society. Much of the change in higher education is being driven by research in technology and market forces. Institutes must take a new look at it, and on mass scale start M Tech and doctoral courses.

Fifthly, Indian Industry can no longer do all the research; it needs to survive by itself. Engineering colleges/ polytechnics, universities in partnership with industry may have to conduct research more vigorously. Leaders in education and leaders in industry must have to walk hand in hand together for national cause.

Last but not the least, Traditional regulations by universities and government in today's stormy weather of globalization do not suffice. Higher and Technical education must remove constraints, and introduce flexibility, and autonomy. Virtual and for profit universities from across the world are on the horizon, and posing a serious threat.

If higher and technical education is not revitalized in the light of above, opportunities will slip out of our hands and economic stagnation may result.

"If you charge education with the spirit of innovation, creativity, discovery then you do not have to do anything else, but if you do not do this and do everything else that is not going to matter much.

References

1. What Business wants from higher education, By Diana. G Oblinger and Anne-Lee Verville published by American Council of Education.
2. The Creation of the Future By Frank H T Rhodes, published by Cornell University Press.
3. Higher Education in Canada, Edited by Charles M Beach, Robio W Broadwayand R Marvin Melnnis published by Queens University press.
4. Universities for Sale, by Niel Tudiver,A Canadian Association of University Teachers Publication.
5. The Crisis in Canadian Universities Petrified Campus, By David Bersucan, Robert Bothwell,J L Ganatsein,Publishers- Random House of Canada.
6. Universities as Drivers of Regional and National Innovation, San Diago's Program for Hi-tech Entrepreneurship, By Julian R Betts and Carolyn W B Lee, pulished by Queens University Press.
7. Globalization, The Impact on our lives, By Rob Bowden, Rain tree Chicago Publication.

8. Globalization and the need for Higher Education Reform, By David E Bloom.
9. Innovation U-New Practices Enabling Cultures By Lous G Tornatzky.
10. Creating Knowledge- Strengthening Nations, The Challenging Role of Education Edited By Glen A Jones, Patricia L McCarney amd Michael L Skolinik, University of Toronto Press, 2002.

Chapter - 3

Adoption of Global best Practices in Universities & Colleges - the only way to Bring Globalization & Internationalization in Indian Higher Education and make it Globally Competitive

Synopsis

The paper outlines in brief the need & importance of adopting global best practices derived from world ranking institutions for adoption in Indian universities & colleges for globalization & internationalization. Thousands of students every year by paying huge amounts of fees are going abroad for higher education. Many of them do not return after studies are completed. It is a big brain drain so also money drain. So as to arrest the exodus of brilliant students it is essential to make Indian higher education globally competitive. In fact, so as to shape India's future in this competitive world the only way is to globalise and internationalise higher education and make it relevant to the jobs. The paper suggests strategies like establishing foreign collaborations and partnerships to immediately upgrade quality of higher education and empower youths to harvest vast opportunities available in world. This however is not an easy job. There are many challenges & difficulties. To meet them ably, requires lessons of experience from world ranking institutions. They need to be discussed, debated for adoption with suitable modifications, if any. Then India and its people will be able to harvest vast opportunities available world over. The achievement of dream of becoming a developed country by the year 2047 would also then become easy. Improving higher education is badly needed for it has a deep impact on trade & commerce, industry and economy. NEP-2020 aims to achieve this. Conclusions are drawn to globalise & internationalise education and adopt global best practices in universities & colleges.

Introduction

Higher education in India after independence in 1947 has progressed well in quantitative terms but in qualitative terms it is yet far too behind the world. Expanding horizons, visions & missions of leaders in universities & colleges through best global practices in higher education to meet local & global challenges is necessary. Strategic visions & missions from the world ranking universities like Stanford and MIT are derived and presented in this paper for adoption and implementation by Indian universities & colleges. Today leaders of Indian universities & colleges are found to limit their visions & missions largely to teaching and do not adequately reach to research, innovation & creativity. Organizational and management best global practices of foreign universities which are relevant to Indian situation and can make a big difference in them are also presented. New knowledge and new technology generation in Indian universities is far too low. Technology transfer from university to human society is far too weak. Marketing of new knowledge and technology from university to human society is almost absent. NEP-2020 has very ably outlined the challenges before higher & technical education in India. Now it remains for Indian universities & colleges to implement them effectively. Government is very serious about implementation, because it is the key to people's capability building. Indian youths in today's globalised world need to be nurtured to face not only local but also global challenges. Effective implementation of NEP-2020 is however not an easy job. It essentially requires the best global practices derived from world ranking institutions. Besides, every university & college must have to cope with global winds of change, welcome them and discuss, debate and adopt them with suitable modifications, if necessary. The purpose of the paper is to develop awareness among leaders in universities & colleges about best global practices. This does not require money but requires visions & missions of current best practices being followed by world ranking institutions. Capability building of human resources takes place in universities & colleges which in turn increases ability of people to see and meet challenges and harvest opportunities at local and global levels. Projects like Atma Nirbhar Bharat, Skill India, Make in India etc will stand to gain if Indian higher education becomes globally competitive.

If all the leaders in universities & colleges adopt the modern visions & missions, best global practices out lined here then Indian education will shoot over the world and undoubtedly Indian higher education will become globally competent and a great hub of education, bringing back past glory of Nalanda.

Should the universities & colleges have to prepare strategic plans?: Undoubtedly yes. Do the Indian universities & colleges have well prepared documents of strategic visions & missions? Are the plans prepared taking in to account aspirations of students, faculty, industry and all other stake holders including available global best practices? Are they well circulated to all ? The article suggests that every institution must after a thorough discussion among its stake holders prepare a written document of strategic plan, and circulate it to all concerned. Every institution should prepare this document scientifically taking in to consideration various alternatives along with possible combinations. Understanding of strategic visions, best global practices presented are also very crucial for effective implementation of the NEP-2020. An institution can adopt the global best practices in part or in full or in combination depending upon institutional situations. They are well proven practices which deserve to be adopted forthwith by each institution. This alone will make Indian education globally competitive and a hub of education as desired by government. There are a few challenges, difficulties in adoption and implementation. Indian institutions could undoubtedly ably tackle them and greatly benefit to make India in today's globalised competitive world a developed nation by the year 2047.

Need and Importance

Reforms in higher education are being implemented in all the universities and colleges. There is an acute need to boost up the exchange of faculty, exchange of students with foreign universities, and arrange many more international seminars and conferences. The progress is however, too slow. The prime difficulty is of mind set of key people which is insensitive. The mind set of authorities in government, UGC, and universities is however not adequately activated. Indian universities ought not to remain only "teaching shops" but become research, innovation and creativity oriented. UGC/ MOE ought now to draw out many schemes for liberal foreign collaborations &

partnerships, to create a country wide tempo for revamping of higher education. How can research be boosted in Indian universities & colleges to meet not only Indian but also global needs? This is a big challenge before Indian universities.

India in the recent past has initiated bold steps, like creating new eco-system for start-ups. This is most welcome. It is giving rich dividends and building a brave new India. However, this is not enough and there is a greater need of emerging technology based start-ups, which requires advanced research.. The bottle neck to become a developed nation is mainly in respect of research & innovation, of higher education in general and technical in particular. If the colleges & universities do not realize this it is less likely for India to become a developed nation by the year 2047. However with the present political able leadership in India it is hoped that it will succeed in effective implementation of NEP-2020

Prepare the Mindset of key people

The basic requirement for global competitiveness is to articulate for a positive change to global standard. Motivate and prepare **"Mind Set"** of all concerned authorities responsible for implementation. The concerned authorities are, namely Government central & state, UGC/ AICTE, University & college management, professors and students. They all need to fall in line and adopt the new thinking in favour of research, innovation and creativity. Indian education today is highly deficient in innovativeness. They should now in changing times not go any more for rote learning i.e. Memorization and mugging up but go for creativity, innovation and discovery. Mugging up should be discouraged. Coaching classes are growing faster than universities & colleges because universities are oriented to rote culture. The mind set of authorities has to be creativity and innovation focussed. NEP prescribes innovations like, product innovation, process innovation, financial and organizational innovation etc. to be undertaken in various projects and programs in partnership with industry. The present policies and practices, systems & procedures, visions & missions of universities & colleges need to be reformed in today's changed competitive circumstances. This is necessary to make Indian universities & colleges innovative, creative and become a world hub of education, as expected in NEP-2020. Education is now required to lay emphasis on teaching of research skills, innovation skills and entrepreneurship skills for which lessons from best global practices are useful. Preparing mindset of authorities and professors is a vital factor for success in implementation of reforms. Changing the mind set of higher & technical education key persons in terms of modern world will undoubtedly bring bright future for youths.

Change the "Mind Set" of key people, in College/ university for global competitiveness, is the central message

Today's globalised world is full of opportunities, truly unlimited. India wants to make most of them. Higher & technical education occupies high priority in Indian families and government. Youths are coming to universities & colleges in increasing numbers. They want better education. If the universities & colleges make use of best global practices given in the article the day is not far, when the institutions will flourish, fulfil the rising aspirations of people, and rise to greater heights to become a hub of education. Much of Indian & global humanity's problem solving potential resides within universities.

Following are the best global practices derived from world ranking universities which need to be urgently adopted in Indian universities & colleges.

1. Best global practice of Triple Helix model needed

Government would have to adopt "Triple helix organization model" in universities & colleges so as to make them globally competent. This model can be useful for more effective implementation of NEP-2020 also. Having NEP-2020 is good but not enough. Government ought to adopt Triple Helix model for more effective implementation. Developed countries like USA, European countries, East Asian countries like Japan, Korea, Hongkong, Singapore, China are using this model. They are greatly benefitted. By virtue of Triple Helix the quality and quantity of research in universities has improved, patenting & IPR has gone up, number of start-ups has shot up, Commercial exploitation of research output has increased, Collaborative research between academia and industry has increased, Quality of education in Universities has gone up. The model strengthens the National Innovation System [NIS]. It proposes that knowledge infrastructure of National Innovation System [NIS} be considered in terms of Triple Helix consisting of, 1. University- 2. Industry- 3. Government. Present isolation and independent working of the three Helices be given good bye.

Governments of various countries in the world are adopting knowledge based growth as a key driver of economic development. Developing economies like India are starting to adopt knowledge based growth. Universities are tending to become not only for teaching but also for research and innovation. Only those nations win in world which use and generate new knowledge, and new technology needed in society in various walks of life. As knowledge becomes an increasingly critical national resource of economic development, traditional knowledge generating organizations such as universities & colleges have gained more importance. So more universities and more colleges in developing countries are being set up. They are set up not only for teaching but also for research & innovation. Government of India now is giving more grants for research projects. Governments expects research results to be commercially applied in industry to increase quality, quantity of products and reduce their cost. National Research Foundation is established by government of India and it has earmarked good amount of money for research and innovation. Corporate social Responsibility [CSR] law is made by Government. Industry in partnership with university is starting innovation centres. Triple helix model of University- Industry- Government relations is observed to be giving boost to the third mission of universities to engage in Intellectual property[IPR] creation and technology transfer activities further downstream in society for human welfare. Via technology commercialization the knowledge bases in universities are effectively networked in to industry and Government sectors of the NIS. These entrepreneurial universities are observed then to be giving education to new generation to become more proficient in using more productive knowledge and bettering people's life. Countries like India may stand to gain. Now that Government is giving more importance to innovation, Patenting and IPR, organization of Hackathons, start-ups etc Triple Helix model becomes all the while necessary.

Who is using the model

According to this model universities in Silicon valley, Research triangle park, Boston area in USA are especially observed to be greatly benefitted. In this model Government gives research grants to universities, who produce research output, utilised by Innovation centres to produce IPR and ultimately used for commercial use in production in industry. Stanford university, MIT Boston and universities like Duke in area of Raleigh use this approach.

Role played by each component

Triple Helix model brings the three helices closer to each other. They share the responsibility and contribute to each other's missions & visions. They exchange ideas, participate in projects, give suggestions to each other to generate jobs, funds, productivity increase etc. The communication between the three increases from time to time, and they synergies with each other. The process is continuous, making each other fit in global environment. Thus the triple helix model of organization refers to a set of interactions between university, industry and government to foster economic and social development, as described in concepts such as the knowledge economy and knowledge society.. Each component plays a distinct role in the innovation process with universities focusing on basic research, industries producing commercial goods and Government regulating funding and markets. As these interactions increase, each component evolves and adopts characteristics of the other institutions giving rise to hybrid organizations. Government plays a crucial role in the Triple Helix model. Adopting this best global practice of using triple helix system will make Indian education globally competent.

2. Best Global practice of Autonomy in each university /college needed

The next best global practice, which urgently need to be adopted is "implementation of autonomy policy". Presently most of the universities and colleges are affiliating type. Wherever autonomy is granted government interferes with them and they fail to achieve the purpose. Foreign Collaborations will enable them for smooth transition from affiliating to autonomous status.

"The government is now willing to grant autonomy, then all universities & colleges must grab it. With autonomy our efforts and investment are likely to be more fruitful".

An autonomous institution signifies its overall ability to act by its own choices in pursuit of its chosen mission. Autonomy is a dynamic participative model of governance based on continuous evaluation of performance. Autonomy means freedom to think and freedom to act, but with accountability and responsibility. An autonomous institution has a inbuilt mechanism for continuous reformation. Autonomy is a world proven model of governance. All world ranking universities & colleges in countries like USA, UK, Canada etc from birth are autonomous. Autonomy has enabled them to achieve excellence. Institutions by practising autonomy over a period of years are found to become innovative and rich in terms of knowledge, patenting and IPR. Creativity and innovation, trust and confidence are the main pillars on which the institution rests. They attract brains from anywhere and everywhere in world. Scholars dream to study in them. Professors in these institutions not only teach and research but think great in global context and provide guidance to government, corporate sector, and public bodies in respect of public policies. It becomes a "Think Tank" for the society.

Indian Experience: For instance, Government College of Engineering Aurangabad, which is 65 years old has recently become autonomous. Now the college has a board of governors. The chairman is from IIT Delhi and 10 industrialists from local and state level industry as members. They meet frequently, and bring new ideas in the institution from time to time. The college is getting live projects from industry for research & innovation. The institution has been showing substantial improvement in quality of education. Research & innovation has been boosted. The confidence of students has improved. The competency of faculty has substantially increased. The burden of college examination on university is reduced. Results are declared in time, which used to be earlier delayed. The image of college in the eyes of state and central government and students has become far better. The college is getting more grants for research from AICTE and from industry. This was possible only because the college could become autonomous.

Do we want education to be relevant and purposeful? Do we want education to be innovative, creative and flexible enough suiting to the current local & global challenges? Do we want it to be qualitative and cost competitive? Should the institutions be producing new technologies, patents & IPR? Do we want education to be job oriented? Do we want to accelerate flow of new knowledge to the Indian people? Government aims high to make India a hub of education. This will not happen unless the colleges and universities are autonomous. Although the college has become autonomous it is not free to recruit faculty and staff. There are far too many restrictions from Government. If collaborations are made then they will use autonomy in true sense. IITs, IIMs were started under collaborations by birth as autonomous, and hence they are too good. Adopting this global best practice of Autonomy policy will ensure global competitiveness in Indian education.

3. Next best global practice needed is to appoint effective Board of Governors: The next best global practice is, authorities ought to have to appoint a forward looking BOG. BOG is ultimately responsible for effective implementation of reforms. BOG chair should not remain inert and passive. The chair has to be active and become a motivating force for principal, faculty and staff. The chair should have high ambition to take institution to greater heights. If the chair does not have ambition, in spite of potential the institution will not rise. BOG may have to learn, how to be further more effective from its counterparts elsewhere in the world. The chair has to articulate and pressurise Government on one side for more resources, and principal & faculty on the other side to upgrade education standard. Conferences and meetings should be held time and again for members of board and faculty to focus on current issues in education at national & international levels. Award winning scientists, industrialists especially those who are familiar with global winds of change in higher education should be given preference for appointment on the BOG.

Indian Experience: Shri Guru Gobind Singhji Institute of Engineering and Technology Nanded, became autonomous in the year 2003. The chairman then was from Pune, Mr Kalyani Chairman of Bharat Forge. He himself is a graduate of MIT Boston, USA. He brought many improvements in the institution, systems & procedures. Syllabi were greatly revised, orientation of courses was improved. He boosted the confidence of Students & faculty. Quality of education and research & innovation got a fillip. Still the BOG does not have authorities and powers like BOG in US universities. BOG is changed every five years.

Another example is of institute, namely " RIT located in Islampur," district Sangli. This institution has on its board of Governors renowned educationists from Bengaluru, Delhi, Pune etc. It has earned a fairly good reputation and stands high enough in NIRF. Students prefer to study here in small town institute than in big cities, like Kolhapur and Sangali. Best global practice will ensure effective BOGs. Adopting this global best practice of BOG is badly needed to make education globally competitive.

4. Best global practice is install Innovation centres to Reduce Unemployment: Unemployment in India is a big problem. Universities & colleges are producing a big army of unemployable graduates. Graduates have degrees in hand but no jobs. They are less knowledgeable, and not possessing necessary skills relevant to do the available jobs. Universities and colleges are supposed to provide relevant knowledge and skills. Education is not aligned with the modern changing globalised world. Universities do not cater to business supply chains, and they do not meet the talent needs of employers. They are diverse from the need of the hour. If the institutions focus on research & innovation, they will be able to envision the problem of unemployment in present & future and it can thus be solved. Professors need to be groomed to be not only teachers but also innovators. Institutions ought to give birth to New Technology Based Firms. Universities in developed countries are doing this and hence unemployment in those countries is far too less. Indian Universities need to be revitalised and made innovative & enterprising so as to ease the problem of unemployment. This is the urgent need of time. Every institution ought to install Innovation centre, Patent & IPR centre, Incubation centre etc in its campus. These centres will lead to creation of new technology, new kind of jobs and wipe of unemployment.

Indian Experience: The author served as mentor for University of Cochin in Kerala. He observed in this university that it started Innovation centre, Entrepreneurship centre, IPR etc. Many innovative projects & processes were developed here. Many students opted for becoming entrepreneur, thus making the problem easy for employment. NIRF of the university went up. Innovative culture is now established in this university. Students are preferred for jobs on global plane.

Best practice of Innovation Infrastructure has made the university more effective. Foreign collaboration may lead to higher degree of success. Adopting this global best practice of creating Innovation infrastructure will reduce unemployment.

5. Global Best practice of Research & Innovation is needed. The next strategy is, universities & colleges ought not to remain only " teaching shops" but in addition become research & innovation centres. Professors should not remain only "Teaching Professors" but become innovative professors. They are now expected to produce not only graduates but also new technology and new knowledge to cope with people's problems at Indian & global levels. Quality of education with research & innovations would then become far better. Professors & students have to depart from conventional policies & practices and adopt new in favour of global competitiveness. The institutions will have to expand their horizons to installation of innovation centres, technology incubators, research parks patent & IPR centres etc as recommended in NEP-2020. Necessary conferences, seminars, workshops etc may have to be arranged on large scale so as to prepare the mindset of concerned authorities in favour of productive jobs. Strengthening the board of Governors and reorienting them may have to be done. Deputing professors and board members abroad to world ranking institutions to learn from their experiences. Intellectual capital of university must be converted in to usable products & processes. Thus far industrial development of India was propelled by foreign collaborations. Now is the time, to develop with research & innovation indigenously. India desperately needs such a strategy to provide new generations with creative inclusive leaders who will come out of such institutions. Then only unemployment problem will go away. Universities & colleges should take Research & innovation seriously. Adopting this global best practice make education of high quality.

6. Best global practice of Start-Up, needed. Waves of technology are sweeping the world. Now is time to dream big, think great and take a jump start in creation of new technology for the future. The mindset of key graduates has to be in favour of "start-ups" in new technology based firms to be competitive at global levels. Institutions will have essentially to be enterprising. Role of colleges & universities in fiercely competitive world are changing. A new enterprising society is coming in to being. Institutions should therefore focus their attention on reorienting students for closer interaction with the world. They ought to become as competent as their counterparts in developed world. Start-ups in India are increasing, is a good sign. How to produce more entrepreneurs and how to encourage more firms to grow on national and global planes should be the main vision and mission of institutions. India needs to introduce entrepreneurship education in universities and colleges. Indian universities today are producing far too less entrepreneurs needed by economy. Hence is the need to adopt this vision.

- Stanford university of USA so far has produced more than 3000 startups. University has a venture capital which is given to entrepreneurs to star an enterprise. University makes an agreement with these entrepreneurs for payment of royalty to university after they may make profit, which is ploughed back for R & D and incubation of new entrepreneurs. This is not unique with Stanford but almost true for all universities. MIT Boston has a full Entrepreneurship Development department in which there are 6 full professors. They teach and promote entrepreneurship amongst young graduates. Will every university have a vision of start-ups? This will decide future of India.
- *Indian Experience*: College of Engineering Poona {COEP} has many alumni working in USA. All these alumni have contributed crores of rupees and constructed a big multi storied building for start-ups. The project is known as "Bhau Project". Every year it has been turning many start-ups. Foreign collaboration will enhance degree of success. Adopting this policy of creating start-up centres will soon make India a developed country.

7. Next best global practice is Accreditation of international standard needed: International education Standard in Indian colleges and universities to ensure recognition, and mobility of students, their career advancement, and availing growing opportunities in the world and to enrich human civilization is the need of the hour. Accreditation by standards of " Washington Accord" would have to be new emphasised. India without international standards is at risk. This affects the competency of Indian graduates and in turn of industry. NBA/NAAC should play a key role in solving problems like autonomy to institutions, commercial exploitation of research findings, marketing etc. and not remain a only inspection body. It should assert and be objective enough Without fear and favour, in public interest. Accreditation by international standards alone will enable India to be a hub of education. Many institutions have been going for NAAC and NBA accreditation. Adopting this policy of International standard in accreditation will certainly lead to global competitiveness.

8. Next best global practice needed is Continuing- Lifelong Education: India's ability to compete in international environment depends on the competency and capability of workforce, which in turn to a great extent depends on lifelong learning [9]. If lifelong learning is left to industry alone, short term profit considerations will dominate and preparation for the future will remain inadequate.. Hence Government's role in lifelong education is vital. Countries like USA, Finland, China France etc are leading in lifelong education. Hence they are far more ahead in the world. Universities & colleges in these countries are offering lifelong education and thus they have achieved and maintained a competent work force so also knowledge society so necessary for winning in world.

Boston university has a corporate training centre, in which courses are run for in service professionals. The author has personally visited this centre. Reading university in UK has also such a centre for lifelong education & training. The author was invited to lecture in this professional development course. Lifelong education should be the prime vision of universities & colleges.

Indian Experience: VJTI Mumbai has started and is running many courses for in service professional engineers. The image of the institution is high up in international global market.

Lifelong education vision made the VJTI shine. Adopting this policy of life long centre in all universities will give strength to Indian economy.

9. Next best global practice needed is" enable faculty in universities to grow to international standards". Next important strategy is to revise the service conditions of faculty and supporting staff. Professors should have an opportunity to travel abroad to attend academic and research meets, Each professor should have budget for research. This is necessary to attract the best talent in institutions. Universities will have to adopt marketing strategy so as increase their outreach and transfer of knowledge and technology to society, local as well as international. But for these strategies universities are likely to be isolated and remain as "Ivory Towers." Restructuring and repositioning of universities and colleges with respect to society and the world is needed .Strategy to convert intellectual capital of university in to usable products and processes is badly needed. India is at risk if professors do not have global visions. Today Indian universities are not counted in world because professors are not innovative and globally competent. Many universities have all the infrastructure needed except world class professors. If India enables professors to grow to world class status, we do not have to do anything else to succeed, but if we do not have this and do all other things, they do not matter as much.. Every institution should have a perspective plan and encourage its faculty to grow to world class standard. Every professor should have one leg in the institution and another leg in industry for innovation. This is to say that synergy ought to be maintained between industry and university. [10] Schemes for faculty growth to reach to higher standard ought to be designed, without which education may not improve. Professors are the active resources and they must be nurtured to international standard. Faculty growth schemes of international standing should be started by India government.

Indian Experience: SGGS Nanded is deputing its faculty to world class institutions like IITs, foreign universities for advanced education. The institution could greatly benefit from such courses. About 50 faculty got PhD from such institutions. Also they brought IIT culture in its working.

Strategic vision to enable faculty to grow professionally higher made SGGS Nanded. Adopting this policy of best global practice of lifelong education will undoubtedly enrich human civilization.

10. Next Best global practice needed is to create technology leaders & pioneers is next important strategy. Institutes will have to think great and dream big. India today does not stand high in world ranking. It is more because of lack of adequate visions & missions. It is not so much because India does not have resources. Professors are not aligned to research & innovation to meet Indian and global needs. Public service of university from teaching has to go far beyond to entrepreneurial activities like technology innovation, patent & IPR. These strategies if implemented will enable our universities & colleges to rank high in the world list. This is necessary to make India a developed nation by 2047. Indian and global needs demand that university leaders "think bigger". Visions & missions of every institution ought to aim at creation of technology leaders and industrialists.

Indian Experience: KK Wagh institute in Nasik has appointed an advisory committee to guide the institute for change in visions & missions. The advisory members are renowned educationists and industrialists. Meetings are held every three months to review the progress. The author is a member of this committee from ten long years. The institute has earned reputation and preferred by students for admission. It ranks high in NIRF. Adopting this policy of producing technology pioneers & leaders will make India shine in world.

11. Best Global Practice needed is using total quality management technique TQM: Indian universities and colleges must have to study the strategies, visions & missions adopted by world best institutions. Internationalism must have to become the trend. Can we create world class centres of excellence? Certainly yes, provided we adopt the strategies of TQM technique in each institute. We have to create a culture and mindset of people in favour of policies stated in NEP-2020.The priority given to S&T in national budget although increasing is far from adequate. Total Quality Management technique[TQM] is not being used in most of the institutions. So also scientific Strategic planning technique is not used. Under these circumstances the institution is not able to reach to its intended goal, even though the resources are abundant and NEP-2020 is good. A vision & mission specially devoted to Total Quality management ought to be provided. This does not cost money but it saves. scientific strategic planning. Strategy of bench marking will enable the institutions to transform the situation in higher & technical education to world class standard. TQM ought to be introduced in all universities & colleges.

Indian Experience: SGGS Nanded is using TQM in its organization & management. It is found to be greatly useful. Students are greatly benefitted and taking jobs in global market. Adopting this policy of using TQM will bring efficiency in Indian education.

12. Next best global practice needed is of Globalization, international collaborations and partnerships.

Globalization and internationalization brings vast opportunities to an institution. Its need and importance ought to be realised by all universities & colleges.

Globalization and collaboration means empowering professors & students. Globalization means making education globally competitive. Globalization means mixing of cultures, shrinking of time and space. Globalization means business at the speed of thought, instant communication, and instant decisions. Globalization means abandoning traditional methods, systems and procedures, in favour of modern which essentially makes higher education fit for today and tomorrow.

Globalization benefits human civilization as a whole. However, some benefit more than others. So as to bring more benefits to the People in India, universities will have to upscale the skills and knowledge of people, young and old. India is yet a developing country. It remained developing because its education so far was more localised and less globalised. Research & Innovation in universities & colleges was less emphasised. India can be a developed country only if the digital divide between India and the developed world is reduced. We must wake up to this reality and act fast to accelerate acceptance of globalization by international standard which demands open mind and higher priority to innovation & research. This kind of mindset alone will give boost to emerging technology and more successful start-ups at national and global levels. So as to harvest them demands hi-tech knowledge and skills besides positive attitude and ability to mix with the people round the world. Survival of the fittest in globalization is the law. There is a great impact of Hi-tech knowledge on jobs and business. Old outdated jobs with primitive skills are going out and new jobs with higher technical skills are coming in. Are Indian universities equipped and having a "mind set" to educate youths to cope with? Are they providing knowledge and skills required in today's global market? Universities ought to be enterprising in creating knowledge based society. There is however deficiency in Indian universities in this respect. So as to increase the priority of globalization Universities and colleges must have to take steps in the direction of globalization and partnerships and make them equivalent to counterpart institutes elsewhere in the world. Adopting this policy of globalization & internationalization will make Indian education globally competent.

13. Next best global practice needed is to attain synergy between industry and institutes is the next important strategy [14]. Industry-institute interaction is expected to become synergistic to enable both industry and institute win in competitive world. Industry is advised by NEP-2020 to go nearer to academicians, and encourage academicians to make innovations to bring India in line with developed world. This is necessary to make both industry and institute globally competitive. Industry is now expected to work with academicians and provide funding for research & innovations. Universities & colleges will have to grow to world class standard if industry & economy has to improve and reduce brain drain. Mediocre universities are more costly than the cost of their upgradation. Policy for industrial development and policy for higher & technical education at national & state levels should be made compatible to each other. Apex bodies like UGC & AICTE need revamping. Tripple helix system, namely integrated approach between Government, industry and university for higher education is suggested. Government has passed a law of, " Corporate Social Responsibility". Both the industry and institute ought to take benefit and associate with each other. UNESCO has prescribed this kind of partnership between the university and industry. It has started a program " UNISPAR" University industry science partnership and many conferences are held world over. Every university & college must have to initiate steps to achieve synergy between university & industry. Government should give awards & prizes to those who achieve synergy.

Indian Experience: University Institute of Chemical Technology Mumbai, has built a good synergy with industry. Almost every professor and many of his students are working on some problems of industry In India so also in foreign countries. Adopting this policy of Global best practice of Synergy between Education & industry will bring improvement in both of them.

14. Next best global practice is "marketing of universities" Marketing is a tool not only for corporate sector. It is a powerful tool even for universities & colleges to attract scholars and funding agencies. Universities & colleges have many strengths, like young scholars, labs, library, knowledgeable professors, and experienced alumni. They have good amount of new knowledge and new technology which is badly needed in society. An institution should adopt a strategy which will accelerate the flow of knowledge/ technology from university to society, young and grown-ups. Universities obtain patents & IPR which are needed by business & industry. They are innovative and they want to interact with business & industry, at global level. World ranking universities are marketing their strengths to the whole world. They are arranging many campaigns in India. They are reaching out to every alumni time and again with new developments in the university. Indian universities & colleges ought to resort to marketing like foreign universities. They have to attract scholars not only from India but from whole world. One day they will be ranking high in world list. Do you want the university ,college to be globally competitive? Then you have to adopt vision & mission of marketing. The author has found that almost all universities in USA, Germany, UK have technology transfer departments, selling patents & IPR. More you sell more you grow is their experience. Universities should not lag behind in marketing their strengths to society. Private universities and colleges in India are doing marketing extensively, but state universities are lagging. Adopting this best global practice of marketing universities will take education to all needed.

15. Next Best global practice needed is to mobilize alumni support: Mobilizing alumni support to the cause of education found to generate money and does not cost money, It gives joy to both the alumni & students. Creativity and imagination of both the alumni & students is enlarged. It also gives economic security to a nation .However, alumni support today is not fully mobilized in most of the Indian institutions. Indian institutions must without delay encash this support readily available at no cost. Foreign universities have gained a lot from alumni support. This requires Institutions to have a shared vision, shared ambition with alumni. Passion to make institution better, world class should be shared with alumni. They can suggest ways & means like in foreign. There is a tremendous strength, energy and global visions with alumni. An institution should not leave this alumni resource untapped. Alumni are the ambassadors of college. They are ready to give support and services to the college voluntarily at no cost. To make an institution world class for offering education to children and grandchildren alumni support is the need of hour. College should encash this valuable resource available at hand. Alumni have contributed immensely elsewhere in the world, they will contribute in your college/ university also.[16] Alumni can improve the universities & colleges to a great extent.

Indian Experience: SGGS Nanded has built a strong alumni network. Alumni meetings are arranged every year in the institution, so also in cities like Mumbai, Pune, also in Silicon Valley, New Jersy, Atlanta where there is concentration of alumni. Alumni have created a fund and constructed a canteen building for students in the institution campus. The alumni are giving feed back to the institution for revision of syllabi, and conduct of courses, to raise the college to meet local & global challenges in respect of manpower requirement and winds of change in technology. Adopting this global best practice of mobilizing Alumni support will strengthen education.

16. Best global practice needed is of Installation of Research Park: The author has visited Research Park at Madison University in Wisconsin state of USA. This park is installed by "Wisconsin Alumni Research Foundation" [WARF]. There are about 150 employees in administration and management. There are many companies in this park. The entrepreneurs & scientists deliver lectures to students in University. Many students work for the companies in the park. This park has given birth to many brand new technologies in association with university professors. The park is bringing out newsletter every three months. Many universities in USA & Canada have installed Research Parks. They are creating innovation infrastructure and making the region innovative.

MacMaster university in Canada has a Research Park, visited by the author. Toronto university has a Park known as "MaRS" Medical & Related Sciences, in which 6000 PhDs work in many companies. Berlin Technical University has a park known as WISTA. In UK parks are there in almost every university like Birmingham, Harriot Watt, Cambridge etc doing good work, and making education in association with alumni globally competitive.

Indian Experience: IITs in Bombay, Chennai, Delhi, etc and a few universities like Poona university have these Research Parks. They are doing good work and the scheme is progressing well. Department of Science & Technology Government of India has sanctioned more than one dozen Science Parks in various Universities. They are progressing well. Adopting this best global practice of Research Park will make Indian society innovative.

17. Best global practice needed is Preparing strategic plan document: Institutions are advised to use as many strategic visions as possible and prepare a document of strategic plan, in an open manner with the involvement of faculty, students and society. Various Indian Universities & colleges presently are in the process of implementation of NEP-2020. Government is pressurising them to expedite. It is hoped that the article will help them. Strategic plan has to be prepared in a scientific way as give in a chapter in the book written by the author published by X-press publishing Notion Press, Chennai "Insights in to Research, Innovation & Entrepreneurship." It is a step by step scientific process taking about 1-2 months. Only common sense is not enough. Adopting this best global practice of strategic planning will make Indian education globally competitive.

18. Best global practice needed is How to set up new Universities: The author has visited Harburg university in Germany. This university was started with the appointment of 15 distinguished professors as advisors "Mentors" to various departments from countries like USA, UK, Japan, Germany etc. The university started innovation centre, Research Park, Patent & IPR centre, technology transfer department from day one. New universities are being set up in various cities In India They ought to emulate the system which Harburg did. IITs were initially set up under the guidance of universities in UK, USA, Russia, Britan. So they are better. New universities in India without such mentors are tending to become far inferior. Renowned Professors as "Mentors" may cost to the university but this alone will ensure the purpose of setting up an university. It has to be realised that Cost is far too less than poorer quality of education, research & innovation culture .

In Berlin FREI university was started by purchasing a developed residential colony. The Government then did not want to spend time on construction of roads, installation of telephone lines, water supply & drainage etc. In India we build compound walls, roads etc. Adopting this best global practice of establishing new universities will bring high efficiency quickly in universities.

CONCLUSION

Adoption of best global practices derived from world ranking institutions undoubtedly will make Indian higher & Technical education globally competent. Foreign collaborations and partnerships is the only way to succeed in implementation .It is also the cheap and best mode. Universities & colleges in India today undoubtedly lag behind not because they are short of resources but because they are short of usage of best global practices. Mindset of leaders in universities is old, outdated and primitive teaching oriented and not research, innovation and creativity oriented. The leaders are inward looking and not outward looking, to winds of change in world. Triple Helix model of organization is needed to ensure success to bring organizational efficiency.. India so as to become a hub of education has to focus its attention on research & innovation. They have also to pay attention to knowledge & technology transfer to local and global society. Unless they adopt the best global practices as stated in this paper they are less likely to become a hub of education and attract students from foreign. Changing the "mindset" of leaders in universities & colleges is very essential to make education globally competitive. India ought to harvest innovation & creativity potential lying idle in youths and professors of the country. Effective implementation of NEP-2020 is key to development. India can hope to become a developed country by 2047 by adopting best global practices given in this paper. The impact of following these best global practices, on strategic visions & missions by Leaders in Indian Universities & colleges is indeed going to be great. India can soon become a developed country. Without adoption of best global best practices derived from world ranking institutions, Indian universities & colleges may miss the bus of globalization & internationalization.

References

1. Report from International Institute of Education planning, 7-9 Rue Engne75116 Paris.
2. National Knowledge Commission, Government of India, 2006-7.
3. American Council of Education, Shifting Ground -Autonomy- Accountability and privatization in public higher education, 2004.
4. NPIU-2012 World Bank supported initiative Good Practice Guide For Governing Bodies.

5. B M Naik, "Is the Role of Universities & Colleges Vital in Employment generation? Can they Afford to Ignore? At what Cost? Who Pays?" i-Manager's Journal of Management, Volume 17, No 4 April-June 2023.
6. James Duderstadt, "A university of 21st century, The University Michigan Press.
7. Naik B M, Higher & Technical education, Book of Knowledge, Gyan publishing House, New Delhi, 2010.
8. WOSA-12 World Summit on Accreditation-2012, New Delhi, March 25-28 Souvenir.
9. B M Naik, "Education and Leadership, Role of Indian universities & Colleges in Nurturing Future Leaders" Atlantic Publication 2018.
10. B M Naik, "How Can Universities & Colleges stand High in World List? I-Manager's Journal of Educational Technology," Vol. 20, No. 4, 2023.
11. Rhodes, Frank H T The creation of the Future, Cornell University Press.
12. Mohanty R P, and Lakhe R Handbook of Total Quality Management, Jaico Publishing House, 2004.
13. B M Naik "India desperately needs Synergy Between University And Industry To make Education Globally competitive" i-Manager's Journal of Economics & Commerce Vol. 4, No. 1, April 2024.
14. US Academy of Sciences, Report, Rising Above the Gathering Storm, 2007.
15. Government of India, NPIU,PIP2009
16. B M Naik, Insights in to Research, innovation & Entrepreneurship Xpress publishing Notion Press 2021, Challenge of NEP-2020 "Strategic Planning to make an institute Innovative and Enterprising" Chapter 10.
17. The Role of Universities in the National innovation Systems of China and the east Asian NIEs: An exploratory Analysis of Publications and Patenting Data By Poh Kam Wong, Asian Journal of Technological Innovation Vol. 23, No. 2, pp. 140-158.

Chapter - 4

Reforms in Governance & Leadership - Need of the Hour for Reimagining Indian Universities & Colleges

Abstract

India desperately needs good governance in colleges and universities so as to create a culture of innovation, and entrepreneurship so as to become & remain competitive in world market.

Synopsis

Poor governance and poor leadership is observed to be the root cause for all ills in university education. Indian students & professors are brilliant but unfortunately they have to work today under poor governance. Governance and leadership both at central and state levels is mainly responsible for poor educational standards. The governing bodies, namely MHRD, UGC, AICTE, Board of Governors, executive councils all, it seems, are not well familiar with the global winds of change. Truly, they are behind time. No wonder if Indian universities in spite of brilliant students and brilliant professors do not stand high in the world list. Thousands of students every year are leaving shores for foreign. To rectify the ills and to ensure educational quality India urgently needs to go first on priority for modernising governance systems, make them effective, imaginative and competent. They ought to engage fruitfully with the vice chancellors, principals and especially listen to the voice of students. In globalization education can best be shaped by adopting role models of only world best universities. National budget allocation to university education which creates vital human capital, which is a driving force for national development, is unfortunately observed to be dwindling. This is a major problem, and a challenge too. So as to build colleges and universities innovative, creative, and qualitative by world standards some suggestions are made in this paper. Strong leadership, distributed leadership and autonomy at the institution level is recommended. What kind of impact a professor makes on society and the profession of his specialization is of vital importance to take the nation to greater heights. Are professors competent by global standards? How can they be? Do the systems enable them to be so? Importance of education is outlined by Dr. Amartya Sen Nobel laurate which needs to be borne in mind. He says there is no better way for economic development of India than to educate people well. If India does not provide better education, and instead even if it implements reforms in all other sectors like food, water, electricity etc. that is not going to matter much.

Introduction

Indian universities after independence in 1947 have made great progress. From just a few, the number has shot up to more than 1000. The progress made quantitatively is indeed good. But qualitatively it is not. Universities in India do not stand high in world ranking. Times Higher Education agency of UK has declared world ranking of universities in 2019. It says there is no Indian university in first 300. Even premier institutes like IITs, IIMs, senior universities like Bombay, Delhi, Madras etc. by world standard are far too behind. Although brilliant boys & girls take admission in them their nurturing is poor. The students are not happy with the type of education they receive (National Knowledge Commission, 2009). They are not happy with the curriculum, teaching system, labs, innovation infrastructure and especially the lack of innovation approach with professors. They aspire to make most of their youthful time on capitalising new knowledge and new technology, but their aspirations are not cared for. They are disappointed. Service conditions and opportunities for growth of professors as followed in international fraternity are not available. They remain primitive, old outdated. Professors are treated as government servants and not as partners in institution building. There is an acute need to respectfully involve them in governance, without which professors are not able to contribute to the best of their abilities. On account of this, thousands of students every year are going abroad, a huge brain drain and money drain. They are going to countries like USA, UK, Australia, Singapore etc. They are spending huge sums of money, by one estimate it is equivalent to capital required for establishment of 3 IITs.

Why India does not have world class universities? Even small countries like Singapore, New Zealand with a population of around 50 lakhs have world class universities. But a big country India in spite of rich heritage of Nalanda, today does not yet have even a single. There is something seriously wrong in governance and leadership with apex authorities like MHRD, UGC, AICTE. Really all these bodies are behind time. This is reflecting on overall economic performance of India and standard of living of people. Often blame is given to shortage of funds. But this is not true. The governing bodies are in reality not managed & maintained by competent professionals. The governance and leadership at central government and state is far too poor, especially systems in governance. Besides, Key people in Governance are not keeping pace with global winds of change. Prime minister long back expressed his desire to bring at least a few institutions to top in world list. He has sanctioned the budget demanded, and full autonomy but still so far none could come up. The problem is not of money but of age old systems and procedures, visions & missions, policies & practices, to which we adhere. Do we have schemes and service conditions to enable a professor to grow to world class level? Secondly, do we have compatibility between industrial development policy and higher education policy? Unfortunately not, and these are two important reasons due to which we remain behind.

World ranking of universities has assumed great significance because those which rank high are found to produce globally competent professional and political leaders needed to manage affairs of a country from local to international levels. World experience tells us that in knowledge based economy of today, prosperity of a nation is driven essentially by leadership in research & innovation, which normally is grown in world class universities. Having world class universities in a nation is now a prerequisite to qualify for achieving developed nation status. Even if a nation is endowed with abundant natural resources, without world class universities, and especially world class professors it cannot become advanced.

Leadership in academics both at central and state levels is far too weak. To illustrate need & importance of leadership, there is a story of two armies. They were fighting a war with each other. One army say -A, had Lion as its captain but the soldiers were sheep. The second army say-B, had Sheep as its captain but the soldiers were lions.

Guess, who would win the war? The strategies drawn by sheep captain - B are like a coward sheep. Although there are so many lions in its army it loses the war. The lion captain - A, with sheep as soldiers wins because it draws bold strategies like a brave lion. The story underlines the role played and strategies drawn by leader. It is the leader that matters most. Today, students and professors in India are intelligent like lion but the strategies drawn by government leaders, its political masters are behind time, For example too low budget. When the new political party comes to power it uproots schemes of the previous government. They have no realization and gravity of the value of education in today's knowledge based economy. They provide so little only 3 % of GDP budget to education, when other countries provide up to 10. Consequently, leadership in various professions and in politics is not up to the mark. India remains behind in brain race and there is an exodus of raw brains abroad. India is importing hi-tech goods from years from foreign countries. Really, education policies should go on and on, regardless which political party comes to power.

One good thing finance minister has announced in recent budget of 2020 is of permitting Foreign Direct Investment [FDI]in education. With FDI coming, in author's opinion It is likely that foreign universities may set up their campuses on Indian soil. It is most wanted. This should have been done long back. But it is better late than never. Now some Indian study in them, as per systems and procedures of foreign. So also these universities may admit students from foreign countries. International mixing of students is possible, which is found to enhance quality of education. Indian universities public and private will have to face competition with them. Competition is said to be the best fuel for progress. Indian universities may then improve, without which it is less likely. Many committees and commissions in the past from 1966 have prescribed Autonomy to universities and colleges but they have not yet been implemented in true spirit, Government interference is rampant, it is pulling strings, causing harm to quality of education.

1. Discussions

1.1 what is Good Governance

An important characteristic of good governance is that of probity, that is to say working honestly, earnestly in a transparent manner with integrity for public good (USA Association of Governing Boards, 2019). Governing body should have to assert and be accountable to the interests of all stake holders. BOG of an institution should be thinking body, sensitive to world dynamics, preparing students for globalized world. A good BOG scientifically evaluates its own performance from time to time. It is a great fund raiser, from alumni, national & international sources. So the institution gets financial strength to implement plans for future.

Successful BOG is that which arranges written feedback from students, faculty, staff, alumni on quality of education, and makes strength, weakness, opportunities and threats [SWOT] analysis, and self-evaluation from time to time. This is a powerful tool to know where the institute stands today, and where it tends to go. The results of SWOT analysis need to be made known to all stake holders.

Good governance contributes to make its institution innovative in character. Innovative institutions produce professional and political leaders with higher imagination to become pace setters. Good governance creates conditions where students, learn not only known knowledge but can enlarge imagination to discover new what is not yet known. There is huge energy in Indian youths, yet too few become leaders in industry and pioneers in technology on global plane, because that is not what present institutes are teaching students to become. Good governance is needed to promote power of imagination of students in ever changing world. This is necessary to make them more compatible to opportunities and challenges arising in globalized world. Good governance is that which ignites the spirit of entrepreneurship, leadership, innovation and creativity.

Strategies for good governance should also include increased privatization but with public accountability and social commitment. Today private institutions in India are in abundance, mostly managed and maintained by political leaders. All is not well with them. A turmoil is breeding for they are exploiting students. Governance in them ought to be reformed for which they should keep in mind deeper purposes of education, should not exploit students but help. Governing body members should show statesmanship and use the institute as means to build national unity and to develop human resources needed by global economy. Another strategy for good governance is that which enables an institute to be technologically sophisticated and community dependent. Good governance builds synergy between institutes and local community. It sensitises institutions as well as local society. Good governance facilitates an institute to be competitive internationally. It is that which adopts policies and practices to address local problems with an eye on international. It provides Increased international mobility especially to professors and enables them to grow to world class level. Cost of providing international exposure is undoubtedly high but much less than hidden cost of not providing the same, for it keeps the human force behind.

Good governance creates academic partnership with many. It is both inward and outward looking, It should make alliances within the academic community, and new partnership outside it with communities such as local state and national agencies, corporations, libraries, museums, publishers and professional associations, scholarly societies and other institutions .It should establish closer collaboration with other education providers and users of knowledge including commercial vendors of education hardware and software, institutions that nurse public private partnership [PPP]. Success of an institution depends on how many partners it is able to carry with.

Universities & colleges will be successful only if the mechanism of good governance is adopted by using scientific approaches at all levels, namely Governmental, University, and college levels. The present orientation of Indian education is still based on rote learning, memorisation, rather than experimentation and creation of new knowledge. It is presumed in present system that knowledge is finite, already discovered and written up, so that a young scholar is needed to study and mug up the established facts. Research, discovery of unknown is not yet integral part of curriculum. This new vision must prevail.

Principal is the most important component of good governance (Naik, 2018). He ought to be a good leader, go getter, a magnificent speaker, a great writer, a good public relations man, a man of iron health, and stamina, married to a virtuous wife, having peace at home. He has to be a great individual, with great spiritual qualities, an experienced administrator, but able to delegate, and a great scholar, a social philosopher, raising pertinent questions to faculty and staff, in national interest. He should have first-hand touch with students in all disciplines. He should be converting negative energy of people in to positive. If you have a good principal then you tend to have good governance.

Good governance gives joy of work, joy of learning to everyone, student or employee. It has essentially to create a learning organization with learning individuals. Learning organizations continuously change with time. Governance has to be not imposing but discussing and debating. Disputation is the core of an academic institution. Dogmatic approach in dealing has to be discouraged. It has to create and continuously elevate its knowledge organization to successively greater heights. Good governance is that which maintains peace on campus.

India desperately needs world class institutions, which will provide coming generations with creative, inclusive, inquiring, engaged and enabling leaders. Brave new India of tomorrow is being created today in these temples of knowledge. Good governance is therefore urgently needed.

1.2 Role and Responsibilities of Board

Board of Governors to an institution is like navigator of a ship sailing in sea, charting the course by long range planning, and essentially using techniques of strategic planning, while the head of the institution is like a captain facing day to day operational problems. Both the BOG & the principal together are the key players to serve the educational interests of society (Glen et al., 2003). If navigation is proper the ship sails smoothly in intended direction. Good BOG ensures quality of education, ensures economic security to India and avoids technological obsolescence. BOG ought to provide adequate opportunities to professors to grow to the level they are capable for. It should install systems to enable them to grow to international standards.

The principal/Director is the link between the board and the campus. The principal is expected to provide leadership for all administrative arrangements for developing budget, admissions, examination, etc and overall effectiveness of the institution. Board & principal both delegate substantial responsibility to the faculty. Vigorous governance by faculty lies at the heart. The faculty, in one sense is the institution. They determine who should be admitted, what should be taught and who should graduate. Professors ought to be granted freedom to experiment in method of teaching, examination, industrial apprenticeship. Standard methods coming from yesterday needs to be questioned.

Faculty governance and responsibility remains at the core. The three, namely BOG, principal and faculty ought to clarify each other's roles, develop trust & confidence and provide able leadership. Differences in opinion some times are however, inevitable. Leadership at each level plays a vital role to bridge. The institutions ought to be granted autonomy, permitting them to swim or sink.

1.3 Effective Governance of the Board

The responsibility of the board is to govern and not to manage. There needs to be an absolute clarity and the distinction between the governing function of the governing board and executive responsibility of the principal and the executive team led by him or her. Governing function is described by the saying, "Noses in- Fingers out" (Rhodes, 2001). This is the tested advice to board members. Whenever and wherever there is foul smell in an institution board is expected to go to its roots, diagnose the cause and evolve solution to stop further rot. It may take help of internal or external agency to evaluate and correct. Good BOG should not tolerate the rot for a long time. Good BOG finds solution for every problem.

The most important single responsibility of the board is the selection, appointment, periodic performance review and continuing support to principal and faculty. The most effective boards are those that have developed a code of conduct and self-assessment practice of their own performance.

The institution is expected to provide salary, professional support, facilities, equipment and protection to academic freedom to professoriate, while the reciprocal obligations of the faculty member are not explicitly spelt out. Effective governance requires creating collective ambition, shared goals, dreams corresponding to counterpart institutions abroad, and that is the responsibility of the principal. Without strong and dedicated leadership of principal no system of campus governance can be effective. He should have the characteristics of a good academic leader. He must bear in mind that tomorrow's leaders, who are movers and shakers of the world, sit today in his classrooms and he should dedicate his efforts in that direction (NPIU, 2012). Following strategies are suggested for transformation to world class standard. People who know the global winds of change need to be appointed on boards. People with political contacts, who have no insight in technical and higher education, and who do not know the current trends should not be appointed.

1.4 Education does not grow where governance is ineffective. Government should orient governing members to world standards. Professors essentially need to be involved in governance (Naik & Kandlikar, 2010).

Universities abroad have installed long back Research Parks, Technology /business Incubators, innovation centres, start-up centres and Patent & IPR centres etc. These are the units which facilitate engagement of industry with institutes. Education in foreign has improved only on account of them. Have we done this? This is the role & responsibility of governing bodies to expand horizons from class room teaching to innovation, generation of new knowledge, new theories & new technologies. Knowledge is infinite. Students should learn to discover, innovate and start new technology based firms. universities have invested in buildings, equipment but not in research. It is mainly on account of the lack of research, quality of education is poor. Professors are engaged more in administrative activities, having no time to concentrate on research and teaching. Can installation of quality assurance cells provide an aid? Is it possible to create a culture of self- discipline and self-assessment? Do the institutions care to increase their influence and outreach beyond class room? Governing bodies have to learn how to be effective, from its counterparts elsewhere in the world. What is the use of governing body if it does not ensure educational quality?

1.5 Stop Political Interference in higher education. State governor should not be the chancellor of universities.

Brave New India of tomorrow is really being created today in universities & colleges (Naik, 2011). In this period of knowledge base economy creation of brave new India, as is aimed by present government largely depends on how well educated, knowledgeable and globally competent its men and women are. Government, is also ambitious to make India a 5 trillion economy. From experience elsewhere in the world it is observed that education of citizens holds the key to such efforts of national development. Nations where people are well educated, nations which have world class universities, develop faster. Universities produce professional and political leaders for various walks of life, such as engineering, law, medicine, education, agriculture etc. including those for politics and industry. They produce leaders to manage affairs at local as well as international levels. What kind of leaders, how resourceful, and how competent globally they are matter?

"Higher Education in India, however is in deep Crisis" [8]. Although thousands of graduates are available for jobs, very few, only 17 % are employable. We must realize that, the solution of virtually all problems with which government is concerned today like housing, environment, crime, low productivity, problems of defence, security etc. all depend mostly on availability of qualified and competent manpower and hence upon health of Indian universities & colleges. Political intervention in education has spoiled the culture in universities. It should be stopped forthwith and autonomy promoted. This is the experience and recommendation of several committees and commissions. Education should go on and on uninterrupted regardless which political party comes to power.

The stakes involved in higher and technical education are now too high. The post of Chancellor of universities cannot be left in the hands of a non-academic, non-professional, and political person, like the Governor of a state. The Governor has to attend MLAs, MPs and other important matters. Howsoever capable and competent he may be he cannot do justice to the chancellor's post. Observations made indicate that the bottleneck lies always at the top. Most of the times problems of higher education reported in many education commissions reports remain inadequately analysed and improperly action taken.

State Governor being a politician, brings politics to university. He does not hold any credentials what so ever in academics. Yet, he being chancellor of universities is authorized to choose and appoint vice chancellors. This is simply illogical. Often he selects V.C. on political considerations, selecting second grade when first grade is available. Higher education is spoiled by such structural defects. Foreign Experience supports this view. This is in the interest of youths of the country and their future. Stopping interference of politicians in universities is a critical requirement to reform governance in higher education, and to build a brave new India.

1.6 Universities have all the required resources at hand, to stand high in world list except good professors. Faculty growth in India is unfortunately neglected. It is necessary to revise service conditions and provide adequate opportunities of growth to PROFESSORS TO ENABLE THEM TO GROW TO WORLD STANDARDS. Do universities have vision and ambition to build great professors?

Professor is said to be the king pin in education (Technical Education Quality Implementation Program, 2009). His standing in his respective field of specialization largely decides the reputation of the institution he serves. Opportunities for faculty growth in India are far too weak, not compatible to enable them to become world class.

Research funds are not available. Sabbatical leave is not granted. Freedom to think and freedom to act is not available. These are the things necessary to enable them to build competency. Today, professors are critical to the success of universities, critical means if this is well attended Indian universities will rank high in world list, otherwise not. India needs to enable the professors to be of international standards and it should design schemes to make it happen. Indian universities without world class professors can never be world class and they will produce graduates only to become not leaders but followers, or copy cats. A professor ought to deserve as a knowledge leader, a thought provider of world standard to inspire both students and practicing professionals for innovation & creativity. They are an insurance agent against obsolescence of society. Professors are not meant to be simple teachers to teach yesterday's knowledge today, but they are supposed to be research scientists to discover new knowledge and new technology to teach tomorrow's knowledge today. Professors by virtue of their knowledge ought to influence the professions and politics to give a higher standing to universities in world context.

Research professors in universities abroad are allowed to continue research till they wish. Many Nobel Laureates are professors even in advanced age actively doing research in universities. They are allowed to guide students for PhD till they wish for example Dr. Amartya Sen even at the age of 80 has PhD students. In India, as soon as a professor retires from university at the age of 60-65 he has to stop taking students for PhD. This should be changed and brought in line with eminent universities abroad. Secondly, the duties and responsibilities of professors need to be well spelt out and given a mandate by law. In the absence of which many times professors are engaged by management in sundry non-academic jobs. Higher authorities mis use them and put a cap on their growth. A law should be passed in parliament specifically outlining the duties & responsibilities, so that professors can focus their attention on their core jobs. Professors should not be treated like other government servants. They are insurance agents against obsolescence of society. They should be allowed to spend one year in research and teaching in world best university once in 7 years. This is necessary to bring good policies and practices from world best universities. Education can reach to global standard only if professors are respected and allowed without diversion to do their jobs of research and teaching. Unless this is done Human Development Index of India which is as low as 130 will not improve. This is in national interest. Professors are not granted powers today which international fraternity is giving. These powers are usurped, and they have become humble servants. Professors, researchers, innovators regardless of age, from industry or state/ CSIR labs, academics should always be allowed to have a chair in college/ university. It is a usual practice in Germany. The author has observed this in Karlsruhe University Germany, that professors have two chairs, one in university and another in national research laboratory, so also researchers in national labs have a chair in university. This brings about integration and best utilization of research capabilities.

1.7 Governing bodies should MAKE GAP ANALYSIS with world best TO UNDERSTAND WEAKNESSES, and initiate corrective measures. Teach students to explore, enlarge imagination.

What is the difference between our institutes and counterpart institutes abroad? (Blom & Cheong, 2010). Why to call Indian universities good, and give them five star rank in accreditation if they can't produce employable graduates? Benchmarking with world best certainly provides a stimulus to creative thinking. Where lies the Gap? Can we not make up? In globalization India should benchmark with developed world. The gap lies in knowledge generation, Patenting, IPR, and Start-ups of New Technology Based Firms, Technology Incubator, Venture Capital Foundation commercial exploitation of technology, knowledge, technology transfer. The above-mentioned innovative and entrepreneurial directions in institutes abroad are found to make education relevant and purposeful. They teach so little, but more relevant. Universities' in foreign countries are found to function like a lighthouse for industry. They show a new way to human civilization. Professor's work hand in hand with students and form a community of learners, discoverers and innovators. It is therefore no wonder if best of brains from anywhere and everywhere in the world go to them. Institutes in foreign provide joy of learning, create impact by doing research & innovation on economy and increase the economic rate of return on investment. The contribution to advancement of human civilization is high. The institutes have come to be known as technology and wealth generating instruments. Nations become strong only if knowledge organizations are strong. Transformation process in India must now focus on producing not just graduates but able leaders, to become pioneers in scientific inquiry, and not mere followers of technologies generated elsewhere in the world.

Getting higher marks in examination is good but not enough. Students must learn to make business plans, finance and start New Technology Based Firms. They must learn discovery of new technology and obtain patents. They must learn to become pioneers of research-based companies like Elon Musk, who started battery operated electric cars, namely TESLA. How innovative students are should be the priority, rather than how much knowledge is stored in brain. When foreign students can learn innovation and patenting why Indians can't? Future belongs to those who understand this. Can academicians and institute's BOG take this as challenge?

1.8 Indian universities ought to play vital role in employment generation. UNIVERSITIES WITHOUT THE SPIRIT OF RESEARCH AND INNOVATION ARE IRRELEVANT, INCOMPLETE AND NONVIABLE IN MODERN SENSE. INSTITUTES MUST CONSCIOUSLY CREATE WELL water SPRINGS OF NEW KNOWLEDGE.

Universities ought to be innovative to play vital role in generation of hi-tech employment. For example, Stanford university in USA has so far given birth to more than 3000 hi- tech start-ups, employing millions of educated men and women, each earning high income. Universities in Australia, China. Singapore, New Zealand are not behind. Stanford University gets royalty, millions of dollars each year from these companies which is ploughed back in research to create further more new technology based firms. On the downstream side of these firms many jobs are generated in low tech. Universities in developed countries actively engage themselves in high end research, innovation and entrepreneurship. They obtain patents and huge royalty on commercialized patents. For example in mobiles, the material cost is hardly around Rs. 500 and the rest is royalty earned by patent holders for patents used in mobile. Besides, a phenomenon is observed, world over, that hi- tech industries especially research based companies are flocking around advanced research & innovation centres in universities for brand new ideas, providing plentiful hi- tech, hi- pay jobs, which creates many more downstream low end jobs like selling, maintenance etc. Do universities in India have a mission to give birth to such hi-tech firms? Do they engage in high end research? Have they installed innovation infrastructure? Why they do not yet have when universities abroad have from many years? Indian universities have high capabilities but unexplored. They lack in global vision, strategic planning, and bench marking with world best counterparts. This leaves education handicapped which is the main reason for low employability of Indian graduates, {only 17%}and consequently India remains a less developed country, in spite of high potential.

World experience tells us that vast bulk of job growth comes from advances in new knowledge & new technology being generated in universities, rather than resources like land, labour and capital [Robert Solow Nobel Laurate]. India so as to generate jobs ought to focus now its attention on hi-tech innovation, research and entrepreneurship. So as to increase much desired employability of students it is essential now in universities to emphasise on innovation on the lines of Stanford. Increase in state budget for research and innovation is strongly recommended. Not investing adequately in higher education is like planning for failure which results in slowing down the pace of Indian economy.

It is a high time to realise that the key factor behind unemployment in India is insufficient innovation and insufficient entrepreneurship. Innovation is a strong stimulant. persons with innovation skills in India are in short supply. This is the major barrier in job generation & economic development. An innovative person has a mission in life, which gives him extra energy and purpose. He consistently strives to improve. He is always dissatisfied with the prevalent. He wants to create new and again new. Innovation is progressing constantly on the efforts of new ideas of such persons. Can our universities produce such innovative graduates more in number? Then graduates will become job generators, and unemployment will go away.

Shall we not adopt strategies in favour of innovation in university education? Can universities afford to ignore this legitimate role? At what cost? Who pays? It is said students who learn innovation in young age practice it lifelong. They become job generators. There is a great influence of universities on innovation capacity of a nation. Nations which lead in innovation take away jobs from those who lag. Innovative students and innovative professors are found to show a lead in start-ups in new technology based firms. According to a study as many youths are unemployed in India so many jobs are awaiting able men and women with requisite skills & knowledge. Today opportunities for employment are growing in one direction and our education is growing in another, resulting in mismatch. Consequently, thousands of dissatisfied students are going abroad, by paying huge sums of money, a huge brain drain and money drain. Indian universities in the absence of innovation infrastructure are behind time, which is very costly. Cost paid is very heavy, it is the students who pay in terms of their future life. India should have to put conscious efforts to avoid this.

The challenge before India now is to reimagine and equip universities & colleges in respect of innovation infrastructure to achieve desired target of job generation. Universities in India should make a beginning to play this role effectively. If they assume innovative character unemployment will be no problem, otherwise it will remain a dream. Governance & leadership in India needs improvement.

1.9 UGC, AICTE, MHRD and UNIVERSITIES SHOULD BE keeping in view WINDS OF CHANGE IN WORLD. THEY HAVE SO FAR UNFORTUNATELY BEEN BLIND TO WHAT THEIR COUNTER PARTS ELSE WHERE IN THE WORLD ARE DOING

The above bodies now being merged in NHERA are empowered by law not only to drive the routine administration, in which they seem to be too engrossed, but also to redesign the engine of higher & technical education from time to time and keeping it competitive and fit by global standards. Have they drawn any circular to promote patenting? Have they set up any committee to set up patent culture? They thought that it is not there business. But they ought now to focus on commercial exploitation of research outcomes. This makes the institutions qualitative and yet financially more viable. This attracts investment from industry. UGC and AICTE in the past have totally neglected these things. Consequently the whole nation is a loser. We have been caught today in the death trap of a too centralized model. The over centralized planning has crippled the innovative thinking of the youthful talent in universities. They don't look to world outside.

1.10 Innovative, creative, accountable & effective BOG is the need of the hour.

Many Indian Universities and colleges have all the resources at hand. They spend money more than necessary, but in return they do not gain quality. Why? Studies show they do not have proper visions, missions & commitment to excel. Indian universities lack systems for quality assurance, quality policy, quality manual, quality planning & monitoring cells, and mechanism for periodic internal & external review. They lack methods and not the resources. They lack force in their action. Professors attention is diverted to non-priority activities Working hard by principal alone is good but not enough.

BOG together with the principal sits in driver's seat. They both jointly with faculty & staff are responsible for educational quality. It is observed that quality of education is as good as the imagination, visions and commitment of the board for the cause of education. If the board is excellent the quality of education is most likely to be excellent. BOG needs however, to envision new goals from time to time to cope with emerging opportunities and challenges in globalized world.

BOG is the chief fund raiser, raising funds with imagination from national and international sources. So far, colleges have neglected alumni as a source of money and ideas. Involvement of alumni to ensure quality education is essential to make institutions world class. Board needs to engage appropriately with the principal, activities in college and alumni. BOGs are increasingly being appointed in more & more colleges private & public, which is good but it is better if board is consisting of visionary, imaginative, and responsible professionals. Nobel Laureates, Bhatnagar award winning scientists, industrialists and Fellows from Indian Academy of engineers [INAE], distinguished professors if appointed on board, they will make a big difference. Great leaders matter. World experience tells us that BOG of an university serves the nation better in inculcating human and ethical values if it is protected by legislation from political and bureaucratic interference. Board chair should be as far as possible an eminent industrialist, educationist, committed and competent for the cause of education. Successful boards have a culture of periodic scientific self-evaluation of college and all authorities including board itself. The paper provides a base for brain storming. It is high time that BOGs are created and activated to become an effective force in enhancing quality of education to world class level.

1.11 Landscape of university education in the world is changing fast. How can India cope with?

Knowledge is becoming the driving force of world economy, obviously so knowledge institutions like colleges & universities are achieving significantly high importance. Providing good governance to them for improving quality and relevance of education has become of paramount importance. Good governance & distributed leadership is important for their own health & the health of Indian economy. It is the prime responsibility of the head of the institution, together with BOG. An institution in spite of all the resources at hand without good board may falter and lead to autocracy and disrepute.

Which government does not want to generate hi - tech employment, high pay international jobs, spur industrial growth, and make education globally competitive? Industries, world over, are seen flocking round the advanced knowledge centres to obtain brand new ideas for global competitiveness. Institutes must have original knowledge springs like well water springs. They must have a mechanism to convert intellectual strength in to usable goods and services. Role of higher education has emerged central to industrial and economic development, in creating India's future. Industry is now research driven. Association with industry, venture capital firms, international agencies who succeeded in this cause is essential. Will governance facilitate to build bridges? A bird can fly high in air if it has two wings. Similarly Indian economy needs two wings namely, industry and institute. The two wings must be equally strong and operating in harmony.

Education does not grow where high end research is absent. The paper prescribes "dream big and think great. They should aim high at technology generation, technology diffusion, which is achieving high significance in enabling a student to win. The paper emphasizes adoption of new organizational inventions like Research Park-Technology Park, which when implemented will contribute to India's international competitiveness. The institutions should have now to look beyond the traditional lines of teaching and learning and adapt to corporate development, and help industry to win. They should have to restructure themselves to become fountain heads of new knowledge and new technology. They should deserve the status of "Light House" for industry. Synergy between industry and academics in this cause is vital. Parks play a middleman's role in this. They have enhanced the scholarship of universities/colleges elsewhere in the world. They jointly can give economic and political stability to India. Will industry- institute interaction become a national priority? The paper recommends especially these roles for BOG for reforms in the light of experience elsewhere in the world.. Practical should prescribe discovery, innovation and not merely to test old theories.

The innovation centres, incubation centres, research parks, patent & IPR centres belong to one family of innovation, for taking new knowledge and new technology to well being of human kind.. They are an asset to university and not a liability. These centres generate income for the university and for the country. Research Parks are a source of income to universities. If the universities have land they can make a source of income to subsidise education. The experience of the world is that, research and innovation subsidise education and education subsidises research & innovation. They together are known as wealth generating agencies The initial capital investment is paid back by these centres in a period of about five years. To illustrate in Toronto university there is a unit known as MaRS {Medical and Related Sciences} which is housed in 17 big multi-storeyed buildings, created out of income from MaRS. There are 6000 PhD degree holders working in this centre. The author has personally visited MaRS, met the founder Professor Dr Evans in the year 2007, the he was 90 years of age. He started MaRS in one room In 1950. What is true for MaRS is true for all such units all over the world. Innovation and entrepreneurship is a forward linkage of the university education. It is found to make education on qualitative and purposeful.

University Related Research Parks Association (URRP) conducts courses for personnel from universities which are intending to start Research Parks. These courses are very useful, so is the opinion of successful persons from research parks in operation. Macmaster university Research Park in Hamilton its chief from Canada expressed this opinion during the author's visit to park.

Conclusion

Grip of government on education should be reduced. Governor of state should not be the chancellor of universities. In public interest, in the interest of young boys & girls government should not fear for taking hard decisions.

Benchmarking with governance systems of world best institutions followed by strategic planning is the need of the hour. This is the only way to build world class Institutions.

Is there a peace on campus? Then the governance is good.

Indian universities have all the required resources at hand to improve world ranking except good professors. Faculty growth so far is neglected, This is the weakest point of governance. Can we make it strong? Mindset of professors in favor of innovation & entrepreneurship has to be built. Enabling professors to be of global standards should be the vision and mission of universities & colleges.

Who is responsible and accountable for raising the educational standard? It is none other than Governance and leadership at state and central levels.

Joint meetings, group discussions and conferences should be held for governing body members time and again to update them on current public issues in education, at national and international levels.

If governing bodies make a commitment to change, change to world class level is undoubtedly possible. Only those who work with optimism and "can do" approach are likely to win.

Are students learning what they need to thrive in 21st century?

Governing bodies should be conscious that tomorrows leaders, professional and political, are sitting in their class rooms. Do they nurture them to become globally competent leaders in their chosen fields of specialization?

What is the next big thing for BOG to do? They have to install Quality Assurance Cell.

There is a tremendous strength in collective wisdom and collective ambition of faculty and alumni. Colleges should harness alumni strength without delay. No institution can provide all the services needed all alone. It must be backed by ideas, experiences and feedback from alumni. They are learned and experienced ambassadors of college. No university has grown to greater heights without alumni participation.

Do the governing bodies provide attractions for researchers, innovators, discoverers regardless of their age, cast creed and place of their work?

Create culture of innovation and attract innovators. Award winning scientists, leader in industry if appointed on board will they take the institution ahead of time. Faculty growth to excel in innovation & research must be ensured. Universities should prescribe laboratory work to generate new knowledge and new technology. It should not limit to only testing yesterday's theories & knowledge

What crucial topics should figure on BOG agenda?

Expanding horizons of the universities & colleges to install research parks, technology incubators, and patent & IPR centres should now be the first and foremost item on agenda. Budget for these schemes ought to increase.

Government should put its full trust and confidence in governing bodies of universities, and empower them to function without government intervention. They may sometimes fail, but we know failure is the high road to success.

References

1. **National Knowledge Commission. (2009).** *National Knowledge Commission Report to the Nation 2006-2009.* Government of India. Retrieved from http://14.139.60.153/ bitstream/123456789/112/1/National%20Knowledge%20 Commission-Report%202006-2009%20.pdf
2. **USA Association of Governing Boards, AGB. (2019).** Newsletter.
3. **Naik, B. M. (2018).** *Role of Indian Universities & Colleges in Nurturing Future Leaders (2nd ed.).* New Delhi: Atlantic Publication.
4. **Glen, A. J, Patricia, L. M., & Michael, L. (2003).** Creating Knowledge, Strengthening Nations, *The Changing role of Higher Education.* University of Torronto.

5. **Rhodes, F. H. T. (2001).** The Creation of the Future: *The Role of the American University.* Cornell University Press.
6. **NPIU. (2012).** World Bank Supported Initiative. *Good Practice Guide for Governing Bodies.*
7. **Naik, B. M., & Kandlikar, W. S. (2010).** *Higher and Technical Education: Book of Knowledge.* Gyan Publishing House.
8. **Naik, B. M. (2011).** Indian colleges and universities need good governance & leadership for the future of children & grandchildren. *Journal of Indian Technical Education,* 34(2), 37-47.
9. **Technical Education Quality Implementation Program (TEQIP) (2009).** *PIP Department of Higher Education. Government of India.*
10. **Blom, A., & Cheong, J. (Eds.). (2010).** *Governance of Technical Education in India:* Key Issues, Principles, and Case Studies. The World Bank.

Chapter - 5

How can Universities & Colleges Stand High in World Ranking?

Abstract

The world ranking of universities has assumed great significance because those that rank high are found to produce globally competent professional and political leaders needed to adeptly manage the affairs of a country from local to international levels. World experience tells us that in the knowledge-based economy of today, the prosperity of a nation is essentially driven by leadership shown in research and innovation, which typically flourishes in world-class universities. Having world-class universities in a nation is now a prerequisite to qualify for achieving developed nation status. Even if a nation is endowed with abundant natural resources, without world-class universities, it cannot become developed and remains a developing country. There are many universities in India that have a good amount of money and excellent infrastructure, yet they do not rank high on the world list. They have all the required resources at hand except for good professors. Unfortunately, in India, faculty growth is neglected. Outdated rules and regulations and service conditions have constrained professors, preventing them from performing to the best of their abilities. This is the main bottleneck. Their service conditions urgently need to be reengineered along the lines of the world's best universities, without which India is less likely to rank high globally and, in turn, become a developed country, as is eagerly desired. Each university and college should have a mission and ambition to build its faculty to a world-class level.

Keywords: World Class Education, Brain Drain, Leadership, Synergy, Research Park, Incubation, Faculty Growth.

Introduction

"Where do you produce global leaders to make a nation developed? It is said, Seeds are sown within the four walls of class rooms"

A small country like Singapore, with a population of about 56 lakhs, less than half of Mumbai, has three world-class universities. Canada, with a population of 4 crores, has 10 world-class universities. These small countries have become developed mainly because of their excellent professors in universities. However, India, with a population of 125 crores, has only mediocre universities and has thus remained a developing, poor country. Why can't India create world-class universities? The government and academicians must address this question and find a solution. India is not short of resources but is short of world-class professors. India lags behind mainly because of its poor education system, particularly in higher education (Naik & Kandlikar, 2010). It lags in the brain race and therefore remains a poor country. Do we realize this? Indian universities, in a global context, are categorized as mediocre; they are not considered, which does not speak well of the government and its academia. Who is at fault? Both. How to correct it? Who is to initiate change? Governance of universities at national and state levels falls too short of requirements. The rules and regulations, stemming from tradition, are outdated and not conducive to enabling a university and its professors to be world-class (Duderstadt, 2009). Professors retire too early at the age of 60, whereas abroad they work much longer. Professors like Nobel Laureate Dr. Amartya Sen were active even at the age of 80. Professors are found to guide students for PhDs until they wish, whereas in India, soon after they retire at the age of 60 or so, they cannot take on new students for PhDs. Truly, Indian universities lack global visions and missions, good policies and practices, and a collective vision, mission, and ambition to make a mark in the world (Naik & Kandlikar, 2008). India today follows technology rather than leads it. Yet, India aspires to be a technology powerhouse in the near future (Rhodes, 2001).

India has initiated schemes such as Atma Nirbhar Bharat Abhiyan, Make in India, Startups, Research Parks, Skill India, Smart Cities, etc., aiming to bolster high-tech, high- income employment opportunities for the younger generation. However, the effective implementation of these schemes hinges on the presence of world-class professors and universities. Universities serve as the bedrock of these initiatives; unless they achieve high global rankings, their ability to produce globally competitive graduates is compromised (Zhao, 2004). Consequently, schemes like Atma Nirbhar Bharat are likely to encounter reduced success. Historically, India's industrial development has been driven by foreign influences. However, the nation now aspires towards nationally-driven import substitution under Atma Nirbhar Bharat. This paper identifies the factors contributing to India's academic mediocrity and proposes strategies to elevate professors and universities to world-class standards. Without enabling universities to achieve world-class status, India will lag behind the global curve, leading to a continuous brain and financial drain as talented students seek education in foreign institutions, potentially never returning home (Naik, 2012).

The Prime Minister and President of India are publicly declaring time and again their determination to elevate Indian universities and colleges, at least a few, to world- class standards, ranking high on global lists. The government is keen and allocating additional funds, presuming that only money is required. However, this presumption is not entirely correct. Many universities and colleges in India have ample financial resources, good infrastructure, and brilliant students, yet they do not rank high on the global list. The UGC and MOE are unable to weed out old, outdated rules and regulations. Indian universities lack an academic culture and mindset that favors professors, especially in terms of their growth opportunities. It is the professors who bring fame to an institution or university, and hence they need to be empowered to excel and reach global standards. The government ought to give more importance and delegate authorities and responsibilities to professors, as is done in the USA, Germany, and other countries.

In this regard, it is worth learning a lesson from the USA on how it made remarkable progress and surpassed European countries. The third president of the USA, Mr. Thomas Jefferson [1801-1804], provided support to universities and their professors to elevate their status globally. He emphasized to Americans that unless USA universities excel and surpass European universities, the USA's economy and industry will lag behind European countries. If the USA aims to lead globally, its universities and professors must first achieve top positions. Today, eight out of the top ten universities in the world are from the USA. The world's brightest minds aspire to study in US universities from all corners of the globe. The majority of the world's intellectual property is owned and held by Americans, making the USA an economic, technological, and political powerhouse globally. India's dream of becoming a developed country will not materialize unless its universities and professors, at least a few, attain world-class status.

The Indian government ought to realize this and act fast to correct it. Any amount of investment in infrastructure, as proposed by the prime minister, without concurrent faculty growth will not work.

1. Why India Needs World Class Higher and Technical Education Institutes?

The strength of a nation or region is measured not only in terms of the size of its army or arsenals but also by the scientific and technological capabilities of its people, which are primarily nurtured in good institutes. World-class institutes are known to produce graduates who pioneer new knowledge, technology, and theories ahead of others (Jones et., 2005). The direction of universities is increasingly geared towards industrial development. World experience tells us that it is these world-class institutes that drive industrial development. Presently, India follows technology rather than leading it. Previously, industrial development in India was largely driven by foreign influence. However, there is now a desire for domestically-driven import substitution. The meaningful implementation of Five Year Plan schemes requires competent leaders across various professions such as engineering, industry, trade, and commerce, who can be nurtured not by mediocrity, but by world-class universities.

Indian institutes are on the brink of becoming redundant, not counted, not preferred, and having less significance globally. Small countries like Singapore, Canada, and Australia, despite their smaller populations, boast world- class universities. It is in these small countries where thousands of students from countries like India go for higher education every year, paying huge sums of money. By one estimate, Indian students going abroad collectively pay enough money to build 20 IITs. They are subsidizing higher education in the USA and other countries. Many Indian universities have good infrastructure, but they lack world-class professors and academic culture necessary for an institute to be considered world-class. In the absence of world-class universities in India, foreign universities are entering the scene, and brain drain is occurring on a large scale. World-class universities and professors are needed to arrest brain drain. Does a university have the vision and ambition to cultivate professors of world-class standard? Are the professors themselves striving to achieve world-class status? Unfortunately, not. Until the professors become world-class, universities, and the Indian economy, despite all their resources, will remain lagging. The per capita income of India is around Rupees 2000, whereas that of the USA is more than 30,000.

India urgently needs to establish world-class technical institutes and universities in order to achieve its dream of becoming a developed nation and a leader in the world. The presence of such institutions has now become a distinguishing feature, setting apart developed from developing countries. World-class universities play a crucial role in producing globally competent professionals across various fields, including engineering, industry, commerce, trade, politics, and administration, enabling them to effectively manage the affairs of the country at local, national, and international levels. It is believed that the seeds of leadership are planted within the four walls of classrooms (Naik, 2019). Effective leaders are essential to expedite the process of national development. Leaders educated in world-class universities are known for their competence in harnessing the physical and financial resources of the country, thereby facilitating meaningful and purposeful development for human welfare. Hence, the establishment of such institutions is imperative. It is the world-class technical education institutes that produce competent human capital, which in turn produces financial capital and other resources. This is essential for removing poverty and increasing the standard of living of the masses. Mediocre institutes produce mediocre leaders, while world-class institutes produce globally competent leaders. Nations, even if endowed with ample natural resources like minerals, land, and water, are less prosperous without the presence of good institutes. People need access to the latest knowledge and technology, which often emerge from world-class universities.

India has remained a low-income economy despite having abundant natural resources. With priority, India must build universities offering education of world-class standards comparable to counterparts in developed countries. The government must take steps to make universities world-class. According to a report published in May 2017, the total research output from 800 Indian universities, IITs, and IIMs is not equivalent to the research output from just two universities, namely Stanford and Cambridge. All the problems in a nation, such as poverty, crime rate, unemployment, communal conflicts, and terrorism, stem from an insufficient education system and its poor quality.

2. Strategies Needed to Make Universities and Colleges World Class

Professors matter most, they are key players. They need to be empowered as a top priority to reach world standards. Professors possess the necessary intellectual potential, yet due to poor service conditions and a lack of world- class growth opportunities, they often engage in politics instead of focusing on academics. For instance, professors often lack adequate research budgets and have limited opportunities to work abroad or collaborate with industries nationally and internationally. Universities lack a scientific approach and autonomy in their planning and governance. How can a good academic culture be fostered if professors do not have access to essential facilities such as sabbatical leave? Professors retire too early, just as they are reaching the peak of their wisdom. The Indian government must reform policies, practices, systems, and procedures, and adopt new strategies to govern universities. India should learn from global experiences. There should be no mandatory retirement age for professors; they should continue guiding students for PhDs for as long as they wish. Indian universities must embrace research-based approaches, not solely teaching-oriented ones. Professors are pivotal in making a university world-class. Their service conditions must be reimagined in alignment with those of the world's best institutions. The enterprising culture, autonomy, growth, and innovation opportunities necessary for professors to excel globally must be promptly provided (Naik, 2021). Research should be their primary focus, supported by teaching, as seen in the world's leading universities (European Commission, 1995).

There is an urgent need to establish synergy between universities and industries, commencing from the highest levels of ministry. Policies governing industrial development and those concerning higher and technical education in India are not aligned; they lack congruence. This misalignment leads to subpar achievements in both sectors. Notably, the interaction between universities and industries in India is glaringly absent. These entities are meant to be mutually supportive, rather than independent or isolated. There should be significant interfacing between the two, yet both neglect this crucial aspect. Consequently, there is a lack of synergy, shared vision, and collective ambition for national and state-level growth and prosperity.

For example, industrial corporations are planned and implemented by the industry department with huge sums of money, without any financial inputs for research and innovation in local universities and colleges. As a result, industries do not get solutions to their problems and have to import technology from abroad, at heavy cost. Consequently, they remain technology followers and do not become leaders, remaining less competitive, and eventually becoming stagnant. For instance, the Delhi- Mumbai Industrial Corridor project is spending millions of rupees on land, buildings, roads, water supply, and electricity but not allocating a single rupee to strengthen research and innovation in local universities and colleges. The skill set demanded by the industry is not provided by universities, and what is provided is not useful to the industry. There is a significant mismatch, which through interaction can be avoided. It is believed that even if the industry and universities have all the resources at hand, but lack synergy between the two, India will lag behind the world. There is no feedback obtained from industries about the education and research conducted by universities, resulting in a mismatch between education and industry expectations. On one hand, there are many educated individuals with degrees in hand, but they are unemployable. On the other hand, industries are not getting the right type of people they are looking for, hindering their growth prospects.

Universities were once mere reflection centers, teaching knowledge imported from abroad. Now, they are expected to be innovative hubs, fostering advancements in knowledge, technology, and the creation of high-tech start-ups in emerging fields. They must serve as idea generators. Without synergy between universities and industry, both will lag behind the rest of the world. The government should initiate an Adjunct Professors scheme, bringing professionals from industry to teach in universities. Twenty percent of professors should belong to this category. This aligns with the global trend of providing students with practical and professional insights alongside theoretical education. Classroom teaching alone is insufficient. Adjunct Professors are crucial for imparting practical experience within traditional educational settings.

We need to install innovation centers, incubation centers, and Research Parks in each university. Innovation-IPR is the key to development. India ought to boost innovation in colleges and universities. Professors should become innovative and not teach in a routine manner. The focus should be on innovation, creativity, and not memorization. They must apply science & technology to real-life problems and reform them. We do not see a university abroad without these centers on campus, but in India, we hardly see a university with such centers. As a result, our brilliant students lack creativity and imagination. They become servants, termed in the USA as technology coolies, to do low-end jobs in multinationals. They are not creators, drivers, architects, or first-mover entrepreneurs. Innovative centers are the only way to educate students innovatively. The students are learning known knowledge and known technology, but innovation skills and research skills are neglected. Indian universities need to produce professional leaders, not followers. India is not short of resources but is short of synergy between the industry and institutes. Developing a world-class university is therefore not only the business of the university or government alone but essentially a joint effort in partnership with industry. India needs these centers to make education and research compatible with employment and growth opportunities. It is to be realized that jobs are not going to come from industries of yesterday; sunrise technologies are needed. Innovation is the need of the time to give birth to new technology- based companies. Colleges must change to create the future (FICCI, 2022).

We should create an Innovation Forum in each university, consisting of innovators from industry, innovators from the university, and representatives from civil society. In today's knowledge economy, the strength of a nation is measured not only in terms of the size of its army and arsenals but also in terms of its people's scientific and technological capabilities, for which world-class universities are necessary. Universities are now expected to not only produce graduates but also to give birth to new scientific inventions and technologies. World-class universities, by virtue of their knowledge organization, have come to be known as providers of economic security to a nation, creating a bright future for the young generation. Without world-class universities, India cannot produce globally competent professional leaders. Nothing is more important for the Indian economy at this juncture than building synergy between the university and industry for faster development. Interaction between the two is now not optional but compulsory. Universities have come to be recognized worldwide as the drivers of development.

Recognizing the need and importance of world-class universities in nation-building, our Prime Minister has announced the government's determination to make a beginning with ten universities classified as world-class in the public sector and ten in the private sector. He declared the grant of extra funds and full autonomy, meaning they will fall outside the purview of UGC and MHRD. India aspires to become a developed nation as early as possible, possessing the necessary potential. To unlock this potential, it requires giving higher priority in the national and state budgets to education. Some time ago, Nobel laureate Dr. Amartya Sen was asked a question by the then Finance Minister, Dr. Yashwant Sinha, regarding the priority India should give in the national budget to education. The Nobel laureate replied, "First priority." When asked what should be the second priority in the national budget, he again emphasized education. Third priority, he reiterated, should be given to education. India today is significantly undereducated. Without a rise in the level of education, it is difficult for India to ascend the ladder and become a developed country. University education in India today, by global standards, is far too weak. However, simply providing more budget to universities does not guarantee their elevation in global rankings. They require funding as well as many other crucial resources. The government should address these needs at the earliest opportunity.

Universities should aspire to think big and demonstrate commitment to implementing such aspirations. They should possess high ambitions and align themselves with counterparts elsewhere in the developed world. Indian universities, however, lack the ambition to achieve world- class status, despite their capabilities. They remain largely isolated from their international counterparts. With vast assets such as land, buildings, faculty, and staff, along with brilliant students, these institutions possess immense potential. Yet, both their physical and intellectual resources lie largely idle, underutilized and failing to yield full economic returns. This is largely due to a lack of an entrepreneurial culture within the universities. Regulatory bodies such as the UGC and AICTE are predominantly administered by bureaucrats rather than by professors, thinkers, or reformers, which is a significant weakness requiring urgent correction. The National Knowledge Commission of 2006-2007 provided recommendations in this regard, but they are yet to be implemented.

Autonomy, like that in foreign universities, should be granted to universities and colleges. Autonomy does not require additional money; instead, it saves. The government has granted autonomy to universities and many colleges on paper, but it has retained control. Boards of governors are formulated, but they do not possess necessary powers. Government intervention in governance is excessive. The type of autonomy enjoyed by world-class universities elsewhere should be granted to Indian universities and colleges for them to meet expectations. Our institutions are too focused on memorization for examinations rather than fostering creativity and learning. Students lack autonomy in choosing subjects they wish to study. The cafeteria approach is absent. Professors lack autonomy in conducting research and teaching; they are overly controlled by authorities. If India grants autonomy to universities and colleges, it will have completed more than half the job; they will manage all other aspects. Conversely, without autonomy, nothing will improve; the situation will persist.

The governor of a state is not qualified to steer the direction of a modern university. Education has become complex, competitive, and global. It requires a well- educated chancellor of universities, supported by a fully- fledged office consisting of visionary, creative, and academic leaders. Many good recommendations from the Kothari Commission report of 1966, such as autonomy, the New Education Policy of 1986, and the National Knowledge Commission of 2006-2007, have not been implemented or delayed simply because of a lack of able leadership from the chancellor's office (National Knowledge Commission, 2009).

3. Discussion

This paper delves into the critical need for India to establish world-class higher and technical education institutes to propel its journey towards becoming a developed nation. The introduction highlights the pivotal role universities play in shaping global leaders and driving economic prosperity through research and innovation (National Academy of Sciences, Engineering, and Institute of Medicine, 2007). Despite India's abundant resources, its mediocre education system, particularly in higher education, remains a bottleneck. The discussion underscores the importance of cultivating world-class professors and fostering an academic culture conducive to excellence.

It critiques outdated rules and regulations that hinder faculty growth and advocates for reimagining service conditions to align with global standards. Moreover, it emphasizes the significance of synergy between universities and industries to drive innovation and industrial development, proposing strategies such as establishing innovation centers, incubation centers, and research parks within universities.

The strategies needed to elevate universities and colleges to world-class standards are outlined, with a primary focus on empowering professors and fostering collaboration between academia and industry. The discussion emphasizes the pivotal role of professors in driving academic excellence and innovation, advocating for reforms in policies and practices to provide them with growth opportunities aligned with global standards. Additionally, it stresses the importance of establishing synergy between universities and industries to bridge the gap between education and employment needs, thus promoting economic growth and development. The need for autonomy in governance and leadership is highlighted, along with the imperative of implementing recommendations from past commissions and policies to foster a conducive environment for academic excellence and innovation. Overall, the discussion underscores the urgent need for concerted efforts from government, academia, and industry to transform India's education landscape and propel it towards global leadership and prosperity.

Conclusion

Having world-class universities is a prerequisite in a knowledge-based economy to qualify for the status of a developed nation. Rich nations with abundant natural resources also need to have world-class universities to be at the forefront. What makes a university great? It is undoubtedly the professors, their research, and innovation output. The Government of India should urgently reengineer the service conditions of professors and make them comparable to the best universities in the world. Professors ought to be autonomous, having the freedom to think and the freedom to act, to create a worthy future for coming generations. Mediocre universities produce mediocre leaders who cannot efficiently manage the affairs of companies at local, national, and international levels. India is a poor country, a low-income economy because it is producing mediocre graduates in the global context, who in turn become mediocre leaders in their respective chosen fields of specialization. Education should be reformed to world standards; until then, India will remain behind. Mediocre universities are far more costly than the cost involved in making universities world-class. National or State planners should allocate more funds for modernization. Roads, railways, electricity, water supply, etc., are all important, but for budget provisions, education should be of paramount importance.

Policy for industrial development and policy for higher technical education should be made compatible. Innovation centers, incubation centers, and research parks should be installed forthwith in each university campus. Institutes and professors must practice innovation. Students should not learn by memorization but through innovation. Industry-institute synergy should be built starting from the top, at the ministry level. Mismatch in education is a result of a lack of synergy. Education should match growth opportunities in globalization. Unless universities become world-class, the region will continue to produce mediocre graduates and leaders. India will lag behind the world, and brain drain will persist. The government should grant more autonomy to universities and colleges, allowing them to sink or swim. They will learn to swim only when they are about to sink. The Indian government must harness the global winds of change in higher education. If we enable professors in universities and colleges to be innovative, creative, and competitive by world standards, we won't need to do anything else to succeed. If we do not do this and focus solely on other efforts, success cannot be expected. If India fails to make universities world-class, its economy can never achieve world-class status. Future generations will undoubtedly suffer, and they will not pardon us.

References

1. **Duderstadt, J. J. (2009).** *A University for the 21st Century.* University of Michigan Press.
2. **European Commission. (1995).** *Green paper of Innovation.*
3. **FICCI. (2022).** *FICCI: Industry's Voice for Policy Change.* Retrieved from https://www.ficci.in/api/home
4. **Jones, G. A., McCarney, P. L., & Skolnik, M. L. (Eds.). (2005).** *Creating Knowledge, Strengthening Nations: The Changing Role of Higher Education.* University of Toronto Press.
5. **Naik, B. M. (2012).** Strategies to make technological universities globally competitive. *Journal of Engineering Education Transformations,* 25(3), 11-18.

6. **Naik, B. M. (2019).** *Education and Leadership: Role of Indian Universities and Colleges in Nurturing Future Leaders.* Atlantic publishers, New Delhi, 2015.
7. **Naik, B. M. (2021).** *Insights in to Research, Innovation and entrepreneurship for Higher & Technical Education.* Notion Press, India.
8. **Naik, B. M., & Kandlikar, W. S. (2008).** Gap Analysis between Indian Institutes and their Counterparts Abroad. *Journal of Engineering Education Transformations* (pp. 1- 9).
9. **Naik, B. M., & Kandlikar, W.S. (2010).** *Higher Technical Education. Gyan publications, Delhi.*
10. **National Academy of Sciences, Engineering, and Institute of Medicine. (2007).** *Rising Above the Gathering Storm: Energizing and Employing America for a Brighter Economic Future.* National Academies Press Washington.
11. **National Knowledge Commission. (2009).** *National Knowledge Commission: Report to the Nation 2006- 2009.* Retrieved from https://www.aicte-india.org/downloads/nkc.pdf
12. **Rhodes, H. T. F. (2001).** *The Creation of the Future: The Role of the American University.*
13. **Zhao, F. (2004).** Academic entrepreneurship: Case study of Australian universities. *The International Journal of Entrepreneurship and Innovation,* 5(2), 91-97.

Chapter - 6

India Disparately Needs University Related Research Parks [URRP] To promote Hi-Tech Entrepreneurship

This is the way to increase regional innovation & growth

URRP is a world Proven Model

Many universities in US, Canada, European countries have advanced in industry making use of this model.

The author has personally visited many like Stanford, madison, Toronto, Berlin, Karlsruhe, Cambridge

Universities have increased scholarship. World class start ups have evolved, disrupting the conventional products and processes. Generation of jobs in emerging skills, and income generation has taken place. On park enterprises are more successful than off park. Industrial development is faster due to URRP. Scientific evaluation of Parks is done and published in a report by AURP & Battelle in 2012.

Research park generates hi-tech employment with high income, and superior job conditions

- It is a joint effort between university and industry for mutual growth
- Research based companies come and park adjacent to university

- They draw benefit of research output of university, and scholar students. University and professors get royalty from them.
- Industry experts in park deliver lectures to students in university
- **adoption of URRPs is far too slow in India, acceleration is needed**
- Research park is innovative complex, located adjacent to university
- **It is planned & managed jointly by university, government & industry**
- Enterprises on park are far more successful than off park.

Research Park is a meeting place for innovative minds both from academics and industry

- University & industry synergies and give birth to disruptive ideas.
- The atmosphere in park is inspiring for students and industry experts
- Seeds of sunrise industries are sown in the minds of innovators
- Technology push matching with market pull is given on sustained basis
- **Lectures of distinguished technology pioneers from world over are frequently arranged**
- **Prof Terman gave this philosophy that- Industry needs access to first class research in university and university researchers need access to industry for commercialising their research.**

All world class universities in USA, Europe, Canada, China, Japan have research parks on campus

- They have increased relevance of education to world of work, and improved skill set of students
- Research skills, innovation skills, & entrepreneurship skills is superior.
- PhD quality and its relevance has become better.

- **Economic value of research done in university has enhanced, funds attracted**
- Industrial development of the country accelerates, so also income.
- China has a massive program 300 parks and this accelerated industrial growth
- It has boosted Start-ups in emerging technologies
- It enabled companies to rise to global standards
- It has reduced time gap between invention & commercial application
- **Thousands of students from India are going abroad, because innovative infrastructure like research park is not available. Brain Drain**

To conclude: India is at risk for want of URRP. Each university ought to have a research park.

- Universities without the parks are not worth the name. A university without park is incomplete, irrelevant and outdated in modern sense.
- **India will win in Atma Nirbhar Abhiyan with parks and not without them**
- Research Parks produce industry leaders, competent by world standards. **STEPs are started by DST, but too few for a big India.**
- India ought to dream big and think great to convert intellectual capital in to usable goods & services for which parks are essential.
- **Research park is a profit centre and not a liability. They earn money for university**
- It generates wealth for nation, it is a cradle for entrepreneurs
- **Indian industry, university & economy will get a face lift with URRPs**
- Thank You.

Chapter - 7

India Desperately needs Synergy between University and Industry to make Education Globally Competitive

Abstract

This paper presents the brief need and importance of synergy between higher and technical education and industry. A win-win game between industry and institute is very essential in raising their respective performances to greater heights. If synergy is achieved, then higher and technical education in India can hope to become globally competitive. India can then become a hub of education to attract students from abroad, as desired by the government. Synergy will also enable Indian industry to be competitive by world standards and enable India to become a developed country with a high rank in the world. NEP-2020 recommends synergy between the university and industry. In the past, many conferences and seminars in India have taken place, but the progress has been rather slow. This paper makes suggestions to bring synergy into practice. This paper is based on observations made during personal visits to several universities in developed countries, like the USA, UK, Germany, and India.

Keywords: Synergy, India, Higher Education, Technical Industry, World Standards, Globally Competitive.

Introduction

UNESCO, for the overall good of humankind, has prescribed synergy between institutes and industry to all countries in the world, both developed and developing. It organizes a program known as the University Industry Science Partnership (UNISPAR, 1993).

Many international conferences on this subject are held worldwide. The Indian government has also passed a law on Corporate Social Responsibility (CSR), aiming to establish a bond between the two sectors (Brainly, n.d.). Industries are required to spend 2% of their profits on social organizations, including educational institutes. Many industrial organizations are undertaking joint programs like technology incubators and scholarships for students. For instance, Bajaj Auto, in partnership with Dr. BAMU University in Sambhajinagar, Maharashtra, India, has installed a technology incubator, which has yielded very good results. However, there is a need to expand these partnerships.

Higher and technical education institutes that rank high in the world invariably maintain synergy with industry. Institutes in developed nations, by virtue of this synergy, offer superior-quality education, job-oriented courses, and attract scholars from all over the world (Duderstadt, 2009). Even institutes in smaller countries like Singapore and New Zealand, mainly through the strength of synergy, rank high on the global list and attract students from large countries like India. A win-win game is desperately needed in Indian industry and institutes for mutual growth and prosperity, with the goal of becoming a developed nation by 2047. The education standards and research output of institutes would then become far more relevant to achieving the much-desired 5 trillion economy.

Higher education institutes without fruitful interaction, i.e., synergy with industry, have become too bookish, irrelevant, redundant, and outdated. This has resulted in graduates being less useful for job placement, rendering a vast number of them unemployed and underemployed. This paper outlines, in brief, the need and importance of strengthening industry-institute interaction in India, as prescribed by the National Education Policy 2020 (NEP-2020). NEP-2020 envisions India becoming a hub of education, attracting students from abroad.

While the government has passed the law on Corporate Social Responsibility (CSR), the industry is still not associating liberally with institutes or sponsoring research and innovation. The industry lacks confidence in the institutes' capability to provide useful solutions to their problems. The industry goes to institutes only for campus interviews, recruiting graduates who they find half-baked and needing retraining to fit into jobs. Institutes expect sponsorship from the industry for research and innovation. Unless a win-win situation occurs, synergy is unlikely to happen. This adversely affects the placement of students in the industry. The growth and prospects of both industries and institutes are hindered. They both work hard but fruitlessly because they do not synergize their efforts, ideas, and resources with each other. Without synergy, India can never hope to improve the quality of education and become globally competitive.

When synergy takes place, institutes benefit from interaction with industry, and industry benefits from interaction with institutes. This mutual benefit creates a win-win situation, leading to significantly higher performance. In synergistic conditions, performance is far greater than when both operate in isolation. Through alliances, they become mutually supportive, adding substantial value to each other. To further explain, one plus one becomes two in arithmetic, but in synergistic conditions between industry and institutes, one plus one can become far more than two, depending on the wisdom and imagination of the innovative people in both organizations to generate desired values.

Why Should an Institute Interact with Industry?

Students demand job-oriented knowledge and skills for innovation and research to ensure placement and prosper in their professions. World experience indicates that unless a professor is involved in industry-oriented research and innovation, there is current and relevant knowledge to teach. Teaching tends to focus on outdated knowledge that is incompatible with global job opportunities (Naik, 2018). Classroom teaching gains force, depth, and sharpness when professors are engaged in industry-oriented research and innovation. They become imaginative, stay ahead of their time, and update their capacities to match their counterparts abroad, which is necessary to capitalize on technology ahead of others. The visions and missions of colleges should essentially include enabling the industry to win in a globalized world. This alone will make education relevant and purposeful.

Why Should Industry Interact with Institutes?

Industry needs new technology and knowledge from research and innovation in institutes on a continuing basis to remain competitive in the global market (Bowden, 2004). While industry conducts some research and innovation independently, it is not enough to achieve global competitiveness. They need the support of public institutes, particularly young scholars. They lack the necessary infrastructure and mindset to achieve synergy with industry. However, institutes feel that the industry is not coming forward to interact with students in universities. Both parties prefer to remain in their isolated cocoons, avoiding outside interference in their functioning. This mutual isolation is detrimental and weakens any nation, including India.

Higher and technical education institutes worldwide are found to be a dominant force in economic development (Jones et al., 2005). Institutes are assuming a key role in global economic systems, where new knowledge and highly skilled people are perceived as fuel for economic and social development. Colleges, as sources of new knowledge and technology, have become a dominant economic force. They are viewed as suppliers of new knowledge and technology and as national and international leaders. Institutes are expected to nurture today's technological leaders for tomorrow. Good institutes and colleges have become prerequisites for a nation to win in a competitive world.

Institutes in India, however, are observed to be far behind their counterparts in the developed world. They are inward-looking and lack adequate interaction with their counterparts abroad. They do not have structural connections or a vision to help industry succeed in the global market.

This paper outlines the need and importance of associating with industry, especially for framing visions and missions and sharing necessary resources. The interaction has to be a win-win game, mutually supportive of each other's growth and prosperity. The education of students would also become more creative and imaginative. If both work hand in hand, the interaction becomes synergistic. It is observed that a higher and technical education institute without a partnership with industry is incomplete, nonviable, and ineffective in the modern sense. Industry cannot perform all the necessary innovation by itself to be globally competitive. They need contributions from young students and academicians in institutes.

The Need and Importance of Synergy in Research and Innovation

The benefits of research far outweigh the associated costs. Research fuels education, making it both high- quality and cost-competitive. It brings a sense of achievement, provides economic security to a nation, and instills confidence in students. It enhances the return on investment already made in colleges and improves campus placements. Research enriches human civilization. Research in universities and colleges is the mother of innovation and creativity. A student learns best by researching (Naik, 2004). The process of researching leads to the creation of brand-new technology, providing a competitive edge in the global market. World experience demonstrates that the progress of human civilization is closely tied to research.

1. World Experience

Prof. Turman of Stanford University said, "Professors, so as to test their laboratory research results, need access to industry, just as industry, to be globally competitive, needs access to first-class research in institutes" (Rhodes, 2001b).

Industry and institutes, by being stand-alone entities, cannot achieve peak performance even if they have high potential. They need to synergize their efforts, which requires synchronization between the two. They must function in harmony and synergy; otherwise, education is likely to remain bookish, outdated, less relevant, and ineffective.

Examining the world-ranking institutes reveals a close association with industry in many activities, such as research and innovation, training graduate students, framing syllabi, appointing industry professionals to boards of governors, inviting industry experts to deliver lectures, and sharing resources. These activities have been observed at MIT Boston, Karlsruhe University, and Toronto University. At Karlsruhe University in Germany, the exchange of experts between the university and industry is embedded in the structural framework. For example, chairs are reserved for industry experts in the university, and chairs are reserved for professors in the industry. This is mandated by the government in the larger interest, although it is not always favored by both the university and the industry. However, it has been found to benefit both greatly (Naik et al., 2009).

The industry expects a continuous flow of new knowledge, new technology, and managerial support to upgrade its competitiveness in the global market. Indian institutes are not equipped enough in terms of research manpower and laboratories to provide this kind of support. The Geographical Positioning System (GPS) was invented at Cambridge University. Genetic engineering was born at Stanford University, and the discovery of DNA was made at Cambridge. Inventions in electronics were made by Prof. Hertz at Karlsruhe University, Germany (Naik & Kandlikar, 2010). Many inventions have taken place in universities and colleges worldwide. Not only inventions, but companies are born based on research output from these universities. Universities and colleges have become the "Maternity Homes" of hi-tech firms. Modern universities and colleges worldwide are not only teaching in classrooms but also engaging in research and expanding their outreach. The impact of university research on human civilization is vast.

1.1 Michael Faraday

There is a story told about Michael Faraday (Rhodes, 2001a). Faraday had demonstrated his discovery of electromagnetic induction, on which the dynamo depends, to the then Prime Minister Benjamin Disraeli, who asked for funding, "What use then is it?" Faraday replied, "As much use as a newborn baby." Years later, another British Prime Minister, Margaret Thatcher, admitted that Faraday's invention had generated huge wealth for the UK, more than the entire capital represented by the London Stock Exchange. This is proof that research is financially much more rewarding to a nation than normally imagined.

1.2 Research and Innovation Generate Financial Surplus

Research and innovation generate financial surpluses and provide economic security for a nation. Experience around the world tells that the benefits of research far outweigh the costs. Studies indicate that the rate of return (ROR) on investments in research is around 25% for universities and colleges and 60% for the public, compared to an ROR of 15-20% for a typical commercial project. Additionally, students acquire research and innovation skills that they use throughout their lives. Research provides protection against obsolescence and offers economic and technological security, keeping the nation ahead in a competitive world. Colleges can better serve the public if they incorporate research into their frameworks. Research does not consume resources but generates a surplus. The dividends from investments in research for colleges and for India are extraordinary.

Universities and colleges have acquired proficiency in teaching, making it the right time for them to switch to research and development. The National Education Policy (NEP) 2020 recommends the establishment of a National Research Foundation with an earmarked budget of Rs 50,000 crores. India needs to double down on this direction to succeed in initiatives like AtmaNirbhar Abhiyan, Startups, and Make in India missions.

American universities and colleges have a high commitment to research, which is why the U.S. economy and its universities rank highly globally. There are around 130 research universities in the U.S. that produce most of the research output and PhDs. Thomas Jefferson, the founding president (1801–1844), believed that if America wants to lead the world and surpass Europe, it must first succeed in higher education. The Bush Commission's report of 1945 further emphasized that research should be the main product of universities, with education as its by-product. Education should focus on creativity, which can be achieved by integrating education with research and industry.

1.3 Characteristics of Universities Abroad Arising out of Synergy

On the campuses of universities like Madison, Cambridge, and Stanford, what we notice is that research companies are flocking around them (Bok, 2009). Incubators, research parks, innovation centers, and patent and IPR bureaus are distinctly visible. Venture capital companies have opened offices on campuses in search of new technological ideas for commercialization. Universities in developed countries have become like magnets, attracting not only scholars but also industry, entrepreneurs, and venture capital firms from across the world. They are globalizing their operations to meet the world's needs in both education and technology.

By virtue of their strong research base, these universities are sources of the latest knowledge, education, and new ideas that enable companies to succeed in the global market. Universities in the USA produce as many as 200 patents per year. These universities sell patents to companies, earning an income that accounts for almost 30 percent of their budget. Young scholars and mid-career professionals carry out research and innovation, which is disseminated through classroom teaching. Every professor is a research scientist in addition to being a teacher. Innovation and research are considered the 'well springs' of economies.

1.4 Participation in Exhibition

The author once visited an international industrial exhibition in Hannover, Germany. In this exhibition, there was a pavilion for universities and colleges, which was the most crowded area. Visitors came from all over the world, and universities from various countries presented their research and innovation outputs. They showcased the patents they had obtained, new inventions, and disruptive technologies likely to dominate future industries. Visitors appreciated this very much, and many financial transactions between companies and universities took place.

A university in India needs to take this strategic direction. The health of Indian industry and the economy depends on the health of higher education. Nations or regions are found to be more prosperous where university-industry partnerships exist. Education in such nations is innovative, creative, dynamic, relevant, and fitting to industrial needs. There is no mismatch between the skills demanded and the skills provided. New technology-based firms are born, and the generation of high-income jobs takes place. Nations where universities and industry go hand in hand are richer, offering a better standard of living to their people. Together, they create brand new technologies, products, and processes, making joblessness rare. Innovators from industry and universities frequently meet at innovation parks to show new ways to industries. Incubation centers, research parks, entrepreneurship centers, and startups grow. The majority of funding comes through venture capital, putting untried, untested virgin technologies into commercial application.

"First-mover entrepreneurs" and "technopreneurs" lead, and foreign collaborators have so far propelled the Indian industry. Indian universities, academics, and researchers are called upon to propel their industry, for which they must synergize. If universities and industry jointly set up a "Corporate Education Center," in-service people will receive nonstop training for lifelong global competencies. The future of the younger generation will be secured, and capacity utilization of installed facilities will be increased. The author has also visited the "Corporate Education Center" of Boston University.

2. Indian Scenario

2.1 Higher and Technical Education and Research

India is a late starter in higher and technical education and research, gaining momentum only after independence in 1947. It was presumed that new technology could only be discovered abroad. Initially, Indian colleges were designed to teach technology imported from foreign countries rather than generate indigenous technology. People were content to follow technology rather than lead. As a result, India has been constantly buying technology from foreign countries.

However, universities and colleges in India have gained adequate experience and made laudable progress. Indian talent has become conscious of its capabilities, and people are ambitious to lead in discovery. Indians in Silicon Valley have made a significant mark, with the President of the USA considering India an intellectual threat and publicly urging Americans to compete. It is observed that students who learn innovation during their college days are better suited to discover the unknown throughout their careers.

Research is the mother of innovation. With the current policy of the Indian government aiming to make India the third-largest economy in the world, research is essential. Students aspiring to become leaders in technology and industry must necessarily be innovative, acquire skills, develop the vision to generate new technologies, products, and processes, and obtain patents.

Thousands of students go abroad each year in search of quality education, spending huge sums of money. Postgraduate and PhD programs are serious weaknesses that urgently need to be converted into strengths. Due to the lack of infrastructure for research and development, higher and technical education in India is far behind. Colleges only teach known knowledge and do not encourage discovering the unknown. Indian universities do not rank highly and cannot reach parity with the world until synergy is built.

2.2 Leaders in Technology and Captains of Industry

India needs leaders in technology and captains of industry, not mere soldiers. This requires synergy. Professors have almost no experience in industry, research, or innovation. Very few institutes, like IITs and NITs, are engaged in research, which is why their standards are high and they are preferred. However, by world standards, they too are behind, especially in the commercial exploitation of research findings.

The vast majority of colleges do not have the infrastructure and technical capability to conduct research and innovation. They are not knowledge generators but distributors of knowledge imported from abroad, functioning like departmental stores. Consequently, their teaching lacks force, depth, and relevance. Colleges are therefore mostly producing graduates as technology followers rather than leaders. Graduates typically find employment as soldiers in multinational companies, but they are expected to become captains of leading industries on national and global levels.

Primarily, the lack of research and innovation in colleges is why the quality of education is poor by global standards. There is less creativity. As a result, investment in fixed property yields more returns than investment in industry. The global economy is undergoing significant structural changes. Synergy between institutes and industry provides a base for progress.

2.3 Long Range View and Sponsor Research

The industry is expected to take a long-range view, sponsor research, and actively participate. A study by the US Academy of Sciences (2007) reported that only a few engineering graduates in India are employable in MNCs; the rest have to make up for deficiencies by attending finishing schools at extra cost and time. There is a huge energy in youth to become technology pioneers or leaders on a global scale because present institutes are not teaching students to become such. Commitment to implementing them is lacking. Synergy will enable both institutes and industry to grow to greater heights.

AICTE, UGC, and the Technical Education Quality Improvement Program (TEQIP) are prescribing the creation of a research ambiance on campus and providing financial support. TEQIP, in association with the World Bank, is investing around Rs 4000 crore in 200 well-performing engineering colleges. It is well realized that research in science and technology has become very important for economic health and national defense.

Industry is expected to take a long-range view and actively participate with colleges in research. Industry cannot achieve peak performance by standing alone. Industrial development is research-driven. Hence, the Government of India has launched the Atma Nirbhar Bharat Abhiyan, reducing the import of technological items in the defense department. Synergy will facilitate the success of government schemes.

2.4 Restructure Higher Education

To become a significant economic power in this century, India must urgently restructure its higher and technical education and integrate it with indigenous research in partnership with industry. Despite a large number of engineers and technicians graduating from engineering colleges each year, India's scientific and technological achievements do not reflect this abundance of S&T personnel. The quality and relevance of education, by world standards, are lacking, making India a technology- following nation.

Expectations from colleges are high, and they cannot meet these demands alone. Alumni, as ambassadors with field experience, should support their alma maters to strengthen them, fostering synergy between institutes and industry. The technology landscape changes frequently, about four to five times during a teacher's career. A teacher cannot impart the latest knowledge without exposure to current developments. Engineering colleges, like their counterparts abroad, are tasked with producing not only competent engineers but also new technologies for the industry. Professors active in research possess the current and relevant knowledge necessary for effective teaching.

There is a notable mismatch in the job market: many engineers are either unemployed or underemployed, while those with specialized skills are scarce. The education system must align with industry needs to improve industrial competitiveness. Industry alone cannot fulfill all its research needs, even with dedicated R&D centers. Collaborating with universities and colleges for research is more cost-effective and introduces fresh perspectives necessary for breakthroughs. Thus, industries should sponsor and participate in college research initiatives, acknowledging their interdependence with educational institutions.

Small-Scale Industries (SSI) and Small and Medium-Sized Enterprises (SMEs) cannot afford their own R&D centers, making industry-institute synergy crucial for mutual benefit. Isolated research remains critically unexamined, untested, and unchallenged. Private knowledge, unless disputed, is knowledge lost. Research conclusions must be openly discussed and debated within the scientific and industrial communities, highlighting the importance of research in public universities.

The power of research is evident not only in isolated innovations but also in creating new technology-based industries, some of which become major economic power drivers. High expectations from colleges require alumni support in terms of ideas and funding. Synergy between institutes and industry is essential to making this vision a reality.

2.5 Education and Industry

Education and industry are complementary to each other. Worldwide, it is observed that research in institutes subsidizes industry, and industry, in turn, subsidizes research in institutes. Stanford University, for example, has given birth to more than 3,000 startups. These startups pay royalties to the university for research, which is used again for new startups. Most importantly, this makes learning joyful and creative, with learners becoming achievement-oriented. Institutes and industry are found to be inseparable and mutually supportive.

Every professor should be viewed as a scientist. Like in foreign institutions, they should be given funds for research at the time of their appointment. Professors should be encouraged to build research teams consisting of junior and senior students, lab assistants, and industry innovators. The culture of institutions must change in favor of industry. This mindset should be instilled among students and staff. Their performance should be measured by their discoveries and patents, not by how much they have memorized. Colleges should be sources of new knowledge, theories, and technologies.

Regions, cities, and nations develop faster where institutions lead in knowledge and technology. No society, region, or nation prospers without good research output. Research brings more money, endowments, and recognition to colleges. They attract funds for research, thereby lowering the cost of education and tuition. Education becomes qualitative and cost-competitive, and the bond between industry and institutes becomes stronger. With technological advancement, awareness of the importance of research is growing in Indian industry.

The experiences of Silicon Valley, Research Triangle Park in North Carolina, Route 95 in Boston, and Bengaluru indicate that knowledge institutions have become key players in regional development. They have moved from the periphery to the center of development. People's development, especially in science and technology, matters most. Therefore, Indian colleges should think strategically and start research and innovation centers in partnership with industry on their campuses, providing world-class education in cutting-edge technology to youngsters. Education, combined with a spirit of research and innovation, is essential for moving a nation forward. This demands synergy.

Industry hesitates to sponsor research in colleges. They ought to think long-term to be more competitive. The industry needs to be innovative and research-minded. They cannot do all the research they need by themselves and should seek the help of academicians and young scholars in institutes. The mindset of key people in both industry and institutes is outdated. Very few institutes and industries have a burning desire to be equal to their counterparts abroad. The full scope of research and innovation in India and their deeper purposes are less understood, resulting in low priority in the state budget. India spends only 0.45% of its GDP on research, while other countries spend 4% to 5%. For India to become the education hub it dreams of in NEP-2020, it must spend more on research in colleges and universities.

Teaching known knowledge and established technology is good, but not enough. Using new knowledge and technology determines competitiveness. Syllabi are oriented towards learning established knowledge and practice, presuming that knowledge is finite. In reality, knowledge is infinite, and students need to learn not only what is known but also to discover the unknown. Education without learning skills for research and innovation is incomplete and irrelevant in the modern sense. This is why Indian institutes today do not rank highly on the world list. The interaction between institutes and industry for research is too weak, adversely affecting the competitiveness of both.

2.6 Systems Matter

The theory of education says that if there is no significant research in a college, then there is no significant quality in education. The quality of education does not grow where research is absent. It is noticed in universities abroad that many research-based industries are located on the periphery of colleges. They draw ideas from research conducted by professors and students. Students work for these companies on research projects, and company researchers teach in colleges. The quality of both research and education goes up, and the cost to a nation is lowered. What they experience is that peak performance in industry cannot be reached without support from institutes, and vice versa. This underlines the need for and importance of synergy.

2.7 Synergy between Institutes and Industry

India desperately needs synergy between institutes and industry. India is at risk due to the lack of institute-industry partnerships. If universities and industries synergize, create a shared vision, pursue collective ambition through Corporate Social Responsibility (CSR), and jointly establish innovative projects like research parks, innovation parks, corporate education centers, incubator centers, patent and IPR centers, and entrepreneurship centers, the Indian economy will undoubtedly rank highly in the world. This collaboration will produce globally competent leaders in various professions, including politics. Job generation for youths in emerging technologies will then grow by leaps and bounds.

India must inspire its key people in both academia and industry with a spirit of enterprise and innovation to move the country forward. University-industry partnerships are critical for growth and prosperity. This partnership alone can provide the "technology push" to match the "market pull." Universities and colleges will then become "lighthouses" for industry. The younger generation will benefit immensely from this approach.

World-class universities produce globally competent leaders who, in turn, lead their respective professions to become global leaders. Others produce mediocre individuals who follow rather than lead. Thus, there is a global race among universities to become world-class. Leaders are crucial for growth and prosperity. If universities and industries jointly establish Research Parks and Corporate Education Centers, possibly with CSR funding, it will make the industry globally competitive, elevate the university to world-class status, and help eradicate poverty. The limiting factor for growth and prosperity in a competitive world is not the availability of natural resources like oil, coal, or iron ore, but the synergy between universities and industries for generating new knowledge, new technology, and competent human resources. Then, India will become a high-income economy.

2.8 Passion for Research

Passion for industry-sponsored research should define the character of a campus. Research leads to industrial development and employment generation. This paper argues that industry and institutes need to recognize the full scope of the innovation phenomenon. The innovation capacity of India, its economic progress, and the generation of employment opportunities depend greatly on students acquiring innovation skills. Professional leaders, to be globally competent, essentially require research and innovation skills. India's vision of becoming a developed nation by 2047 depends on the value it attaches to industry-oriented innovation and research in engineering colleges and polytechnics. Low aim is a crime. "Passion for research" is crucial. It must be the campus character. This is the way to succeed in the world economy.

Many innovations are taking place in Indian institutes too. Hackathons are arranged every year, and start-ups are emerging in increasing numbers. Students and professors in colleges have designed racing cars with new shapes and tested them aerodynamically. Awareness of research among Indian youths and the "can-do spirit" is growing. This is a positive change.

3. Suggestions

3.1 Compatibility between the Policies

Compatibility between the policy for higher and technical education and policies at state and national levels is essential. All world-class universities have research parks on campus. Research parks are built by institutes in partnership with industry and the government. New technology-based firms are born in universities, such as Yahoo, Google, and CISCO, with more than 3000 companies originating from Stanford University. Universities in China, Australia, and Europe are not behind. They have generated high-tech employment with a high income. The Anil Kakodkar committee recommended this to the Maharashtra government, but there has been no progress. Recently, China has established more than 300 research parks. China's progress is greatly attributed to these research parks.

American industry, in association with universities, helped transform its economy by establishing research parks and research centers. The Indian government has launched ambitious projects like ATMA NIRBHAR BHARAT, Make in India, Digital India, Smart Cities, Smart Villages, and the Delhi-Mumbai Industrial Corridor Project and is raising funds through two percent of profits in corporate social responsibility. Their prime role in today's knowledge-driven economy is to jointly produce globally competent leaders, both professional and political, for industry and various walks of life. No one in isolation is empowered to achieve this.

They essentially need a partnership with industry. Mediocrity in universities prevails, leading to a mismatch between what is taught and what is needed. The Mackenzie report states that only 17% of graduates are employable. This is a result of the disconnect between universities and industry. When industry and universities come together, they stand tall. In isolation, they cannot achieve peak performance. Companies are attracting the best talent from anywhere and everywhere in the world by offering attractive salaries and perks.

The university, in partnership with industry, propels industrial growth. Universities and industry are interdependent. They cannot be mutually exclusive and must support each other. No industry, regardless of size and strength, can conduct all the research it needs alone. It has to depend on public research done in universities. Industry needs access to first-class research in universities, and researchers in universities need access to industry for the application of their findings. The growth and prosperity of a region depend on the presence of world-class universities.

Universities are globally competitive only if their professors are globally competent, regardless of the infrastructure. Industries and universities should take a long-range view, come together to attract globally competent professors, and enable local professors to grow to a world-class level. The government ought to emulate foreign universities, especially in service conditions, enabling professors to be world-class. Present job conditions do not grant the necessary autonomy and opportunities for professors to grow to global standards. AICTE and UGC will have to examine and conduct comparative studies with the world's best universities.

3.2 World Class Institutes Synergizing with Industry

Cities and regions grow faster and on a sustained basis only when they have world-class institutes synergizing with industry. This growth does not occur even with abundant natural resources if these institutes are lacking. The Indian industry needs to conduct research and innovation in association with colleges to compete in a knowledge-driven world economy. Cities and regions in India are underdeveloped and trailing behind the world not because they lack resources but because their institutes lack a shared vision with industry to create world-class institutions that nurture globally competent professional leaders. Therefore, the world ranking of universities has assumed great significance worldwide. It has become a determinant factor for a region's economic prosperity.

The differentiating factor between developed and developing nations is the presence of world-class technical institutes synergizing with industry.

Industries want to be globally competitive. They must emulate the Industry Institute Interaction Model of "Institute Related Research Parks" from abroad. What is observed differently in higher education institutes abroad is that R&D units of private companies flock around and park on the periphery of universities in search of new knowledge and Intellectual Property Rights (IPR). These R&D units draw on the intellectual capital of the university, using the expertise of professors and young innovative students, and research infrastructure such as labs and libraries. Experts from private R&D units deliver lectures to university students, creating a continuous exchange of knowledge and innovative ideas between companies and technical institutes. This interaction enriches both the university and the companies. By doing this, they subsidize each other's costs of education and research. This system especially triggers students' imagination and inspires creativity. The author has personally observed this at many universities, such as McMaster University in Canada, Karlsruhe University in Germany, the University of Wisconsin at Madison in the USA, Stanford University, and several others. This practice has been widely prevalent in many universities for years.

Industry and universities ought to have a shared ambition to create an enterprising culture. Ambition on the part of only the university or industry in isolation will not suffice. It is hoped that Indian leaders in industry, academia, and social and political systems will come together, work together, use collective wisdom, and give proper shape to industry-institute interaction to build India into a developed nation. A study entitled "Driving Regional Innovation & Growth," conducted by AURP and Battelle in the USA in 2012, reported that university-related research parks in partnership with universities have accelerated industrial development and generated high-tech, high-paying employment.

3.3 Corporate Education Centers in Partnership with Industry

Establishing corporate education centers in partnership with industry by institutes is the trend worldwide. The author has visited Boston University's corporate education center, which runs many courses for in-service personnel throughout the year. India's ability to compete in the international market now depends on the competence and innovative mindset of its workforce. Lifelong, continuous education is the trend elsewhere in the world. This has enabled people in developed countries to keep pace with changing technology, avoid obsolescence, and remain competitive in the global market.

In Japan, it is believed that employing people without continuing education and training is a mistake on the part of employers. A company is only as good as its people and their lifelong training. In China, training is both a right and an obligation. Corporate training institutes are developed to cover 100% of the workforce every year. This has become essential for all serving personnel in India as well. A university, in partnership with industry, ought to create a learning society with learning individuals for 100% of the workforce in the region. It should provide an opportunity to upgrade their skills, knowledge, and attitudes. This alone will lead to an increase in productivity.

Conclusion

Leaders in academia and industry should form a forum to meet frequently and create synergy. The forum should be at national, state, and institutional levels. The government should give rewards and incentives to those who achieve synergy.

India can become a five-trillion-dollar economy and a hub of education, as envisaged in NEP-2020, only if synergy is developed. Joblessness, a serious problem in India, will be alleviated only if institutes synergize with industry. Projects like ATMA NIRBHAR BHARAT ABHIYAN, Smart Cities, Make in India, Digital India, startups, and incubation centers initiated by the government need synergy between industry and institutes to succeed. Without this synergy, these projects will be less effective.

Both industry and universities must change their traditional mindset of remaining in isolated cocoons in favor of cooperation, especially for research and innovation. They must become 'idea generators.' Success in a globalized world, characterized by fierce international competition, depends on turning intellectual capital into marketable commodities faster than one's competitors. Without joint research parks, corporate education centers, patent and IPR centers, and entrepreneurship centers, India will fall behind in international competition despite hard work in isolation.

Students need innovation centers on campus, in partnership with industry, to enhance their skill sets and power of imagination. World experience tells that any company unwilling to commit the funds and efforts required for synergy and strategic alliances for research and innovation with academicians in universities or colleges will not likely reap the benefits of new technology and new knowledge. Such companies, despite their high potential, will not be major forces in the industry. Nothing is more important to the Indian economy at this juncture than upgrading its universities by synergizing with industry. No investment from the government, especially under CSR, such as in roads, housing, and electricity, is more rewarding than investment in research and education in universities and colleges.

References

1. **Bok, D. (2009).** *Universities in the Marketplace: The Commercialization of Higher Education.* Princeton university press.
2. **Bowden, R. (2004).** *Globalization: The Impact on Our Lives.* Raintree.
3. **Brainly. (n.d.).** *Corporate Social Responsibility is Compulsory for Every Industrialist.* Retrieved from https://brainly.in/question/33213232
4. **Duderstadt, J. J. (2009).** *A University for the 21st Century.* University of Michigan Press.
5. **Jones, G. A., McCarney, P. L., & Skolnik, M. L. (Eds.). (2005).** *Creating Knowledge, Strengthening Nations: The Changing Role of Higher Education.* University of Toronto Press.
6. **Naik, B. M. (2004).** Needed innovation and entrepreneurship in higher education institutes. *Journal of Technical Education,* 27(1), 27-32.
7. **Naik, B. M. (2018).** *Education and Leadership: Role of Indian Universities and Colleges in Nurturing Future Leaders.* Atlantic Publishers & Distributors (P) Limited.
8. **Naik, B. M., & Kandlikar, W. S. (2010).** *Higher and Technical Education: Book of Knowledge.* Gyan Publishing House.
9. **Naik, B. M., Kandlikar, W. S., & Shirkhedkar, M. P. (2009).** Expanding horizons in higher and technical education to adopt new visions of new world: A challenge. *i-manager's Journal of Educational Technology,* 6(2), 20-29.
   https://doi.org/10.26634/jet.6.2.798
10. **Rhodes, F. H. (2001a).** *The Role of the American University: The Creation of the Future.* Ithaca, NY: Cornell University.
11. **Rhodes, F. H. T. (2001b).** *The Creation of the Future: The Role of the American University.* Cornell University Press.
12. **UNISPAR. (1993).** *UNISPAR: University-Industry- Science Partnership.* Retrieved from
    https://unesdoc.unesco.org/ark:/48223/pf0000144315

CHAPTER - 8

Gap Analysis between Indian Institutes and their Counterparts Abroad

Synopsis

Where does India stand in the world list in higher education? Why thousands of students every year go abroad? Have we failed as a society to provided adequate opportunities to our youth to be educated in world class manner? Have we failed in creating a vibrant educational ecosystem that supports cutting edge research? How are their institutes different from Indian? What do they teach which we do not? Where do we go wrong? Teaching profession in India is a grim affair. Where as it is prestigious in foreign. We have too much of rote learning. They have more of innovation, creativity.

Why coaching industry in India is booming? Nalanda and Taxshila were the first universities of the world, where scholars used to come from abroad. Now why a shift in culture has taken place and our scholar students going abroad? Is it due to inadequate value attached to discovery of new knowledge, new theories? It is essential at this juncture of time to make introspection and learn from the world experience in science and engineering education. The future of youths depends on knowledge, rather than resources. Status of India in world, in leadership, income level, and well being of people depends on its scientific and technological capability. India, to cope with challenges will have to enlarge the scope of institutions to cover research, innovation, creativity, generation of theories, technology creation, patent and IPR, creation of New Technology Based firms etc. What value we attach to above in national budgeting? How can we bring back the past glory of Nalanda?

Students studying today in universities are tomorrow's leaders, in politics, industry, academics etc. They sit in parliament, board room, write books, become creative thinkers, and drive the society to progress. For India to win in world economy they have to be competitive by world standards. To be able to have world class leaders tomorrow we have to have world class professors and world class institutes today. They have to learn not only known knowledge but learn to discover unknown.

The article presents in brief, the gap analysis in respect of visions and missions; policies and practices; organization structures, systems and procedures in India and their counterpart institutions in developed countries. They are critical to the success. IITs were set up under foreign collaboration. Their visions missions, policies and practices are molded on foreign lines. Hence they could shine. The paper observes that rest of the Indian higher education is far too behind. India will have to capitalize on emerging technology to fulfill people's needs. Institutions will have to have wellsprings of new knowledge like in developed countries and not remain mere reflection centers. The gap analysis presented here makes an attempt to find answers to the questions raised above.

Importance of academic institutions in today's volatile time is very high. It is the institutions which are furthering human civilization to greater heights. It is the academicians who provide new knowledge, new theories new technology and competent manpower to industry, leaders to government and leaders to the total economy. This in turn creates wealth and comforts. Industry, society and government in return ought to provide funds to academics to make it grow. India and for that matter any nation can be richer only by use of advanced knowledge. There is no other way. What kind of leaders our institutes produce matter

This is a time characterized by change. The world under the forces of globalization is changing fast. Institutions would have also to change. Only those who change to innovate and again innovate tend to educate the youths on correct lines. Students now demand world class education. Institutions in India will have to be competitive by nothing less than world class so as to remain in service. Other wise foreign universities will come here and capture major share of education market, and our students like in the past will keep going abroad.

People in India are as intelligent and hard working as else where in the world. However, today their efforts do not bring fruits as much as their counterparts. We work six days a week as against five days in foreign. Yet per capita income is around only 1000 dollars where as that of USA is 30,000. It is 30 times more. They work less and earn more. 25 % people in India, live below the poverty line. It is mainly because of the lack of new visions of new world. It is due to lack of dedicated effort to realize the vision. We lack vision of research based education, relevant to the current needs.

The systems employed in India in education and all other walks of life are less efficient than those in developed countries. Indians when they migrate abroad they are found to contribute far more. It is the systems efficiency which enables people to contribute more. We are spending resources and efforts on education but because of outdated systems output is less. Indian students study so much with less relevance. Foreign students study so little but with high relevance. This makes them more competitive. Our visions and missions, policies and practices, systems and procedures need examination in the light of world proven policies and practices. They need substantial improvement. Hence is the importance of gap analysis.

Identification of Gaps, and Their Analysis

The paper presents only critical gaps which demand immediate attention. They are presented with a constructive criticism.

Creativity, Discovery, innovativeness is the character of institutes abroad. Is it so in India?

I was reading an article written by an American author in the journal, "Fortune". The writer was addressing the question, "Can India ever compete with US in software business?" To answer the question he made an analysis of higher education in both countries, and recorded that Indian system is rote learning that is to say mechanical, stereo type based on memorization and not creative thinking. Students are taught sunset knowledge. Institutions in India do not produce new knowledge, new theories. Students are not learning innovation and hence they do not know how to discover unknown. They are reflection centers teaching that knowledge which comes to them from developed countries. It does not focus on creativity, discovery and innovation. He came to the conclusion that Indian institutions can produce at best followers in technology but not leaders. On the other hand, thrust of US universities is on producing leaders, discoverers, creators, who obtain patents and intellectual property. It is US which are pumping new technology most in the world market.85% 0f IPR is held by Americans. He said student's education in universities and colleges is an enabler to competitiveness of software industry. A nation creating followers can never compete with a nation creating leaders, unless in future it improves. Universities in India need to incorporate creativity in syllabi and aim to produce leaders.

Another study from Duke University was examining if there is a threat from India to US competitiveness. It observed that today the quality of Indian universities and engineering schools is by and large poor. The number of M Tech and PhDs who are crucial to technological innovation are too few and so India is far too behind in innovation. It concludes by saying that India on account of poor higher education does not pose a challenge to US competitiveness in near future.

Universities abroad have been upgraded as birth places, [maternity homes], of New Technology Based Firms. How many of our universities do this?

MIT Boston is giving birth to as many as 50 companies every year. Microsoft was born in Harvard. Tesla electric car was born in Stanford.. There are more than 3000 companies which owe their origin to MIT. Australian universities [Fang Zaho], each one is giving birth to 40 companies every year. Chinese universities of late are also doing the same. Why Indian universities can not? How many companies are born in Indian universities? They can do this. But they need to have this vision. Where do our institutes stand in comparison with their counterparts? In the recent past IIT Mumbai has set up a Technology incubator, Business incubator. It has started spinning off hi-tech enterprises. Employment and income generation depends on New Technology Based Firms. It is these companies which provide new life and blood to industries and keep them technologically up to date. This gap needs to be filled up with priority. Indian Universities need to take a drive to adopt new visions as their counterparts to install a mechanism for spinning off companies. It is reported that IISC Bangalore has recently made collaboration with MIT Boston in this respect.

Institutes abroad display patents for sale in Industrial Exhibitions

Do we do that? Patents are almost unknown to institutions in India. It is good to do research but it is essential to make commercial exploitation of the findings of research. This makes research financially more viable, and attracts more funds. Today, the economic returns obtained from research done in India are far too few. This has been our weakness, and so actual funding for research does not grow.

A few years back I happened to visit Hannover industrial exhibition. There was a pavilion meant for universities and colleges. It was most crowded by the visitors. Students were explaining the new researches, emerging technologies like, patents and IPR to visitors. Universities had come from world over to display. Visitors wanted to know the technologies of tomorrow. In India how many institutions have obtained patents and participated in industrial exhibition? Students do research for PhD, M Tech. Thesis remains in library. It is published in journals and is being harvested by foreigners for obtaining patents. We do not exploit research done commercially. Even the traditional knowledge like Haldi, Turmeric, Ayurvedic medicines, Wheat etc are converted in to patents by USA. We need to build this culture in our education. If the young students learn this they follow in future career. If they do not learn they do not practice. Attempts by Technology Information and assessment Council [TIFAC], New Delhi a government of India body, are being made to popularize patent, IPR. It has yet to reach universities and colleges. We need to protect our research findings before publication by patenting and convert it in money. Research is a wealth generating mechanism provided it is converted in to patents, IPR. When shall we realize this? [Naik 2004]

Institutions in India today are distinctly a technology follower. They do not lead; do not give birth to new technology. They are by and large inward looking, restricting to class rooms and not going beyond. They lack the world vision. They are not enabled to think and act in this direction, the situation needs correction.

We need to install patent IPR centers in each institute and display patents in exhibitions. Industry is keen on knowing emerging technology. Institutes should aim at that. Visions of our institutions need to be enlarged, to go beyond to what their counterparts else where in the world are doing.

Institutions abroad are in driver's seat. Indian institutions are followers like bogies of a train

A friend of mine 25 years back went to USA. He studied MS, PhD and then started a company in Silicon Valley. He returned to India after a gap of 25 years, we received him on the airport at Mumbai. He was curious to know about the progress made by India. We were driving by car to Pune. He was happy to see the new high way, as good as in USA. When we came to Pune I was telling him now we have entered Pune. He was not able to see any signs of his time on roads. He would not believe that this is Pune. He said how Pune can change so much, beyond recognition. We came on Deccan Gymkhana, yet he was not ready to believe that this is Pune. Then we came on Laxmi road. He did not see a single bicycle, which at his time used to be crowded. Then we came on railway station. He did not see a single horse tanga. He refused to accept that it was Pune. Then we brought him to the college where he studied.. He saw the same old labs, class rooms etc. Immediately he exclaimed, now I can not refuse. He said whole city has changed but his college has not. He said in USA Cities change because of institutions. In India, institutions are followers of change.

Institutions in India, instead of becoming an engine have become bogies. This he said is an unfortunate situation. Legitimately institutions should have to initiate changes in society. Institutions need to have attitude to shape the development. Only those cities are well developed where universities are having such visions.

Institutes abroad have Innovative Character. They produce far more captains and Generals [M Tech, PhDs]; we produce more soldiers, graduates. Teaching Assistantship and Research Assistantship in India are almost absent

I have visited more than two dozen universities in Germany, China, UK, US. I found that they are in the pursuit of discovery, research and innovation.[3] Their center of gravity is on post graduation and Doctoral studies. They produce far more graduates of advanced degrees. They produce more captains and generals. We produce more of soldiers. There are no schemes like Teaching assistantship and research assistantship in many universities, to attract the fresh scholars. This is a serious short coming of our education.

It is on account of advanced courses offered in the institute that the quality of UG becomes superior. They teach sunrise knowledge and sunrise technology. According to the report of G Bush Commission, namely "Science the Endless Frontier", research is the main function of university and teaching is a byproduct. Teaching with out research leads to irrelevance, and obsolescence. In India this is the status.

Many universities in India teach sunset technologies to students. Institutions are behind the time. According to Mckinsey report published recently only 30 % of the engineering graduates are employable. Government has now proposed, From NASSCOM to CII, every body is crying hoarse about the quality of our technical manpower.

Education to policy makers to make policies enabling institutes to become innovative like abroad is necessary. Policy makers should enable the professors to be innovative and produce more of M Tech and PhDs that is to say captains and generals. This is a major point of difference between Indian institutes and their counterparts abroad.

Size of Institutions abroad is large and hence economical. In India it is pigmy, uneconomical

National University Singapore has 350 acres of land but it has 1900 professors and 32000 students. MIT Boston has about 500 acres of land and 40000 students with 3000 professors. Georgia Tech University has 20000 students and 1000 professors. It offers 130 different courses. Karlsruhe University in Germany has 30,000 students and 2000 professors. Our universities by and large are pigmy in size. They have big land of the order of 1000 acres but students and professors are far too few. Pankaj Jalote [2007] in one of his articles has advocated scaling up the strength of students in IITs from 4000 to 10000. Courses offered are stereotyped besides too low in number. Most of the universities like Pune Mumbai in their campuses have too few students and faculty. Aurangabad University for example has 500 acres of land, has 1000 students and has only 100 faculty strength. The size of our institutes is uneconomic. They are over capitalized in terms of land and buildings. Universities abroad open at 8 in the morning and remain open up to midnight. We open at 10 in the morning and close at 5 pm. There is a big difference in libraries. They are far too behind. Capacity utilization of installed facility in India is too small. Private colleges in engineering are like small "pan shops" with out PG and PhD education. There are no well springs of knowledge in the institutions. They depend on borrowed knowledge. The scope of our institutions needs improvement. They need to see what is happening elsewhere in the world and do benchmarking. Continuing education is a popular trend abroad. Mid-career students are large in number registering in universities. Almost 20% students are mid-career students. This trend is almost absent in India .Corporate education centers is a common trend in all foreign universities. Why it is not in India?

They have Built Visions for patent IPR culture for the year 2015. Have we?

How many of our universities and colleges have patent culture? MIT Boston every year obtains around 100 patents. The institute has a Technological Licensing Office with 200 people working in it. There is a trend of commercialization of new technology in almost every university. It is a source of income to the professors, students and the institute. Many universities in Germany, UK have patent departments. In fact their performance is measured in terms of how many patents are obtained and the revenue earned. They have Technology Incubators, Business Incubators, research parks and Venture Capital Firms available in campus. Students develop skills of innovation and patenting in them. This is our serious weakness. This is one of the important reasons why Indian students go abroad. We need necessarily to learn from international experience abroad.

They give high priority to education in national budget. What priority we give?

Professor's profession is very important, but the profession is not made attractive. Education is not accorded the priority it deserves in national budget. It does not get budget as their counterparts .India spends around 3% only where as developed countries spend around 10% of GDP. Budget allocation to R&D in India is only 0.8% of GDP where as in China it is 1.5%. Papers published and patents obtained in China are ten times larger. Less number of people and that too poorly are therefore educated. This adversely affects the quality of leadership in all walks of life. Technological content in economy is far too low. It is to be realized that it is education which makes a man competitive. Without education man is less than an animal. It is like training a cook to prepare food. A trained cook uses less material yet prepares tasty food. A untrained cook consumes more material and spoils the taste. Untrained man is unfit to live a worthy life. Nobel Laureate Dr Amartya Sen recommended increasing budget on education. The then finance minister Mr Yeshwant Sinha asked him what should be the first priority in budget. He replied Education. Then he asked what should be the second priority? He again replied, education. Then he asked, what should be the third priority? He replied again Education. Should the Government care for his advice?

Policy Makers in India are not galvanized with new ideas

Foreign universities galvanize their leaders from time to time with new ideas. Do we? Strategies employed in India are far too behind the world. The strategies have almost no strength to take the nation forward. Research subsidizes education and education subsidizes research. Research and education are complementary to each other. This world proven fundamental strategy is not adhered to. Strategies adopted in India are not strong enough in world comparison.

There is a storey of two armies which were fighting a battle with each other. One army had a lion as its captain, but the soldiers were sheep. The second army had a sheep as its captain and lions as soldiers. The lion captain employees bold strategies. The other captain, a sheep designs strategies like a coward and loses even though his soldiers are lions, because the soldiers have to follow the strategies drawn by captain. It is the strategies which enable the army to win.

Situation of India is something like sheep as captain. We have a strong base of intellectuals, and academicians but strategies which are drawn by leaders in bureaucracy and leaders in politics are weak. Academic leadership as a result at national/ state/ institution levels is crippled. Students of today are tomorrow's leaders. To have good leaders tomorrow we have to have good institutions today. Kauravas had a much bigger army than Pandavas. But the strategies suggested by Lord Krishna to Pandwas were far superior. So Pandavas could win. Shivaji had much smaller army than Aurengzeb but still he could win, because he employed better and bold strategies like a lion.

There is a greater need to shed the mental weakness in academicians. They need to be enabled to grow at par with their counterparts abroad.

Brain Power is nursed abroad. It is wasted in India.

Brain power is said to be more powerful than any other power, like money power, political power, electrical power etc. Demand for knowledgeable people in globalize world is sky rocketing. SEZs and industrial development plans demand people with skills like research, innovation, entrepreneurship, patenting and IPR. Nations which understand the dynamics of world market and match it with institutions will win. Others may work hard, spend resources but will lag behind in brain race. Those who take strategies in favor of nursing brain power are only to win.

We have to recognize the importance and work with knowledge, IPR rather than muscle. Salaries of only a few in industry are sky rocketing. Many on the other hand are jobless. They have brains but under nourished. The dichotomy can be resolved only by upgrading the institutions.

Academic freedom is the legal right of students and professors abroad. In India professors are servants without any academic freedom. They have to teach what is given in university syllabus. They can not teach based on personal research. Students have no choice than to learn what is handed over to them

Institutions also do not have academic freedom. This is proved from IIM-A case. They have become puppets in the hands of Government. Independent free thinking and decision making is not allowed. CAFETARIA approach courses are not run, although badly needed. Industries are varied in nature and so are their manpower needs. Courses ought to be unique. Standardized stereotyped courses are giving birth to mediocrity. Hence coaching classes industry is booming.

Academicians are being exploited by governing boards. The students and public at large are also being exploited. Academicians however, ought to work in only public interest. Some times the government, institute and industry are too selfish damaging interest of public at large. Academicians therefore ought not to work to further in the foul interest of institute, industry or government. They must behave fully in a professional manner. For this they have to be autonomous by law although they receive salary from institute, and from government or industry. World experience tells us that nations grow best only when academicians can function in autonomous manner.

Academicians Generate sunrise knowledge and educate people to use. They essentially should not have to go too close to education barons, industry or to government. They should have academic freedom to be able to play their legitimate professional role including that of a critic. Academicians have to work in larger public interest, for maintaining a healthy national economy. They should not have to bend before education barons, industry or government. They work in the pursuit of new knowledge.

Indian economy is a low income economy mainly because of lack of application of new knowledge. All institutions and professors should forth with be made autonomous. Parliament and State assembly should pass laws in national interest empowering professors for the cause of education.

Universities, institutions and private colleges have become the prisoners in the hands of Government. Non educational principles and strategies of government are guiding the people in universities and colleges. In fact it should be the other way round. Higher education institutes have become slaves of whims and fancies of government. They change every five years when new party comes to power.

The scheme of contract appointment of lecturers on fixed low salary of is introduced in Maharashtra state. UGC and AICTE have objected. It has no backing of any academic body but only of bureaucracy. Mediocre are getting in. Although cheap, quality of education is deteriorated. Can the entry of professionals in teaching be protected? How can we produce globally competent leader professionals?

Government is not best qualified to govern education. Government should make only legislation for which it is meant. Long range policies and practices in education in India need be made by professionals considering the trends in world.

Research is main focus abroad. In India it is lacking

Research is given back seat in higher education. Professors have no research grant. Institutes and universities have become teaching shops. Professors and students have no budget for research. Professors teach sunset knowledge coming from abroad. They have no research skills. They learn parrot like that which was taught to them ten years before. Neither the teachers nor students are trained to learn to discover what is unknown. Unfortunately teaching and research have been segregated from each other. This leads to weakening of both. This is not the way to build a nation. They therefore remain followers. Research must become the core function of an institution.

Institutions are governed in India by those who have low value for Academics

Privatization of education is good provided it is governed by those who have value for academics. In most of the cases it is the politicians who do not understand it, and sit on the governing board. Today, education barons have usurped the powers of academicians. Professors have become humble servants. [5] They have no freedom to think and freedom to act. They have no budget for research. While money earned in colleges is siphoned for political purposes. This is too damaging for the future of children and grand children. That is one of the main reasons why brain drain from India is rampant.

Education barons have brought unethical commercial trends in education. Government is a party to it. Thinkers have no place in education. Nobler aims of education are thrown to winds. Bottoms 50% of population, because fees are high, do not have access to higher education. Upper 50% population is mediocre but wealthy and so gets access to higher education. India with such policies will stand to lose in brain race in long range. [6] The fabric of Indian culture is likely to be damaged. At a time when the level of education needed for productive employment is increasing, opportunity to go to college to bottom half population is decreasing. The common man is getting a feeling of betrayal, causing resentment which may lead to discontent, instability, even riots, which may be very costly. The present policies are an aid to Nexalite movement. Education institutes can not and should not be run on commercial lines like General Motors. Public interest is being sacrificed by both government and industry. When shall we realize this?

There is no affiliating system abroad. In India it is rampant. It has killed the innovation capacity of students. Chancellor of universities should not be Governor. He should be an academician. Policies are at fault.

Inbreeding in higher education is taking place. University Acts are obsolete. Governor of a state who is not an academician but a politician is at helm of affairs, as the chancellor of universities. Chairman of UGC, Chairman of AICTE are academicians. How come chancellor of universities is a politician? This is not so abroad.

The chancellor of universities is the appointing authority for vice chancellors. He does appointments mostly on political considerations. Most of the VCs are misfits. He inducts politics in universities. The situation perpetuates down below. This has resulted in politicization of higher education. Blame is wrongly passed on to professors. Policy makers and the chancellors are truly at fault. The situation demands immediate change. We need to adopt international visions to improve.

Unless the change is brought in chancellor's post as suggested above, the affiliating system may not go. There are no affiliated colleges in developed countries. Every college from its beginning is autonomous.

There is more number of technical universities abroad. India has very few

Almost half **of** universities in US are technical. Germany has more than 84 technical universities. [7] So is the case in Japan. It is observed that those nations which have more of technical universities have capitalized technology more effectively. [8] India has more multi faculty universities, which is an outdated model. In these universities Technical discipline does not get a deal it deserves. Hence it lags behind the world. AICTE has recommended establishment of exclusive technical universities. However in most of the states there is only one technical university and many colleges are affiliated to it. It creates monopoly, bureaucracy. Efforts, investment done by colleges, students as a result do not get fruits they deserve. Agriculture Universities which were set up in sixties developed new varieties of seeds, which have resulted in increased food production. Technical Universities should not be only examination bodies awarding degrees but should generate new technologies and improve industrial production [.9] Future of children is linked up with creation of technical universities.

Innovation theorists must learn to live with controversies. Innovators disturb the present equilibrium. Till next equilibrium is brought to order they may have to face rough weather.

Innovations based on S & T advances have become a major contributor to national well being.

Researches in US lead the world in publication of articles. One third authors are from US, 32 out of 50 world best universities are from

US. 20% of world doctorates are in US. US are a country with only 6% of world population.

Research funding of US is 2.72% of GDP, 2.98% in Japan, 2.49 % in Germany, 1.85 % in UK, 2.18 France, and only 0.8% in India.

Industry- Academy- and Government is a self reinforcing triangle.

Conclusion

Good ideas are available not only in India but also abroad. We should not close our eyes and ears to them. We should not miss to benefit from them. Foreign collaborations are necessary. It is too costly not to interact with the counterparts elsewhere in the world. Mobility of professors to world best universities at any cost must be planned in a big way on priority. This is the only way to build good leaders and to take India on world map. [10]

We lack visions and not the resources. We lack interaction with our counterparts elsewhere in the world. We lack dedicated efforts. Institutions, universities need to show new visions of new world which inspire students to become leaders on global level. Institutions ought to shift their culture in favor of creativity, IPR and discovery. India's growth rate can be sustainable only if academic institutions adopt innovative character. Visions drive the national economies forward. [11]

In this time of knowledge society it is the intellectual capital that matters. People work with hands, but it is the brain behind which gives inspiration. Government should have to attach more value in national budget to create and use new knowledge.

The paper has identified only a few gaps, which are critical and need to be attended to forthwith. Without which higher education will not be up to the mark and fulfill the growing aspirations of people. Opportunities do not last longer. They do not wait. Achieving the declared dream of India to become a developed country by the year 2020 depends on how ably and urgently we initiate steps to make up the gaps.

We must not forget to recognize the importance of IPR. Creation of favorable environment for the same should be our top priority.

Rapid up gradation of higher education institutes and universities in the light of experiences in the world should urgently be taken up.

There is nothing more urgent for India at this juncture of time than reviving higher education

References

1. Fang Zaho, Academic Entrepreneurship, Case study of Australian universities, Published in International Journal of Entrepreneurship and innovation, pp. 91-97, IP Publishing Ltd. Vol 5 number 2 2nd May 2004.
2. B M Naik, Needed – Innovation and Entrepreneurship in Higher Education Institutes, published in Indian journal Of Technical Education, January- March 2004 Vol 27, number 1, pp. 27-32.
3. Green paper of European Union on Innovation and technological transfer Enterprise Unit DG, EUFO, 2295-2920 Luxemburg.
4. Pankaj Jalote, An Opportunity To Scale Up the IITs, Economic Times, 26 April 2007.
5. B M Naik, Privatization of Technical Education, Identification of Risk factors, and their Management- making Education affordable, Journal on Engineering and Technology, i-manager publications, volume 1, No. 2.
6. James J Duderstadt, A university for twenty first century. The University of Michigan Press.
7. Derek Bok, Universities in the Market Place, The Commercialization of Higher Education, Princeton University Press Princeton New Jersey.
8. Clark Kerr and Marion L Gade, Association of College Boards of Universities of America., "The Guardians, Boards of Trustees of American universities and Colleges, What They Do and How Well they Do It.
9. William G Bowen and Derek Bok, Princeton university press, "The Shape of The River, long Term consequences Of Considering race in College and university admissions.
10. B M Naik Book, "New Vistas in Technical Education, Vivek publication, Aurangabad.
11. V Raghunathan, "India Needs More quality PhDs", published in economic Times.

Chapter - 9

Colleges / Universities need Research Parks to Make Education Globally Competitive

Synopsis

Research Park is a joint effort between an academic institution and industry. It provides a common platform to both industry and academic personnel for innovation, creativity, technology generation, and product/ process development. It binds together the two namely industry and institutes for mutual growth and prosperity. It is a place where innovative minds of students & professors on one hand are matched with innovative minds in industry on the other.[1] Establishment of Research Parks in universities & autonomous colleges is recommended by Anil Kakodkar committee in its report to government of Maharashtra. The report says China in the recent past has installed more than 300 Research Parks. It is more on account of them that the institutions have become innovative in character. They are playing a driver's role in development of China. is found to be a means to convert intellectual capital of both the university and industry in to usable goods and services.

Research Park is a Profit Centre. It generates wealth and employment. Research Park is a source of income. It is not a financial liability. As is fees from students so is Research Park an income source for college. It increases the rate of return from investment in college. Besides, it is a mechanism to build synergy between industry and institutes. In addition it enables university to upgrade quality of UG, PG, and PhD programs. It converts research output in to patents & IPR, and makes their commercial exploitation. It generates surplus after meeting all the expenses and plough it back on continuing basis to further research. It enables university to be the "Light House" for industry. It facilitates students to earn & learn hi-tech in knowledge environment and become globally fit for future. Innovative students, professors and industry personnel are the key players and drivers of park. It believes in, "Look ahead to stay ahead". Research Park enables a university to keep progressing in research and its commercial exploitation, from generation to generation. It increases the rate of return from investment in universities and industry both.

Institutes and industry are interdependent. One without the support of other cannot stand high. Research Park is a project to be established in partnership preferably with the alumni entrepreneurs and industry. All the partners, namely colleges, alumni and the industry could share development & its management besides the costs and benefits. Research, innovation and testing of materials labs which are costly could be established as common facility centre. The capital cost could be borne by all the partners. Grant from DST Government of India and Rajiv Gandhi Commission for S & T of about 4 crore is available. More than 15 parks in various institutes have obtained grants from them. Thousands of parks all over the world are successfully contributing from the last more than 50 years. They are improving quality of education and simultaneously giving fresh technology inputs to industry to improve competitiveness.

Good teaching in class rooms and labs is necessary but not enough. It has to be supplemented with learning innovation and research skills for which a Research Park is necessary. It increases imagination; creativity of students makes them innovative leaders. The paper explains how to go about.

Research Park is a meeting place for innovative minds: Research Park is a common platform, where innovative minds from industry and innovative minds from academics meet. Professors of university and colleges along with scholar students meet industry personnel to exchange each other's progressive ideas and stretch imagination to bring them to reality. It is a place meant for cross fertilization of ideas in addition to giving feedback for making education more relevant and purposeful. Research Park is meant more for giving birth to new technology based firms.[2] Research Park is a mechanism to commercially exploit the research output of PhD, Masters, and Bachelors thesis in to usable goods and services, and simultaneously give feedback to improve their quality. It converts intellectual capability and technological strengths in to new products and processes. It is a wealth generating mechanism. The city/region can be industrially advanced and economically more developed only if it establishes and runs successfully a Research Park. Research Park gives boost to industrial development. It facilitates learning of research and innovation skills by students. Presence of Research Park in campus inspires students to be creative. Research Park on campus puts more confidence in them. Research Park is a mechanism to earn dividends that is to say economic returns on its intellectual capital. It contributes in turn to improving financial condition of university. Technological contribution of a university through Research Park gives technological strength to industry and makes the city/ region economically better.[3]

Research Park is an innovative industrial complex adjacent to an institution/university, having close links with the innovative professors and scholar students. Researchers, innovators, discoverers are known drivers of research park. It provides a vibrant and creative atmosphere which converts intellectual strength, and technological capabilities of the students and faculty; as well as of innovators in industry in to commercial products and processes. Alumni of the university who are important stake holders derive further inspiration from Research Park and so in larger interest they are found to take active hand in its establishment.[4]

Seeds of sunrise technology based entrepreneurship are planted here in the minds of young students. Innovative industry personnel come here to interact with young scholars. New technology based firms, and research based companies take birth due to cross fertilization of ideas of innovative people in the park. Leaders in academics and leaders in industry provide close guidance to young scholars. Parks facilitate giving Technology Push matching with Market Pull on sustained basis. It is a breeding ground, it is an incubator of talent, and it is an engine for development of SMEs SSIs, in sunrise technologies.[5] It is a magnet attracting bright people from industry and bright people from academia, besides NRI to make important things happen. It is a technology cluster for research, and discovery. Innovation skills which are needed lifelong by students are germinated and acquired in park. This adds strength to the national economy. It generates new jobs and new companies. Should we not then jump start the world proven innovative project like Research Park? Which political leader then not likes to have research Park in his constituency? Research Park from experience in developed world is found to produce leaders in engineering and leaders in industry competent by world standards.

Way back, it is the success of projects like Cornell's Centre[6] for advanced technology that has led many universities and colleges world over, to establish research parks and incubation centres on their campuses. In these parks, space is rented to small, developing companies-often headed by recent graduates-and the college provides infrastructure facilities, as well as scientific intellectual inpuys and business advice and support.

Firms which are born out of research become competitive internationally: Secondly, a major reason for the success of the US computer industry has been the development of a host of small firms in Silicon Valley and in Boston. These firms grew directly out of research in neighboring universities. Professors have acted as consultants to these firms, new grads have provided the workforce, and research projects funded by government have provided ideas.[7] The companies benefitted, so also the nation with new products, new jobs and new market strength. MIT Boston alone obtains as many as 100 patents each year, which earns almost 25% of its annual budget. Around 30 firms are born each year in MIT, and around 3000 firms owe their origin, over a period of years.[8] Chinese universities are not behind, so also Australian. Can the Indian universities not do this? You need a swimming pool to learn swimming, so you need a technology transfer department to learn and practice entrepreneurship.

Teaching and learning in class rooms and doing research in labs is good but not enough. It is essential for students to learn innovation skills for commercial exploitation of research done at doctoral, masters and bachelors levels. This is to increase the scholarship of the university and transfer new knowledge, new technology from university to masses for their welfare. Experience of western schools in this respect is worth emulation. Majority of the western schools convert research in to patents & IPR and transfer them to industry through well defined systems and procedures. Economic returns from investment in universities then increase, which brings more money for further research and makes it sustainable. Public service, carried out chiefly through teaching, was the motive for the creation of the earliest universities. Even today teaching remains the core of the university's public service. But now in competitive world university's public service extends far beyond, to entrepreneurial activities like research park, technology innovation, patent & IPR. Intellectual capital of university which is so critical for national development is required to be converted in to usable goods and services. For a country like India that aspires to be an economic power house all the while it is more important. What use is of research, new knowledge, new technology if not exploited commercially? Universities along with industry and alumni ought to think big jointly in global context and establish on campus a research park, like their counterparts in developed countries.

All world class colleges/ universities have research parks on campus.[9] Quality and relevance of education in universities has become superior because of park. Studies indicate that enterprises born on park are observed to be more successful than those born off park. A university can become centre of excellence only if it ventures in innovative efforts as this. So as to obtain innovative character it is essential that the Indian universities adopt this new strategic direction.

National Knowledge Commission 2006 and Yesh Pal committee report of 2009 both have recommended innovative projects like Research Park, so as to create new knowledge, new technology, discoveries and creative endeavours to be the integral components of the university.

FICCI Higher Education Summit in its report of 2008 has recommended their creation and urged the colleges to show a lead.[10] It suggests PPP mode for implementation. In a nutshell

- Research Park is a cradle for entrepreneurs
- Its output is in terms of New Technology Based Firms, patents & IPR
- It makes commercial exploitation of research done in various departments in university and colleges like in PhD, M Tech, M Sc, B Tech etc
- Research Park converts intellectual and technological capability in to usable goods and services.
- It inculcates research and innovation skills amongst students
- Research Park produces Indian brands of technology
- It increases financial rate of return from investment in university

- It creates entrepreneurial culture in campus
- Facilitates synergy of university and industry
- Research Park generates employment in hi-tech of high income
- It produces world class leaders in industry, leaders in technology and First Movers in industry.

The Indian Universities ought to dream big, think great to create new capacity to succeed in competitive world. Research Park attracts great people from across the society with the possibility of great success.

Research Park increases universities/colleges out reach far and wide in world:[11] Universities world over with Research Park are observed to be enriching them and augmenting new ideas besides budget support for future growth. They are getting well integrated with society and industry. Universities by virtue of Research Park and knowledge in it have moved to the centre of development, they have become drivers of economic and social prosperity. The visions and missions of the universities then become dynamic, adaptive based on sharing experiences with people at large, and not only giving off the shelf irrelevant prescriptions. UGC/ AICTE in various projects in the past have invested good amount of money on research. How much is the financial return obtained from them? In the absence of research park returns on investment are too little. Replenishment of funds for research because of low return slows down. Research Park is designed to generate economic benefits for people in the region, by bringing intellectual discoveries of scientists, professors and students to the world. It accelerates the speed of research and makes it more focused and effective. It brings risk taking entrepreneurs, investors, expert advisors, youthful scientific minds together in the same place at the same time. Can Indian universities afford to neglect?

Programs and events in the park are consciously designed to encourage networking among innovators, entrepreneurs, and investors. Thought provocation speakers from around the world are invited on the park to inspire and inform new ways of working. Entrepreneurship programs aim at inventor- entrepreneurs and leadership teams of emerging companies, to help bridge knowledge gap. Creative people with brand new ideas are a great resource. Can university/ college become a light house for industry without it? How can globally successful companies come here in search of new ideas and technologies? Establishment of Research Park is the answer.

Prof Terman of Stanford University gave the following philosophy,

"An industry to be globally competitive needs an access to first class research in universities. So also universities and professors/scholar students need an access to industry to commercialize findings of their research."[12]

Industry and institute, by being stand alone cannot achieve peak performance even if they deserve. They need to synergies their efforts for which Research Park is essential.

Research Parks are found to have given stimulus to increase the scholarship of the university and colleges, made the education at UG PG and Doctoral levels more relevant and purposeful. Universities have thereby become innovative in character. Research Park is a place to sharpen ideas and to connect with business advisors to explore market potential of these ideas. It is a launching pad for spin off companies to world market. More and more application of knowledge leads to more discoveries. Universities can acquire much desired innovative character by installing Research Park on campus. They get a feel which way the industrial world is moving and orient them to enable youths to harvest opportunities.

Harness the competitive Advantage: Universities are offering UG, PG and PhD programs in science, engineering, arts and commerce etc. Students and faculty are brilliant. The University continuously generates new knowledge, new theories through research at PhD, masters and bachelors level. The theses most of time remain on cupboards in library. No worthwhile use is made of the research findings, except a few publications. If Research Park is established the research done can be most effective to obtain patents & IPR, spin-off companies in hi- tech, taking technology to masses for their welfare. Full capacity of intellectuals in the university and surrounding area can be utilized only when platform of such a park is available.[13] Similarly there are innovative people in industry, for want of infrastructure and synchronization their capacities remain unfolded. Can the Universities aim to be equal to world class? Should we not expand our visions and missions? Low aim is a crime.

Purpose

To provide an organizational base

To Transfer Technology through Start-Ups in Hi- Tech

To attract and create new companies to use intellectual capacities

To accelerate and stimulate research, innovation, patent & IPR and centres of excellence in close collaboration with industrial world.

More commercial exploitation of research is an incentive to researchers. It stimulates young minds to be more innovative and creative.

To develop entrepreneurship culture, research and innovation culture

To generate innovation and research skill set amongst scholars. Students tend to become creative and not remain parrot like mugging up

To generate employment of hi- tech, hi - pay and bring about economic development with higher productivity.

Returns on investment in university/college increases, which attracts in turn more investment.

To enable students to reach out to industry at global level

To reduce time gap between invention and its application

To conduct strategic research in conjunction with industry

To make both the University and industry more enterprising

To develop bond between institute and industry

To apply findings of research done in industry

To create knowledge based society that is to say technological society

To enable university graduates to start companies.

Visions

An institution/University of 21st century to be successful must adopt new visions of new world. It should not function like yesterday.

It should along with all neighbouring colleges synergies its efforts of development with industry. No university, in spite of potential, can become excellent all alone by its own internal efforts and ideas. It must take the support from industry, give birth to knowledge and research industry. Alumni should put their full strength in terms of ideas and money behind academics for long range gains to themselves industry and student's community. The University/ institute essentially should have to show lead. An institution has knowledge strength. It should attract like a magnet knowledge industry around.

Do we want to initiate a project to create Indian brands of technology? Or follow the brands like in the past from foreign? Do we aspire to make most of our abilities and become a technology leader to sow the seeds of development and not remain copy cat? Research Park is then the answer.

How can we create world class institutes/universities? World class universities produce not only graduates but more importantly produce new technologies and new technology based firms [14]. They create a new industrial society, fit for future. Universities elsewhere in the world are doing this. Many companies are in continuous contact with MIT Boston. They derive technological strength, like blood supply to our body. We can if we envision. Low aim is a crime. We should dream big and think great.

China, one time behind India, is now way ahead, producing two times more PhDs and M Techs. They have adopted a vision to produce 100 hi- tech firms/ start ups each year. Does it present an example to Indian universities and colleges? Should we emulate this world proven model

Present status: Around 15 Indian universities, like Poona University [Dr Jagdale], IIT Channai, Cochin University have set up research parks under DST program called as Science and Technology Entrepreneurs Park [STEP] and are also spinning off hi-tech companies. As you need a swimming pool to learn swimming, so you need a Research Park to learn innovation skills. A university /college with out Research Park in modern world is incomplete, irrelevant, nonviable, and outdated. It is W:icapped to perform its legitimate operations.[15] The conventional wisdom of It handicapped which once served well is not fit for today and tomorrow. They must transfer new college to society, for which Research Park is a means. India needs many more of them to be globally competitive.

Missions

To contribute to technology development, patent & IPR in the region

(a) To facilitate new knowledge transfer to society,

(b) To make commercial exploitation of research, of M Sc, MA, M Tech, PhD thesis and enhance their quality and relevance

(c) To convert intellectual capability in to usable goods and services.

(d) To spin off Hi-Tech firms

(e) To inculcate innovation and discovery skills amongst students

(f) To increase scholarship of courses

(g) To enable grads to start enterprises

(h) To provide a platform to industry and alumni to contribute.

All world class universities/ colleges have innovative and creative character. Can we envision?

Incubating Talent for Global Competitiveness

Why thousands of students every year go abroad? They have been going from Gandhi- Nehru period. How long they will have to go? Can all students go? What do they learn, which is not available in Indian university? Have we failed so far as a society to provide adequate opportunities to our youth to be educated in world class manner? Have we failed in creating a vibrant educational eco - system that supports cutting edge research? How are counterpart institutions in developed countries different? We have too much of rote learning. They have more of innovation, creativity. Students abroad are challenged to create, to discover and innovate.[16]

Universities abroad essentially have Research Parks, Science parks, incubators, Patent & IPR centres, entrepreneurship centres, which yet majority of universities in India do not have. In the absence of which, innovation talent remains idle, and underdeveloped. Returns from investment in university and colleges are less. We are importing technology and foreigners are exporting. Bright students are migrating to greener pastures. Knowledge IPR has become more important than resources. Indian enable universities may like now to be more innovative in character and become enterprising. It should enable the talent to grow to the level it is capable for. Do we lack visions or resources?

Research Park is like a magnet to attract and retain talent. It has the potential to arrest brain drain and bring back previously gone, to convert it in brain gain.

Organization for Research Park —

Public private participation Model consisting of some or all of the following is recommended

Local Industry Association

State Industrial Corporation

Leading banks

Leading industrialists

Leading persons from IIT incubator, STEP IIT KGP, UICT as advisors

Organizational head and professors Municipal Corporation

The university may have to plan, install and monitor the progress

Steps involved

Develop awareness among industry and academic personnel

Prepare a project proposal

Discuss and make critical analysis of the proposal

Obtain Approval from government, obtain grant

Appoint head Collaborate nationally and internationally

Appoint expert advisors

Appoint a separate governing Board

Depute people to attend international conferences of Association of science/ research parks.

To recapitulate,

World experience tells us that institutions/regions/ cities develop faster which have established Research Parks in universities and colleges.

Research Park brings long range thinking, long range planning and advanced high end research so badly needed in a university and in Indian industry. University and industry to remain globally competitive ought to carry out jointly functions of research & innovation to keep them fit for future.[17]

Today success in the global market place means creating and applying new knowledge- which is to say new technology- faster than one's competitors. World winners will be those who develop talent, technologies, techniques and tools so advanced that there is no competition.

Innovation potential of youths in the absence of Research Park today is wasted. It enables it be unfolded and put to fuller use.

How to produce more entrepreneurs and how to encourage more firms to grow are the main visions and missions of this project.

A university to create and maintain its leadership position needs forthwith to establish the park.

The park works as magnet to attract best and brightest from anywhere and everywhere in the world.

One of the essential ingredients to generate hi-tech jobs, well paying jobs, industrial cluster is the creation of Research Park.

Research Park if established will make a big difference for industry, economy and university.

Without a Research Park the university, industry and institutes, so also cities and regions howsoever hard people may work will remain behind in international competition.

A university with park will turn out leaders in industry and leaders in technology with knowledge qualitative by international standard. It will create technology pioneers. The quality and relevance of education would become fit for future. Why students will then migrate elsewhere?

The University without park will remain incomplete, ineffective and outdated in modern sense. When shall we realize this?

The Region can win in global competition by establishing Research Park and not without it.

"Success in international competition depends now on turning intellectual strength in to marketable commodities"

Let us dream big, think great to make college in long term a world class institute.

Every Engineering Institution may like to install Research Park, patent centre, innovation centre, in campus in partnership with alumni association, to make education Globally Competitive

COEP is in the process of installing, IIT CHannai and many others have already done, Anil Kakodkar committee has recommended to Maharashtra Government, Institutes in foreign are having from many years, DST Government of India and Rajiv Gandhi Commission on S & T provides funds

References

1. The role of Science Parks in the promotion of innovation and transfer of technology, Proceedings of the Science Parks Association, annual Conference 6-7 April 1989.
2. Ibid.
3. Creating Knowledge- Strengthening Nations, the Changing Role of ones, Patricia L McCartney and Michael L Education, Edited by Glen A. J Skolinik University of University press 2002.
4. Wisconsin Alumni Research Foundation, Research park, website.
5. Green paper of European Union on Innovation and Technological Transfer Enterprize Unit DG, EUFO, 2295-2920 Luxumberg.
6. H T Rhodes, Role of American university- the creation of the future published by Cornell University press 2003.
7. Ibid.
8. Fang Zaho, [2004] Academic Entrepreneurship, case study of Australian universities, published in International journal of Entrepreneurship and innovation, pp. 91-97, IP publishing Ltd, Vol. no. 5 number 2.
9. James Duderstadt, a university of 21' Century, the university of Michigen Press
10. FICCI, website
11. B M Naik, "Strategies to make universities Globally Competitive, Published in University News Vol. 49, No. 26, July 3, 2011.
12. Op Cit Ref 6.

13. B M Naik, Needed Innovation & Entrepreneurship in higher education institutes, published in the journal of Technical Education, January- March 2004, Vol. 27 No. 1, pp. 27-32.
14. B M Naik & W S Kandlikar,[2010]" Higher & Technical Education- Book of knowledge," published by Gyan publications, Delhi.
15. Government of India, National Knowledge Commission 2006-7.
16. B M Naik, Gap Analysis, Between Indian Institutes and their Counterparts Abroad, published in University News.
17. US Academy of sciences "Rising above the Gathering Storm," report, 2007.

Chapter - 10

Strategic Planning to make an Institute Innovative & Enterprising

Introduction

Making an institute innovative, creative and enterprising requires essentially strategic planning with global visions & missions.

Strategic planning requires following inputs, for what the institution exists, where it is today, where it intends to go, what are its present capabilities, what is the road map, does the institute have strategic partnerships with industry, what is the mandate, what is the vision & mission statement, what are the core values of the institute, are they matching with visions and missions? Preparation and usage of strategic plans is found to result, in optimal utilization of the available resources, motivate and unite the faculty, staff and stakeholders to focus on college mission and make graduates fit for innovation and entrepreneurship, for today and tomorrow.

Conclusions are drawn so as to make it easy to prepare and implement the plans effectively. The paper observes that at present the quality of education, innovativeness and its relevance to world of work, is not up to the mark. It is not due to shortage of resources but because the institutions and government are not using strategic planning effectively. They are giving just lip service. The article presents the scientific method, which when adopted culture for innovation & entrepreneurship is created. The author further says, **If the colleges & universities introduce strategic planning they would introduce innovation & entrepreneurship and undoubtedly shine in the world list and take India to greater heights. If they do not use strategic planning they are sure to fail in their mission of innovation & entrepreneurship.**

The paper out lines in brief need and importance of strategic planning for upgrading universities & colleges to cover innovation & entrepreneurship. It provides effective planning and management, and optimizes the use of physical, financial and human resources working for institutes. It renders the institutions more effective, competitive, relevant and purposeful for the situations of today and tomorrow. Most of the Indian institutes now have enough resources, qualified faculty and brilliant students yet they do not rank high in the world list. They get first grade students as raw material but they are not nurtured well in innovation & entrepreneurship. It is mainly because they are not using strategic planning. Strategic planning is a missing link and so they are not innovative and enterprising. As a result thousands of dissatisfied students are going abroad every year for higher education, by spending huge sums of money, a huge brain drain and money drain. By one estimate the fees paid by students amounts to capital investment needed to establish 4 IITs. Colleges normally do, planning in a routine manner but not strategic and so they miss the target. The colleges do not do benchmarking with counterpart institutions elsewhere in the world, they do not have global visions & missions. The institutions are observed to be having a strong will to improve. But mere will and enthusiasm, although essential are not enough. They ought to follow right method and right strategic thinking to make institute innovative and enterprising. The critical need is of **Strategic planning**, covering new visions of new world, SWOT analysis [Strengths, weaknesses, opportunities and threats] and Benchmarking...AICTE, UGC, TEQIP and MHRD with a view to upgrade higher education are now demanding for **accreditation** not simple plans but strategic plans from institutions. It is observed by the author working in the committees of UGC/AICTE, accreditation etc. that most of the institutions do not do strategic planning in a right way. They get them done from management consultants. or do it by common sense. It is not done in real spirit. So the purpose of prescribing strategic plans by authorities is not fulfilled.

The paper describes the procedure for preparation of strategic plans. It essentially prescribes two of its vital ingredients, namely

1. Benchmarking with role models, with a view to envision high aims and
2. SWOT analysis. Both are vital integral parts of scientific strategic planning.

Challenges

Universities/ colleges / polytechnics, in India in the present time of globalization are observed to be ambitious and wish to outwit in local and global market. They want to become most preferred by students in admission.. Private institutions, have initiated vigorously, critical examination of old values, institution visions and missions, work methods, needs of education, attracting students from foreign etc. and demanding a change in. the perceptions of people. They generated a much needed competitive environment for themselves as well as for Government and aided institutes. Colleges now have developed a strong will to get a good grade in NAAC and NAB. But, mere will, enthusiasm although essential are not enough. **They ought to have the knowledge and skills of strategic planning, monitoring, and evaluation without which they will not be able to improve and rise to higher standards.** Foreign universities are also coming in India, and are posing both a threat and competition to Indian colleges. To be able to face the competition ably and win, Indian universities/ colleges/ polytechnics are forced by circumstances to use the technique of strategic planning.

Strategic planning is a tool for top management, principal of college, and BOG, to transform the institution to higher standard. They have to have the knowledge and skill not only to do planning but also to use it with commitment. **The strategic thinking needs to be imbibed in the minds of all employees especially BOG members, senior professors & key stakeholders of the institute.** It is only then that the plan becomes relevant to institutional needs and full benefit of the strategic planning as desired realized. Many institutions in India deserve higher standing in national and international levels, they have all the resources needed at hand but actually they fail to make a mark, because they lack in presenting scientifically done strategic plan.

This is not now an option but compulsion, without which they will become dysfunctional. Strategic planning technique is widely used in universities and colleges in developed countries like USA from many years and in fact so these institutions have become superior. Now is the time for Indian universities and colleges to use it to shine. .

The article presents, in brief, what is meant by strategic planning, what is a vision statement, how to arrive at it, who are stakeholders, how to assess their expectations, how to prepare strategic plan and how to implement it. Forces which Hi – JACK the planning process are identified. Some strategies which have worked well in India and abroad are also presented

WHY STRATEGIC PLANNING

In the absence of strategic planning our institutions are lagging in quality education and are far too behind the world. Most of them have become teaching shops, like coaching classes. They have very little innovation and entrepreneurship. They have almost no contact with their counterparts elsewhere in the world. They are stagnant, status quo minded, they continue to teach old, outdated, and irrelevant. Employment statistics indicates that only 17% of the graduates are employable. They have almost no ability to teach the state of the art. The attainment of students is far too less by international standards. The faculty, students & staff have much higher capabilities but they fail to utilize them for institutional upgradation because they do not have a well prepared strategic plan**. In the absence of a common strategic plan, commitment from stakeholders in bringing about a change is lacking.**

Government of India so also all the states after independence .have adopted five year plan approach for development in various departments like education, agriculture, industry etc. They. have prepared five year plans for budgeting and implementation. On the same lines colleges also ought to have a five year plan, sub divided in to yearly plan. The colleges/ polytechnics make routine plans but not strategic plans. If a college does not have a common strategic plan, progress in intended direction does not take place, resources are underutilized, resulting in lack of motivation, coordination, and students remain dissatisfied, their attainment is far too low.

The interaction between institutes and industry is far too weak. There is a mismatch between the two, leading to high unemployment of educated graduates, besides low productivity in both the industry and institutes. The syllabi, laboratories, library and other infrastructure of Indian institutes are far too weak by world standards. The output from our institutes in terms of quality and quantity is far too low. Our institutions, students and faculty are working hard but output is too less. So the students in increasing numbers are going abroad for higher studies. This is mostly because we do not have scientifically done strategic plans.

If the institutes are not performing as they should, if they are not coping with the change, and changing world, if they cannot understand the global winds of change, and satisfy the educational needs of youths it is largely because they are lacking in method of preparation and usage of strategic planning. **It is observed that the limiting factor for better institutional performance is not the availability of resources but the strategic vision of people to use optimally available resources. Key drivers of institutional development could become more effective if they use strategic planning.** Many institutions want to bring about organizational change and take them to greater heights but they simply are not able to reach, because they have not practiced scientific strategic planning.

It is very nice that the institutions want to rise up from present level and reach in future to higher level. They have to describe their present status, where it is, how it is today, what are the strengths and weaknesses. It has to answer the questions like, **why the institution exists? where it is today? where it intends to go? what is the institution core value system?** etc. for which it has to chart a road map. The road map has not to be in head of only top people, but has to be put on paper, and make it available to all. This motivates everyone who works for the institution and binds them together.

In the absence of a common strategic plan, different people think and act differently in inconsistent directions not knowing that they are operating at cross, nullifying each other's' efforts. Often, people remain unprepared for changes, unprepared for competition and hence they lag behind. New strategies and new directions are badly needed without which Indian Institutes, the industry and economy as a whole cannot have good future. Adoption of strategic planning is found from experience to develop a competitive spirit amongst the employees, make them oriented to goals, targets and global opportunities. Today in, the absence of strategic plans, most of the institutes do not have well defined visions and even if they have they are not connected with activities they perform, hence their performance is low in spite of high potential.

What is a Strategic Plan

Strategic plan is a written document of declared intentions. It is a depiction of consistent actions for tomorrow, detailed on 5 year and yearly basis. It projects the image of the college vis-à-vis the total environment, global Competitors-Society-Region etc. with risks and opportunities. It is always accompanied by a contingency plan to take care of deviations, if any. It is a written document of declared intentions for future. It is a 5-6 page document, made short on one page for students.

- It shows a combined plan of actions for all people working for college
- It is a plan for one year, five years and long range
- **Strategic plan essentially presents a picture of trends in global environment in higher & technical education, competitors, and expectations of stake holders**.
- Plan is prepared considering strengths, weaknesses, opportunities and threats, so as to make it fitting to needs of institute. Strengths are utilised to harvest opportunities Bench marking with the role model institution is done, and presented.
- Strategic plan makes a mention of Mandate & present mission.
- Strategic plan is prepared in consultation with key stakeholders, especially faculty, industry and alumni.
- Strategic plan depicts the deployment of new skills like innovation skills, research, robotic, AI [Artificial intelligence] skills, widening imagination, increase **Kalpana shakti**, make students not teacher puppets, but discoverers, entrepreneurs, innovators with wider global imagination, risk taking, finance skills, human relation,& communication skills.
- Strategic plan presents new methods of teaching, practical, research, and innovation.
- Strategic plan ought to address the quality and relevance of education to industry

Strategic Planning Process

The steps involved in the strategic planning are as under. The process talks about one month.

First of all the BOG of the institution has to make a decision to prepare a strategic plan, after the decision is made it has to appoint a strategic planning group [SPG] of 3-4 professors. This SPG then prepares SWOT analysis of the institute. Simultaneously it scans global winds of change. An institution which prepares strategic plan without SWOT analysis and scanning global winds of change is like preparing irrelevant strategic plan. It is going to be ineffective.

SPG prepares mandate and mission statement, of present status. It presents why the institution exists, where it is today, what are the present activities.

It scans worldwide trends and disrupting forces in higher & technical education, which when adopted institution can show better performance.

It makes an assessment of stakeholders expectations, like students, professors, employers, government development needs of region etc. It mobilises the energies and thinking of all. The assessment is done through pre designed questionnaire. Appropriate proforma will have to be designed, got filled up, from the concerned and then analyzed. This is an important step. In following this step they are found to focus on institutional mission.

SWOT analysis- SPG then prepares bench marking with role models within the country and abroad. SWOT analysis is required to be done throughout the organization; starting from a small laboratory to a big department and ultimately aggregating for the college as a whole. It has to be participative, top down and bottom up. Every individual and department has strengths. We have to be aware for our strengths and apply them to harvest the opportunities. If an institute does not do and use SWOT analysis in strategic planning, the strengths are likely to remain unutilized and opportunities missed. Good ideas of all faculty and staff should essentially come in plan.

While doing so we have to guard on our internal weaknesses and the external threats. Observations of every faculty on weaknesses of the institution and method of conducting the course, need to be recorded. Are our internal systems and procedures matching with objectives? Are they up to date? Are internal people co-operative? Is the external competition manageable? What are the forces which may Hi-Jack the people and organizational strengths? These are some of the questions which need to be answered. It accounts for existing strengths and use them to make most of the opportunities

The institution has to take in to account internal weaknesses, minimise and possibly remove. Envision opportunities at global and local levels to encash them., scan the local environment, state, world best institutes. It anticipates external threats and disruptive forces during implementation, and threat from foreign universities? Every organization has strengths, weaknesses, opportunities and threats. Strategic plan needs to be prepared matching with SWOT and not in air. It further develops long term and short term visions, goals & objectives, identifies relevant strategic issues. To make education creative, innovative, imaginative. SPG develops options. How to increase "Kalpana shakti" of students. reduce rote learning, reduce exam focus, promote creativity. Institutes abroad are always innovating and innovating. Next and the most important thing is to assess the Global environment, to know, who are the competitors, what strategies they are adopting.

Various options will come out from the exercise above so as to meet the stakeholders' expectations. These options will have to be carefully studied by all and the best ones selected. What comes out from this exercise is a strategy or strategies which can turnout our vision into reality. People in the organization at various levels develop a vision and also ability to actualize the visions. There is a saying "seeing a problem is half solving it". Minds of people are energized right from planning stage and they all know where they are heading. Vision formation in people of the organization is a very important step and without which the organizations tend to perish. Procedure for preparation of strategic plan is very important. Those who follow proper method of open debate and discussion with in the organization they strengthen organizational capacity during preparation itself to transform institution from present level to higher level. Those who do not follow they make an improper strategic plan and miss the way .An institution may take guidance from management consultants but it should involve internal faculty and staff.

Many times big visions, promises are kept in view but they are not adequately supported by physical and financial resources. For example, many colleges have a mission of research and development but have no staff, no funds, no systems and procedures. The value system required for R & D is just absent and hence no financial resources, earmarked to permit the academic staff to attend international conferences. How can they become world class without attending international meets?

Therefore, "Strategic Audit" of the plans needs to be carried out before they are firmed up and declared. It must be ascertained, through strategic audit, whether there is a will at the top to carry it out or not, whether there are adequate finances available or not. Otherwise, it results into frustration. Especially in Govt. institutions, strategic audit is a must. We often want to build Taj Mahal with resources not enough even for a small house.

Vision Statement

Vision statement has to be stimulating, unifying, guiding and distinctive, & unique for the institute. It is the vision which touches the hearts of people, inviting their emotional involvement, provides a rallying force, it invites commitment of work forces to achieve goals and targets. Vision statement provides a sense of purpose, for which the institution exists. Key values of the college for today and tomorrow are communicated by vision statement long term debate and discussion may be necessary

Some sample Vision statements for institutes are given below. The list is not exhaustive institutions have to develop their own vision statements which have to be unique. They are to be evolved by consensus amongst all the stakeholders. Vision statement is prepared after comparing with role model institutions. The suggested visions are:

- To provide job oriented innovative education to Diploma, B.E., M.E., Ph.D. students reaching up to employment, self-employment.
- **What benchmarking means to college? What this college should do? Depute professors to world best institutions once in 7 years for one year. They will bring many new ideas to improve to become innovative & enterprising.**
- To provide employee's security of working with job satisfaction, acknowledging the right to be informed and consulted in all matters which affect them.
- To conduct education with due care for the environment.
- To remain on forefront in technology and transfer the same to industry to maintain them competitive by global standards.
- To provide testing consultancy to industry.

- To provide continuing engineering education to in service engineers and maintains them competitive.
- To bring about regional development, community development.
- To provide equal opportunity in education to all.
- To provide new technology to industry to improve its productivity.
- To generate employment and income of the people.

Vision statement has an effect in involving people, gaining employee-commitment to achieve goals and targets. It however, necessitates a process of education, to continuously upgrade the quality of people.

The vision statement is an outcome of a long drawn process of debate and discussion amongst the stakeholders, over a period of months.

SOME CURRENT STRATEGIC ISSUES OF EDUCATION INSTITUTES TO MAKE THEM INNOVATIVE AND ENTERPRIZING

The first and foremost issue is how to increase the competency of people working for colleges and bring them at par with their counterparts in developed countries. There are teaching staff members, administrative and laboratory staff, whose capacity needs to be upgraded by undertaking suitable schemes. If schemes are drawn out and colleges make investment in their employees this is likely to increase their commitment and loyalty. Today, big institutions are in the hands of small men.

Secondly our institutes and people are too inward looking so also the students. They lack in international perspectives. The issue is therefore how to orient them to Global standards.

It is not enough, if only a few employees and management people think strategically. All employees have to acquire the mental skills to think strategically in their own respective fields. Ways and means will have to be devised to promote strategic thinking, introduce a culture of strategic planning in favor of innovation and entrepreneurship in whole organization.

Developing a style of management suitable to local culture and bent of mind of the people is an important issue. The style of management would have to be different at different places flexible and participative to achieve the goals. It will have to provide relevant information to all at appropriate times. Systems would have to be designed fir for the purpose.

One of the important issues is how to increase relevance of education to regional needs. How to make curricula oriented to people's needs? How to bring innovation and entrepreneurship in teaching? In this case, the participation of industry is needed which is quite difficult and is a challenging issue to be resolved.

Today, the institutes are highly deficient in technology transfer, research, continuing engineering education, innovation, patenting, start-ups etc. How to develop an innovative character, and outreach for the institute is the big issue to be addressed by key persons. One of the prime issues is yet how to meet growing needs of technical education of the vast masses of people, in terms of quality and quantity. The priority given by Government in budget to education is too low, only 3% of GNP is allocated as against 10% by many countries. It is said that lack of budget to education has failed the nation.

How to make education creative, enterprising, innovative is an important issue. Today the education is based on memorization. This aspect ought to be discussed and debated with alumni, faculty and industry. Different models from USA, Germany, Japan may be examined and considered for adoption.

SOME STRATEGIES SUGGESTED

One of the successful strategies in institution development is to tap the innovative and creative talent of employees especially the professors, its alumni, and industry where students aspire to go for jobs. It is predicted that knowledge based organizations will lead in future and hence our strategy should be towards usage of new knowledge, intellectual capital is a valuable asset which a knowledge organization should try to possess. Networking of knowledge workers leads to synergetic conditions, and now the organizations should take special efforts to create networking.

Next, the institute should adopt a strategy of listening to students, industry personnel and people. Listening means obtaining a feedback, positive or negative, which is very useful to maintain equilibrium?

Proforma may be designed and got filled at regular intervals, analyzed and corrective action taken wherever necessary.

Thirdly, the learning ability of the individuals and the organization as a whole is very crucial to make the organization flexible enough to adopt to change. If there is no learning, the people become stiff and often resist change. If they are continuously learning they are more susceptible to change and remain in tune with time. Lifelong learning is a very important aspect to be attended to reduce inertia of people. This strategy may be adopted especially for non-teaching employees, who tend to be neglected, and they create bureaucratic hurdles.

Fourthly, grant of autonomy to people keeping a minimum control is a good strategy to motivate more knowledge workers, less of hierarchy, less of departmentalism, more interdisciplinary working helps to succeed and hence these strategies are suggested.

Making the work measurable of each and every employee in the organization has to be tried. What is not measurable remains uncontrolled leading to waste and less efficiency. It is not easy to achieve this, but still it has to be aimed at, and given a fair trial.

Students in developed countries are assigned research assignments by their professors, for example, in Purdue University of USA students from second year are involved in research which the professors are doing. The professors do contract research paid either by government or industry, part of which is shared with students.

CORE Values needed

If the values possessed by the organization are matching with the vision & mission, the progress takes place at a faster pace. If the values are not matching it hurts the progress. The organization may possess the values, adopt new if necessary, given below all or some of them. Value system of the institution is very important for development of institutional culture.

- Transparency
- Corruption free
- Global competitiveness
- Depute professors for improving research & innovation skills of professors.
- Equity

- Quality
- Integrity and commitment
- Professionalism
- Whether the institute cares for every individual student, enable him to bloom in to a good professional
- *Whether the institution cares to enable faculty to grow to their full potential.* ***Does the institution have ambition to enable faculty to world class level? Do the professors wish to rise up and work for?***
- *We intend to generate technology leaders, not followers. Innovators, pioneers.*
- *What value the college attaches to technological research, innovation & technology transfer to industry.*
- *How innovation is promoted through curriculum and laboratories?*
- *Are the systems for job oriented learning?*
- *Does the institution learns from world best counterparts elsewhere in the world*
- Does it have a system to bring about interaction of students with world innovators.
- Does the institution limits to only government authorities?
- Do you have systems to consciously promote interaction of faculty and students with world best?
- Does the institution promote strategic thinking with key stakeholders? Do they hold seminars and conferences?
- Give internship training in foreign

WHY STRATEGIC PLANNING FAILS

All strategic plans are not implemented as they are, partly implemented and partly not. This is due to a variety of reasons, such as political disturbance, natural calamities, and non-availability of funds, organizational bureaucracy and departmentalism. The plans prepared are often HI-JACKED. The managers, however, should not feel frustrated. The management may not attach adequate value to strategic planning.

Often the plans are inadequately documented, & communicated to students, faculty and staff.

Hidden Agenda, invisible strategies, in the minds of people is yet another potential danger. Key persons make strategic plans out of formal process, with the help of the sixth sense.

It also fails when top management and strategic planning group get engrossed in current problems and spend insufficient time on long range planning and the process become discredited amongst other staff. It is also on account of the failure of the management to create a favorable climate, and mobilize support.

Conclusion

Strategic Planning is the only way to transform universities & colleges to improved education landscape of innovation & entrepreneurship. As is necessary for any Government to have five year plans, so is essential for a college to have strategic plans for its future development. Does an institute have a plan for upgradation? Does it have a plan for statuesque? If there is no strategic plan, quality of education is less likely to improve.

This article has presented how urgently Indian Institutes need to adopt scientific preparation, to install culture of innovation and entrepreneurship in the strategic plans. It has outlined a few visions, issues and suggested possible new approaches which the institutes are required to follow. The institutes have to take a stock of their capabilities, short-comings, policies and practices, and do benchmarking with their role model counterparts. They have to share the same with the people, who work for them. This is the way prescribed in strategic planning to improve performance and productivity of institutes. **If an institute does not use the technique of strategic planning in a proper way, it is less likely that the institute will grow to the best of its abilities even if they have ample funds. Most of the Indian institutions today have competency and capability but they do not hold visions and missions, and do not do benchmarking, SWOT analysis and so they do not make a mark in world list**.

Chapter - 11

Research, Innovation & Creativity- the New Agenda for Higher & Technical education For creation of Brave New India

Synopsis

Indian higher education institutes, where do they fall short, with respect to world best? Research, Innovation & creativity is our structural weakness. Colleges should not ignore rather make it strong. Otherwise future generations will not pardon us. "What drives employment in 21st century is the Research & Innovation. Resources in research ,innovation and education are the most important growth stimulating instruments today. Research and innovation, the world over, is found to disrupt the existing knowledge & existing skills in ongoing professions and vocations. Not only machines become obsolete but men also. Technical Institutions must have to upskill and build capability of working people to ride over and win in emerging high end jobs. "

The article presents in brief, an Introspection of higher & technical education institutes in India, vis-à-vis world best institutions. Research, innovation & creativity in curriculum of Indian universities & colleges is far too less and a major, structural weakness, on account of which they have become almost go downs i.e. store houses of old outdated knowledge and technology They are not the fountain heads of new knowledge and new technology, much needed to win in competitive world. Why thousands of students every year are going abroad for higher education, by spending huge sums of money? Indian universities & colleges after 1947 have made a good progress but still they lack infrastructure like innovation centre ,Research Park, start-up centre, incubation centre, entrepreneurship centre, IPR etc. If the centres are developed then much desired high quality, high tech, high income, high end jobs in India will be generated, which is the need of the hour. In the absence of which India will be trapped in low tech- low income – low wage driven category of economies of the world, instead of innovative. So as to make India a developed country by 2022 as declared by government, it is essential to reform higher and technical education to world class standard, without which our human work force will not have skills and knowledge to be able to face world competition. Mediocre institutes cannot make India a power in the world and a developed country, as is eagerly desired. Suggestions, like professors need to be deputed to world best institutions to study their policies and practices, visions and missions and adapt them in India, as early as possible, are made.

Introduction

Indian higher & technical education institutions today do not stand high in the world list. Thousands of students every year go abroad for higher education to improve their knowledge and capability by spending huge sums of money. They are rejecting best of Indian universities and even IITs. Can Indian universities not be revamped and be brought at par with world best? Where do the Indian technical education institutes fall short with respect to the world best? What needs to be done to improve**? We have too much of rote learning, they have more of research and innovation. So they are far too ahead in brain race.** Universities in foreign have become birth places of New Technology based Firms [NTBFs]. For example, Stanford university has given birth to as many as 3000 firms, and they get royalty from them in millions of dollars, which is ploughed back in research from year to year.

UGC and AICTE, honestly are behind time, and in fact so India is failing in creating vibrant educational ecosystem that supports cutting edge research and in turn high end jobs. Service conditions of professors are primitive

Consequently, professors are behind in the state of the art in knowledge and do not grow to world standard. Professors are not having research fund. They have become teaching professors, mostly teaching stale outdated yesterday's knowledge today. Consequently, graduates have degrees in hand but no jobs. Educated unemployed is a major problem. They work hard, acquire knowledge, mostly irrelevant. Research, innovation and creativity are our weaknesses.

They need to install Innovation centres, Incubation centres, Patent and IPR centres, Research Parks, Technology Transfer centres, Life

Long continuing education centres, start-up centre etc, This has to be the main agenda for new India. Should the Government ever ignore it at what cost, and who pays?

If they install them then they will produce creative & innovative engineers, technology pioneers, leaders in engineering who create high end jobs. Such colleges will be more in demand both from students and industry. Industry will flock round such colleges to acquire new ideas, new products and new processes, besides employing graduates.

These centres are existing in foreign institutions from many years and it is more on account them that they have improved the quality of education, productivity and became developed. They have improved the living conditions of people. India must have to learn from foreign, preferably through collaborations to go in a massive manner. **No reform is more urgent for India than this today.** If we fail in doing this in spite of having plentiful natural resources future generations will not pardon us. Installation of all these centres on campus costs, but not installation is far more costly. Youths are bound to remain less competitive in global competition. Can the youths afford to remain behind?

Indian institutions are not short of money, they are short of *new visions of new world.* A paradigm shift in universities and colleges in respect of research and innovation is the need of the hour. Can youths make bright future without transforming universities to world class level, i.e. going in higher orbit? Are technical education institutes behind time? Honestly they are far too behind. Lack of Research and innovative culture so far led to brain drain and also money drain. Lack of innovation in the past has thrown India behind in development race. India remained a developing country, low income economy, in spite of all things in its hands, due to the absence of world class universities and colleges. How can India strengthen, research, innovation, creativity in higher education? The article explains the things in details.

2. Discussions

2.1 Research is a wealth creating activity. Benefits from scientific, technological and industrial research far outweigh the costs. Nations are flourishing which lead in Research and Innovation, others trail behind. Research is not a fancy affair. It is the seed corn for the harvest of benefit.. Research provides fuel for education and makes it quality and cost competitive. Research gives joy and sense of achievement. **It provides economic security** to a nation and confidence to youths. It enhances the rate of return on investment made in colleges and generates jobs to educated graduates. It enriches human civilization. Therefore it is advisable to provide Industry oriented research and Innovation skills to students:

Without research & innovation base in universities and colleges, students although educated have become misfit for jobs present and future .If India does not introduce research in universities and colleges in a big way, higher and technical education in India is impossible to be competitive by global standards, in turn India will continue to remain a poor developing country. Students then in spite of high potential will lag behind. Those who can afford will continue to go abroad to receive higher education**. Research is a profit making activity and not a financial liability. Research creates wealth for the nation,** enables college, professors and India to earn wealth from world over, besides credit. It creates joyful atmosphere in an institution, and improves the quality and relevance of education. It goes far beyond to improve competitiveness of industry. A student learns best by researching. He learns to create a brand new technology which gives him competitive edge in global market place. The mindset of the key people in both industry and institutes is behind time. Full scope of research and innovation in India, and their deeper purposes are less understood, resulting in low priority in government budget. India is spending only 0.45 % of GDP on research, when others are spending 5% i.e. ten times more. No wonder if the Research output from 800 universities in India is equal to only two universities in USA. India to become technological power, which it dreams of, ought to spend more on research. **Education without learning skills of research & skills for innovation remains incomplete and irrelevant in modern sense**. The interaction between industry and institute for research in India is far too weak adversely affecting competitiveness and growth of both. That political party which will care for reforms in R & D in universities will win election. Dr Saraswat, a member of NITI Aayog is planning to increase budget for research in coming time. If it is done it will do good to youths, and arrest brain drain.

What is innovation? Innovation is different from research. Innovation uses known knowledge and known technology to earn

more money. Research creates new knowledge and new technology. Innovation is a wealth creating activity.

2.2 All developed countries have world class universities and colleges. Nations are developed only when they have world class universities and colleges, not otherwise even if they have all other things. In other words India is behind because its universities are behind and human force is less educated and less skilled. India can go ahead only if universities go ahead. Do we realize this? Capability and competency of graduates coming out of universities matters most. This increases productivity of all walks of life and the nation as a whole.

Third American president [1801 to 1809] Thomas Jefferson gave a message to USA that US universities would have to go ahead of European universities, if it wants to be better in respect of economy, industry than Europe. He started many schemes to modernize universities. From the time American universities went ahead of European, USA became a power in world. Today first eight universities out of best ten are American. That is the prime reason that USA is a world power. 90 % of the patents earned in world are from USA. **India would have to transform its universities to world class standard, if it wants to go with the world.**

2.3 World Best Universities and colleges are fostering cultures of innovation, creativity, entrepreneurship and risk taking, They are creating ecosystems for "Disruptive Economic Development" which works as "Powerful Engine of Change,". This is the latest world development trend which India must have to adopt. Human capital is produced in these universities competent by global standards to harness opportunities anywhere in world. Many leaders, many Nobel Laureates, and technology pioneers from many countries have received education in US universities. US universities are attracting best talent from world over and Universities are categorized as world class only when they stand high in world ranking. Necessarily they have to be generating high quality research output and technologies for the welfare of human kind providing competent men with path breaking knowledge and skills to whole world. Regions, cities are developed where people are educated and universities are world class, not otherwise even if they are endowed with abundant natural resources. Silicon valley is developed mainly because of knowledge center, research center at Stanford university. Industries are developed in Boston because of MIT at Boston. Research Triangle Park at Raleigh is developed because of Duke University. Most of the universities in all east and west developed countries are always innovating and innovating like doing organizational innovation, technological innovation, and financial innovation etc.

It is observed that innovative nations take away jobs from less innovative. Small countries like New Zealand, Singapore, Switzerland have world class innovative universities, and by virtue of them they could become developed. Why India a big country cannot? Money is not in short supply. Many universities have ample money. What is not available is the global visions and missions, policies and practices. Our rules and regulations, in respect of research and innovation are backward and outdated. For example Professors retire at the age of sixty, they are then disconnected from students for PhD. In foreign they guide up to the time they can and wish. So many Nobel Laurates are in age of 70-75years.

2.4 Do Indian universities have innovation centers? Why Indian universities are not taking lessons from world best universities? Why UGC and AICTE are closing eyes towards these developments in foreign? Why our campuses although huge are dull and behind time in advanced knowledge. By one estimate it is said, five IITs could be established by the foreign exchange students spend each year in foreign universities. There is a huge drain of money besides brain drain. It is reported that research output of our more than 800 Indian universities is equivalent to only two universities of USA. Government and universities do not attach due importance to research and innovation. They feel expenditure on research is unproductive, whereas in reality it is most productive.. Students learn only known knowledge, mostly yesterday's knowledge coming from abroad and do not widen their imagination, beyond text books. Indian universities do not yet have knowledge and technology springs like well water springs.

2.5 Research Park is a proven model in developed world for hi-tech job generation and high income. Research based universities have become a magnet for high tech Industries. *Industry so as to remain competitive globally needs access to first class research in universities. So also the first class researchers in universities need* *access to industry so as to commercialise their research findings. This is the underlying principle of Research Park.*

The author has visited many university related research parks [URRP] in USA, Canada, Germany, UK etc. Every university has a research park. There is a University Related Research Parks,[URRP] Association in USA which gives guidance to universities to install parks and to bring efficient working. They are running courses and holding conferences every year There is almost no university abroad without a research park. In India, only a few institutes like IIT Chennai have recently established research park. This model must have to be adopted in every university, without which research and innovation culture and in turn employment is less likely to grow. Research and innovation is found to pave the way for high end and in turn low end jobs.

They generate high end jobs, with high pay and lucrative job conditions. Industries need new knowledge, new technology, new ideas to win in global competition. Where are they available? They are generated by young talent in research based universities. So the industries are flocking round innovative universities. A new phenomenon is observed that new industrial complexes are growing around research universities.

2.6 Research Universities have become "Light House" for industry. New knowledge based industry is flocking around research universities to obtain new ideas for commercially exploiting technology. Which government does not want to generate hi - tech employment, high pay international jobs, spur industrial growth, and make education globally competitive? Then it must install research /technology parks, incubators, Patent & IPR to facilitate commercial exploitation of sunrise technologies. Class room teaching is good but not enough. Industries, world over, are seen flocking round the advanced knowledge centers to obtain brand new ideas for global competitiveness. Institutes must have original knowledge springs like well water springs. They must have a mechanism to convert intellectual strength in to usable goods and services. Role of higher education through research has emerged central to industrial and economic development, in creating India's future. Association with industry, venture capital firms, international agencies who succeeded in this cause is essential.

The paper prescribes "dream big" for universities and colleges. They should aim at technology generation, technology diffusion, which is achieving high significance in enabling a nation to win. The paper emphasizes adoption of new organizational inventions like Research Park-Technology Park, which when implemented will contribute to India's international competitiveness.

The institutions should have now to look beyond the traditional lines of teaching and learning and adapt to corporate development, and help industry to win. They should have to restructure themselves to become fountain heads of new knowledge and new technology. They should deserve the status of "Light House" for industry. People demand world class education. How can this be done? Synergy between industry and academics in this cause is vital. Parks play a middleman's role in this. They have enhanced the scholarship of universities. They jointly can give economic and political stability to India. Will industry- institute interaction become a national priority? The paper recommends reforms in the light of experience elsewhere in the world.

2.7 Universities Abroad have transformed themselves in to Birth places, maternity homes of New Technology Based Firms. MIT Boston is giving birth to as many as 60 firms every year. Microsoft Bill Gate company was born in Harvard university, Tesla Electric Car company of Elon Musk was born in Stanford, There are more than 3000 firms which owe their origin to MIT Boston, and another 3000 companies born in Stanford university. These universities have their own Venture Capital Firms, giving financial support to start-ups. When these companies become big and earn profit they pay royalty to the university, which now amounts to millions of dollars. This royalty is ploughed back in research and innovation. Australian universities are giving birth to 40 companies every year. Chinese universities are not behind they are giving birth to 40 New Technology Based Firms. Why Indian universities cannot? They can also do this, but they have to have this vision. Bombay IIT has recently started doing this. It is giving birth to research based companies, generating high end jobs, hi tech, high pay, ultimately leading to many more low end jobs. It is these research based companies which provide life and blood to the Indian industries, and keep them technologically up to date and enable them to be globally competitive. A new mechanism to **spin-off NTBFs** has to be installed in each university. This requires a massive program for research and innovation. Educated unemployment will then be wiped out or substantially reduced.

2.8 Service conditions of professors must improve. World experience tells us that unless a professor is involved in industry oriented research, he has very little current and relevant knowledge to teach. He tends to teach otherwise, sunset knowledge incompatible to global opportunities. Class room teaching gets a force, depth and sharp edge if professors are engaged in research and innovation. They become imaginative, remain ahead of time and update their own capacities, which are needed to capitalize on technology ahead of others. How long Indian industry can be run on borrowed knowledge and borrowed technology? Visions and missions of universities and colleges should essentially include corporate development to make industry win in globalized world. This alone will make education relevant and purposeful. If all the professors of college decide and make effort in this direction, undoubtedly quality of education will be superb. Indian professors ought to be deputed to world best universities to study their service conditions.

2.9 Shortage of research and innovation skills in teaching of universities and colleges is a major barrier in employment generation. The key factor behind unemployment, excessive dependence on foreign is insufficient research and insufficient innovation. Shortage of people with research and innovation skills is a major barrier in professional development. Universities and colleges have a major influence on India's capacity for innovation. Colleges therefore should have to resort to these new strategies to induct research and innovation skills in economy. They would have to adopt **corporate development** as a vision and mission. They should provide new ideas and new technology to keep industry competitive in world market. They are like heart to our body, which pumps new fresh blood to keep body alive. **Indian higher education would have to recognize full scope of research and innovation phenomenon. They must provide captains and professional leaders of world standard to industry, and all walks of life.**

Those nations which introduce research and innovation are found to win jobs in competition from those who lag. Can Indian professors not teach innovation skills by international standard. Can they give birth to NTBFs? We essentially need a swimming pool to learn swimming, i.e. innovative culture.

Conclusion

There is no reform more urgent in India than the reform in higher and technical education .Future depends on knowledge and technological capability of men and women, rather than availability of natural resources. A realization that universities and colleges are the main drivers of development and not driven, is lacking in the minds of planners. Will the Indian planners attach due importance to higher education and research and innovation in universities and colleges? Future of India depends on research and innovation in universities and colleges.

1. Key people in government, AICTE, UGC who matter most would have to care and see the opportunities in world market, and take steps to educate and impart relevant skills to people.
2. World is changing fast but most of our people are working with traditional skills which are of low productivity, & hence no more in demand, and so they are becoming job less, common man is suffering,
3. Many people as a result live below poverty line, rich students are going abroad for studies by paying huge sums of money. India remains a technology follower and importer.
4. Research and innovation centers, Research Parks etc. are our weak points. So as to strengthen, India must depute its hundreds and thousands of professors to similar centers in world best universities for six months period to study establishment and functioning of these centers. Association of University Research Parks is offering courses of 3-4 week duration to those who wish to start the centers. We must take advantage of these courses.
5. **If research and innovation reforms are carried out India will win in globalized market, otherwise it will lose in spite of its efforts of development. This is a bold writing on wall.**
6. **If India installs centers for innovation, it will be a home for research based industries, and high end jobs will grow**

in the absence of which India is likely to be trapped in low wage, low tech, low income type of industries, instead of innovative and creative like those in developed countries.

7. Educated unemployment is a big problem, solution for which lies in installation of innovation centers and Research Parks.
8. If India succeeds in transforming some universities to world class status, then India will have better future, it will be categorized as developed nation. otherwise it will continue to remain a developing country, with low income economy.
9. World class universities and colleges are very critical to wellbeing of people. They produce globally competent leaders for professions, politics and all walks of life.
10. Quality of education can be enhanced to world class standard by introducing research and innovation in universities and colleges. Colleges must have to become light house for industry.
11. Impact of research on life of individuals can be huge. It is in these colleges that the impact is discussed, debated and openly tested by opposing groups.
12. **If India does not create research based universities and colleges, if industry does not synergies with academia, the colleges will be providing graduates far too low by international standard to ably run its national and international affairs**. Indian people are then destined to lag behind in world brain race.
13. Research, innovation, and creativity is **today's Guru Mantra**.
14. How to produce more entrepreneurs and how to encourage more firms to grow should be the main vision and mission of universities.

References

1. Book by B M Naik, " Education & Leadership- Role of universities and colleges in nurturing future leaders" published by Atlantic publishers and distributors, New Delhi, second edition 2018
2. B M Naik, Enhancing, employability, innovation entrepreneurship, and creativity in changing world, University News, 6th March 2017.

3. B M Naik, What government ought to do to stand high in the world list? Need of the hour. AAYAM, A KGIM Journal of Management, Volume 7 issue 1, January – June 2017.
4. Book, "Creation of the Future, The role of American University" by Frank Harold Trevor Rhodes- Cornell university USA, 2001.

Chapter - 12

India Desperately needs International Collaborations and Partnerships to Accelerate University Reforms

Abstract

The paper presents in brief, need & importance of International Collaborations and Partnerships so as to accelerate the implementation of NEP-2020 and many other reforms beyond that, available from world class universities. The paper brings out shortcomings of the Indian universities and suggests that urgent steps like collaborations need to be taken so as to achieve the goal of becoming a developed nation by 2047. Characteristics of universities in other developed countries which made them effective, competent and forerunner in the world, are presented in brief. Government has now allowed foreign universities collaborations and even set up campuses on Indian soil. However, the progress is far too slow and India needs to double up in this direction. Collaborations will expedite reforms and make them more purposeful. Start-ups are increasing. This is a good sign. So as to achieve the target, budget available for education & research in universities is however, far too low. This is a gross failure on the part of government. It is holding back even faculty recruitment. Setting a tone of discovery, innovation, creativity, patenting, start-ups in emerging technology, create technology pioneers etc. is the challenge posed by developed world before Indian universities. Is India ignoring these global winds of change? Globalization & internationalization of higher education are essential to keep pace with the changing world.

Need and Importance

Indian higher education by international standards is far too behind the world. Best of Indian universities and even IITs do not rank high in the world list. Thousands of brilliant students are leaving shores and going elsewhere in the world. Government is worried about brain drain. Attempts are being made to revamp the higher education. NEP-2020 gives the policy changes. Reforms in higher education after NEP-2020 are being implemented in all the universities and colleges. There is an acute need to boost up the exchange of faculty, exchange of students, and arrange many more international seminars and conferences. The progress is however, too slow. The prime difficulty is availability of funds. The mind set of authorities in government, UGC, and universities is however not adequately activated. As a result budget allocation to education for reforms falls too short of the purpose. Faculty recruitment in almost all universities central and state is held back. In Maharashtra faculty in universities and engineering colleges of state is only around 50%. This has crippled the quality of education. secondly, Indian universities ought not to be only teaching shops but become research and innovation based. UGC/ MHRD ought now to draw out many schemes for liberal foreign collaborations & partnerships, to create a country wide tempo for revamping of higher education. India in the recent past has initiated bold steps, like creating new eco-system for start-ups. This is most welcome. It is giving rich dividends and building a brave new India. However, this is not enough and there is a greater need of emerging technology based start-ups, which requires advanced research. How can research be boosted in Indian universities & colleges? This is a challenge before universities. Country wide tempo needs to be built up to achieve the goal of higher education at a time when India completes its hundred years of independence @ 2047. India by this time aspires also to be a developed nation. All this essentially requires a well-educated citizenry, and knowledge based economy, in which not only latest knowledge is used but also generated. The bottle neck to become a developed nation is lying in education in general and technical in particular. If the government does not realize this it is less likely for India to become a developed nation by the year 2047. Who can play a important role to make it happen? It is none other than universities and colleges. Future if India depends on the ranking of universities in world list. This underlines the importance of reformation in higher education.

Globalization and internationalization brings vast opportunities. But they are not easy to harvest and risk free.

Globalization means mixing of cultures, shrinking of time and space. Globalization means business at the speed of thought, instant communication, and instant decisions. Globalization means abandoning traditional methods, systems and procedures, in Favor of modern which essentially requires higher education to men and women. Keeping the risks to a minimum and harvesting opportunities requires education. Who can provide this education and increase capability of people for harvesting opportunities available in globalised world? It is none other than the universities & colleges..

Globalization benefits human civilization as a whole. However, some benefit more than others. So as to bring more benefits to People in India, universities will have to upscale the skills and knowledge of people, young and old. India is yet a developing country. It remained developing because its economy so far was more localised and less globalised. The role of education and research in development is less understood by Indian planners. India can be a developed country only if the digital divide between India and the developed world is reduced. We must wake up to this reality and act fast to accelerate international trade and commerce, which demands open mind and more education, more innovation and more start-ups in emerging Technology.

More uncertainties and more risks are associated with harvesting global opportunities. So as to harvest them demands hi-tech knowledge and A.I.skills besides positive attitude and ability to mix with the people round the world. Survival of the fittest in globalization is the law. There is a great impact of Hi-tech knowledge on jobs and business. Old outdated jobs with primitive skills are going out and new jobs with higher technical skills are coming in. Are Indian universities equipped and having a "mind set" to educate youths to cope with? Are they providing knowledge and skills required in today's global market? Universities ought to be enterprising in creating knowledge based society. There is however deficiency in Indian universities in this respect.

What are the deficiencies

Indian universities by world standards are far too behind their counterparts in developed world. They are not counted, since they do not rank high in world list. They still operate on old lines as if they are an extension of high school system. They function today largely as teaching universities, teaching that knowledge which is old outdated and less relevant to the jobs. What is wanted is not taught and what is taught is not wanted. This is rendering many graduates unemployed. Whereas universities in developed countries like USA, Germany, Japan are primarily research based. Research output, especially need based, is their main contribution and education, is their by-product. Bush Commission Report, "Science the endless Frontier[1945] gave this philosophy to universities of USA and which is adopted by many developed countries. National Science Foundation of US has reprinted this report again and again and re-circulated.

The report prescribed that universities main output should be research, patents, new technologies, intellectual property rights. Higher Education should be their by-product. Students learn best by researching, and then it is found to be more relevant and up- to- date. Then the graduates tend to become professional leaders fit to tackle challenges of fast changing world. It is because of this philosophy that the education in universities of USA is observed to be innovative and creative in nature. They produce leaders for professions, they produce technology pioneers. Without research, it is believed that education remains stale and outdated. Normally, good amount of budget of a university in USA goes to research. In India, far too less budget is allocated for research and innovation. Research funding needs to be increased.

CHARACTERISTICS OF UNIVERSITIES ABROAD

On the campuses of universities like Madison, Cambridge, Stanford what we notice is that research companies are flocking round them. Incubators, research parks, innovation centres, patent and IPR bureaus are distinctly visible. Venture Capital companies have opened offices in campuses in search of new technological ideas for commercialization. Universities in developed countries have become like magnets that attract not only scholars but also industry, entrepreneurs and VCF from across the world. They are globalising their operations to meet the world needs both of education and of technology. Brilliant students from many countries in the world aspire to study in them. So also industries from across the world are coming to their campuses to recruit the talent and they feel proud of the same. By virtue of strong research base they are a source of latest knowledge and education and a source of new ideas enabling companies to win in global market. It is well realised in developed countries that the knowledge that is to say new technology, is an important source to bring about economic change. USA has doubled its industrial output from 1909 to 1949 and that 85 percent of credit is attributable to technology change, so said Nobel Laureate Bob Solow.

Universities in USA are producing patents as many as 200 per year. The university sells patents to companies and earns an income which is almost 30 percent of their budget. Young scholars and mid-career in service personnel carryout research, innovation, which is disseminated best through teaching in classes. Every professor is a research scientist besides a teacher. Innovation and research are considered as 'well springs' of economies. .

If India does not create research based universities, synergising with industry they will be providing mediocre graduates far too low by international standards to run its national and international affairs. Indian people in spite of potential are then destined to lag behind in brain race. Do we realize this danger? Countries like Japan, although not endowed with rich natural resources are developed far more because they have many world ranking universities. A new enterprising society in the changing world is coming in to being. Universities are called upon to produce not copy cats, teacher puppets but graduates with higher imagination to lead and take a active hand in creating knowledge society fit for today and tomorrow. This essentially requires international collaborations.

Need & importance of research is less understood by Indian politicians and planners. So too low budget is allocated in national budget to education & research in universities and colleges. research however, is not a fancy affair. It is the seed corn for the harvest of benefit. Benefits from research far outweigh the costs. It provides economic security to a nation. Research is a wealth generating, job generating activity. It is not a liability but an asset. India ought to introduce research & innovation in universities on great scale. Can this happen without international collaborations?

Helping Business to Win

Every university in a developed country has a patent and technology licensing department engaged in knowledge and technology sale.

The author during the period of his recent visit to Germany, UK and USA, studied in depth the organization and management practices of universities along with their visions and missions, systems and procedures. Universities in general have huge campuses, with student strength in the range of 20 to 80 thousands and faculty strength from 1000 to 10,000. For example MIT, Boston has around 30,000 students and 3,000 professors, Karlsruhe University in Germany has around 25,000 students and 1,000 professors, all teachers possess Ph.D. and post-doctoral qualification. Faculty represents a wealth of talent and knowledge, which is exploited to the benefit of both faculty and university financially**. Our universities are far too less innovative in character, and bright students in India are being taught by lowly qualified and less innovative teachers.**

Spin off of companies from universities from universities in foreign is a common phenomenon, so also spin- off of technologies. The companies like that of Bill Gates were conceived and born in universities. Project ideas were based on their research. A foundation is set up in MIT, Boston with the facility of venture capital fund enabling professors and PhD scholars to start new ventures based on technologies; which they develop during the period of their research. Every year as many as 15-20 new technology based firms (NTBF) are born in MIT Boston. The university gives consultancy on retainer basis to as many as 3,000 companies. This is not unique with MIT. It is true with almost all universities in developed countries. They have created Technology Incubators and business incubators to enable raw project ideas to be innovated to marketable stages. The entrepreneurs and professors are thrilled when they see their theoretical ideas being converted in to practical projects. Thereby they are earning wealth for themselves so also for the university besides credit and satisfaction. Universities have thus become 'Maternity Homes' for safe birth of new enterprises. Such enterprises that are based on brand new technologies help to reduce mortality rate and sickness of other industries. **Innovative networks in Research Parks aim to coordinate and amplify start up culture. Professors matter most in reformation of education. Apex bodies like UGC and AICTE need revamping.**

India must harness the global winds of change. Success in globalised world, which is characterised by fierce international competition, depends now on turning intellectual capital in to marketable commodities, faster than one's competitors. Future belongs to those who understand this. Can Indian universities have these activities without foreign collaborations and partnerships? Certainly not. The visions and missions and necessary mind set with universities and colleges is just absent. Reforms like in foreign are less likely to happen without international collaborations.

Institutes abroad display patents for sale in Industrial Exhibitions

Do we do that? Patents are less known to institutions in India. It is good to do research but it is essential to make commercial exploitation of the findings of research. This makes research financially more viable, and attracts more funds for research. Today, the economic returns obtained from research done in India are far too few. This has been our weakness, and so actual funding for research does not grow.

A few years back I happened to visit Hannover industrial exhibition. There was a pavilion meant for universities and colleges. It was most crowded by the visitors. Students were explaining the new researches, emerging technologies like, patents and IPR to visitors. Universities had come from world over to display. Visitors wanted to know the technologies of tomorrow. In India how many institutions have obtained patents and presented in industrial exhibition? Students do research for PhD, M Tech. Thesis remains in library. It is published in journals and is being harvested by foreigners for obtaining patents. We do not exploit research done commercially. Even the traditional knowledge like[Turmeric, Ayurvedic medicines, Wheat etc. are converted in to patents by USA. We need to build this culture in our education. If the young students learn this they follow in future career. If they do not learn they do not practice. Attempts by Technology Information and assessment Council [TIFAC], New Delhi a government of India body, are being made to popularize patent, IPR. It has yet to become a culture in universities and colleges. We need to protect our research findings before publication by patenting and convert it in money. Research is a wealth generating mechanism provided it is converted in to patents, IPR. When shall we realize this? India badly needs international collaborations to make such things happen.

Institutions in India today are distinctly a knowledge & technology follower. They do not lead; do not give birth to new technology. They are by and large inward looking, restricting to class rooms, making students teacher puppets, and not going beyond. They lack the world vision. They are not enabled to think and act in this direction, the situation needs correction. We need to install patent & IPR centres in each institute and display patents in exhibitions. Industries are keen on knowing emerging technology. Institutes should aim at that. Visions of our institutions need to be enlarged, to go beyond to what their counterparts elsewhere in the world are doing. Institutions abroad are in driver's seat. Indian institutions are followers like bogies of a train. Can they become engines without foreign collaborations? Collaborations will bring such reforms at a much faster rate.

New Model for Universities

Does Indian economy need such universities? Can we do without them? At what cost? Without such innovative schemes our investments are being made in sunset technologies. Obviously so they cannot be competitive globally. National Council for Applied Economic Research, New Delhi has published the results of a survey which found that of the 657 Indian companies in the study sample that started up a few years back, 57% were manually operated and 38.7% were semi-automated. In the same period, according to the study, 80% of the startup companies in Japan were fully automated and 20% were semi-automated. It seems then that substantial investment in India is being made in companies which are based on less competitive technologies, and which are therefore handicapped right at birth. Such companies cannot hope to be competitive on global scale. In USA, 36% of capital investment is in new technology based firms (NTBF) where as in India NTBF are far too less. Very recently just a few NTBF are being born in IITs. This is a good sign. It has to become a regular practice in universities, which today are just teaching shops.

However the shift from old technology to new technology industrial base is not easy to achieve. It presents many technological, social, economic problems, as well as resistance from trade unions. People must unlearn old methods and skills and adopt new technologies and knowledge. Universities must reorient themselves; prepare to offer courses and interact with people in learning and becoming more competent. Without this research and innovation strategy by universities, industries and industrial estates will languish and become sick, which would be looking for foreign collaborators. Can Indian universities dream of propelling industrial growth? They must do so forthwith. Otherwise universities may become dysfunctional and economy will run into difficulty. The rate of absorption of new technology in various walks of life depends much on knowledge of people and their scientific and technological capabilities. Can Indian universities propel hi- tech industries like in developed countries without foreign collaborations?

New Vision for New World Needed

What Indian universities lack today, is the new vision of new world? They ought to develop connections, collaborations & partnerships with best known universities in the world and correct their priorities and strategies. It is no doubt a long journey. Yet, it must begin somewhere. Is it not that thousand miles journey begins with a single step?

Prof. Terman of Stanford University in USA observed in 1950 that industry so as to remain competitive globally needs access to first class research in universities. So also the first class professors, researches in the universities need access to industry so as to commercialize their research findings. This is equally applicable to Indian universities at this juncture. They cannot become and remain competitive without the support of each other. Will our universities care to follow today what others did years before? Can Indian universities synergies with industry? Then both the university and industry will grow by leaps and bounds. Collaborations will facilitate such innovations.

It is important to know how universities are conceived and started in those countries. The author visited a newly started Harburg University in Germany. This university started a few years before under collaboration from 15 best universities in US, UK, Japan and Germany. Today this university has 20 thousand students and two thousand professors. It started with a research park, which today contains around 1000 research-based companies adding strength to the economy of the region. University is not planned in Germany without an industrial estate, and research park and industrial estate is not planned without a university.

The author also visited Harriot Watt University at Edinburgh, which is located on 600 acres of land and has Research Park on

600 acres surrounding the university. The University of Madison (USA) has a strong Alumni Association known as Wisconsin Alumni Research Foundation [WARF], which is managing and maintaining a big research park, always innovating.

Taiwan has set up a 'Science Town' at Hsinchu with some 13000 researchers in two universities, 6 national laboratories and around 150 companies specializing in electronics. Tsukuba Science City near Tokyo is another example of university technology park collaboration.

On the other hand Indian Universities are engaged more in teaching as if they are primary schools. **The vector direction of our universities is wrong.** They are largely teaching and examining bodies without research and innovation base and hence they are not effective to cope with global challenges. Will they learn themselves and adopt what best universities in the world are doing? Will they do correct bench marking? Foreign collaborations alone can give India more efficient methods in reduced time and with accuracy. The Frei university in West Berlin after second world war was started by purchasing the existing townships. This saved time on construction of roads,watersupply system, electricity, phones lines etc

Lifelong Education

Universities in Germany have opened continuing education departments, more from 1980, for in-service personnel. They are offering short-term refresher courses leading to PhD. The research work done by employees in their work places is counted for the award of degree. They have a flexible model Cafeteria Approach in which students can choose a wide variety of options. A combination of economics, engineering and music is also possible. Now new Indian National Education Policy NEP-2020 has emphasised this aspect. It is hoped that India will progress fast on these lines.

The credit transfer system, from one university to another is common, world over. A student can study for the same degree course in a number of universities. The credits earned in one university are approved in another. European Commission encourages the mobility of students and professors. It has drawn a program known as Leonardo-da-Vinci to provide financial support to promote such mobility. The students are allowed to get degree from any one university, which they have visited.

Life Long Education keeps the people fit and competitive

Continuing education has become so common that the in-service, mid-career part time, and on line students studying in universities are ten times larger than the full time students. We see three generation students in campus. Learn while you earn lifelong is very common. It is observed in an OECD study that Europe, Japan and USA together represent 80% industrial global outputs. The main contributing factors to this dominance include continuing education policy and practices of universities in developed countries. Continuing education facilities and better management of technology add significantly to economic success. **It is believed that, not only machines become obsolete but men also. Even the gold medallists of universities, if** they do not learn on continuing basis they would soon go out of job .UNESCO in its policy paper has projected high demand on lifelong education. Individuals perceive it as an essential thing to remain in job. In USA continuing education is quite an old hat. Most of the universities have opened special departments exclusively for the purpose. **The author has visited, "Corporate Education Centre" of Boston University. It is a centre where four courses at a time are run. Full time faculty is less and part time faculty from professionals is more.** USA is producing a learning society, and lifelong learning individuals. In China, Government has made it obligatory to employers to offer an opportunity of retraining of one month in one year. It is both an obligation and a right of an employee. In Japan, continuing education enjoys not only support but also leadership and active participation of top management in the conduct of programs. They believe employing people without an opportunity of retraining is a blunder. **It is their firm contention that a company is as good as competency of its people. In Germany Lifelong education is an established practice from hundreds of years. Many CEOs have started their career with craftsman** school termed in Germany as" Beruf Schule" and rose to top position. Finland through lifelong education in universities has created a knowledge society and thereby are winning in world. People in India need to sharpen their job skills again and again for which they need universities to start lifelong education program. There is a joy of learning in lifelong learning. There is a tremendous possible gain in competitiveness.

Many Indian universities yet do not have continuing education departments, patent and technology licensing departments. Technology Park and incubators are conspicuously absent. **They have almost no connection with industry and industries have almost no confidence in universities. They work in "stand Alone" style. The industrial progress** in India is propelled by foreign collaborators. Indian Universities have not gone nearer to them, nor have industries established links with universities. Universities have become corporate offices bureaucratic and political in nature. Consequently what is taught in universities is not wanted and what is wanted is not taught. There is serious mismatch between demand and supply. Rather than motivating and preparing students for the world of work the universities have become organizations which tend to thwart and impede the potential of their students. The National Education Policy way back in 1986 recommended autonomy to colleges to enable them to respond to the needs of industry in terms of research, training and technology transfer. However progress has been too slow. **Innovation is an essential precondition for growth and for generating employment and improving competitiveness**. Those nations which lead in innovation tend to lead in world. Taking a lesson from Silicon Valley it can be said that a strong university system with research, innovation, and entrepreneurship is very essential for a nation to win in competitive world. **University as an innovator, a magnet of innovators, facilitator for innovation a partner for innovation, is a precondition for growth and prosperity. Silicon valley** has not only wealthy entrepreneurs but techno-entrepreneurs. How can India adopt such proven systems for growth of entrepreneurship? We need collaborations. Indian universities & colleges are not yet aligned to world dynamics. They are observed to be poorly equipped and woefully unsuited to the demands of globalization

The traditional affiliating system of universities in India has become a problem rather than a solution. It has stifled the innovation potential and is a hindrance in academics and the public is unhappy. Attempts for improvement are being made. Lack of mobility of Indian academic staff and research staff to world class centres is seen as major problem. Why is India unable to upgrade its universities and make them innovative? **Do we realize that the cost of mediocrity is higher than the cost of upgrading? Why do Indian institutes not transfer**

knowledge/ technology to industry through the use of patents and IPR?

Universities need to be modernised urgently to create leaders of world class standard, lest India is bound to get mediocre leaders.

India is missing all such possible opportunities, Because India does not have many collaborations and partnerships unemployment of graduates is large. Indian universities do not yet have global visions & missions.

Knowledge / Technology Transfer, from university to Societys

Many western schools are having well defined and perfected knowledge transfer systems and procedures. They are not only educating young students to keep them competitive lifelong but practically generating and marketing new knowledge and new technologies and transferring their full capacities to the benefit of society in their vicinity and all over the world. The outreach of universities and feedback is far and wide. Thereby they are enriching themselves and augmenting new ideas besides providing budget support for their own future growth. Such universities exist in Germany, Japan etc. By virtue of knowledge they have moved from periphery to centre of prosperity, and taken the nation to greater heights. They have become the drivers of innovation, social and economic development. The visions & missions of universities are dynamic, adaptive based on sharing of experiences with people at large, and not only giving off the shelf irrelevant and outdated course prescriptions. They are responsive to world dynamics. Restructuring and repositioning of the Indian universities with respect to society and the globalised world is needed. India is at risk for want of innovation based and enterprising world class universities.

So as to go with the developed world India ought to interact closely with world class universities, for which International collaborations alone will make this easy and cheap. International collaborations are not a liability but an asset. Without collaborations India will not be able to create universities fit for tomorrow. When shall we realize this?

To conclude,

Future of India in today's knowledge based society depends on how good the universities & colleges are.

No reform is so urgent as the reform in higher education.

MHRD/UGC authorities seem to ignore the "**global winds of Change, which is so costly**"

Outdated universities are more costly than cost of their modernization. They need essentially to take in to account the experience from abroad, for which only collaborations can help.

If India dares international collaborations & partnerships undoubtedly it will succeed in elevating education standard and relevance.

Making Indian universities innovative, and enterprising is the pressing need of time. Redefining their scope, missions and visions in the light of worldwide changes ought to be carried out forthwith.

The **mind set required** of politicians and planners is undoubtedly not for catching global developments. They need to provide enhanced financial allocation, to education in public interest.

Education does not grow where research is absent.

Will Government and UGC depute more professors to world class universities? without which we cannot get universities & professors of international standing.

No society, region or nation will prosper without world class institutes of higher & technical education even if they are endowed with abundant natural resources. India must take steps to create world class universities. Today India ranks far too low in global list.

Institutes build knowledge society. They are a "**Think tank**" They should not remain merely teaching shops but influencing public policies and society.

Research & innovation in universities is the most cost efficient and cost effective model for employment and income generation. It should therefore become the focus of university.

Universities ought to dream big, think great and must produce able captions, that is to say political and social leaders.

Universities to a nation are like heart to our body. It is they who build capability in youths and make them competent.

The speed and direction of change in universities in coming years matters most. It is hoped that with the given will and skill of

leaders in academics, leaders in industries and politics, we will be able to achieve desired goal.

The prime Minister has expressed his desire to bring at least a few universities to the top in world list. He has granted necessary budget and autonomy. But till today it has not been possible.

If you solve the university education problem, then you do not have to do anything else. If you do not solve education problem and do everything else, nothing is going to matter as much.

References

1. Government of India National Education Policy-2020.
2. Green paper of European Union on Innovation and technological transfer Enterprise Unit, EUFO, 2295-2920 Luxemburg.
3. B M Naik Book, Higher & Technical Education- Book of Knowledge 'Gyan Publishing House, 2010.
4. B M Naik book, "Education & Leadership- Role of Indian universities and colleges in nurturing future leaders" published by Atlantic publishers, New Delhi. 2018.
5. B M Naik book "Insights in to Research, innovation & Entrepreneurship, Challenge of NEP2020," published by Xpress publishing Notion Press, Chennai, 2023.
6. Rising above the gathering storm, report published by National Academy of Sciences, US, 2007, Government of India, National Knowledge Commission Report, 2006-7
7. Book by Rob Bowden, Rain Tree Chicago Publication "Globalization, Impact on our lives" Lous G Tranky, Book, "Innovation of New Practices Enabling Cultures."
8. Glen A Jones, Patricia L McCarney and Michael L Skolinik, Book, "Creating Knowledge-Strengthening Nations, The Challenging Role of Education" University of Toronto Press, 2002.
9. USA report, "Driving Regional innovation & Growth by AURP and Battelle [2012]

Chapter - 13

Role of Universities & Colleges Critical in Entrepreneurship Education Can Universities close Eyes? What it Costs? Why Youths should Suffer?

What drives entrepreneurship in knowledge based economy is the research,innovation & start-ups. Resources for research, innovation and start-ups are the most important instruments today. If they are not provided future generations will not pardon us.

Summary

The paper out lines in brief need and importance of educating youths in entrepreneurship development in universities and colleges so as to enable them to win in competitive world. Young graduates today leave institutes with their minds set on becoming well paid employees. Their role models are the big managers, CEOs, instead of entrepreneurs like Narayan Murthy, and Elon Musk. Lucrative opportunities due to lack of innovative entrepreneurs are either dying or being taken away by foreigners. Our engineers are working for foreign masters, as humble servants. Universities ought to educate youths to become captains to capitalize on emerging technology giving *Technology Push matching with Market Pull. Industry today is technology driven.* The present frame of universities & colleges without innovation centres and start-ups is not competitive enough to produce entrepreneurs of world class standard. *They are producing good soldiers and not captains ,who are necessary but not enough.*

Indian entrepreneurs today in international market are very few, it is because in the past we were not teaching them to be become so. Now in globalization, liberalization Indian youths aspire to make a mark in international market. So as to enable young graduates to become global players in entrepreneurship, universities and colleges are called upon to educate students like in foreign. For example, MIT Boston has six full professors in entrepreneurship, to do promotion, teaching, and research. Various aspects of education are discussed in this paper.

Conclusions are drawn so as to generate more enterprising graduates to harvest vast available opportunities. Role of universities & colleges is critical in entrepreneurship education, which means when not done entrepreneurship will suffer a serious set back, India then may remain a developing country with 20% people living below poverty line.

1. Introduction

On one hand it is observed that there is so much of unemployment and underemployment amongst educated youths and on the other hand there is shortage of entrepreneurs to develop innovative enterprises. There is abundance of natural resources on one hand and shortage of finished goods and services on the other. There is an influx of goods and sevices from east west countries in Indian market. Indian industry and SMEs are far too behind the world, they stand as low as 48th in world ranking. This is because human work force in India is far too less enterprising. Is it the responsibility of universities & colleges to educate youths in entrepreneurship so that they become commpetitive by world standards? Undoubtedly yes.

The key factor behind lack of entrepreneurship is insufficiency of research, insufficiency of innovation and insufficiency of start-ups. Lack of Research & Innovation education in universities & colleges lies at the roots of insufficiency of entrepreneurship. As a result education is going in one way and opportunities are going in another way. Thousands of youths in search of enterprising education are migrating to developed countries. In the year 2021-2022 students going abroad have increased by 19%.

1.1 Innovation is a driving force for entrepreneurship. There is an acute shortage of innovative people in India. This is holding key to growth in entrepreneurship. The paper suggests that research skills, innovation skills and entrepreneurship skills must be included in teaching of curriculum in universities & colleges. So as to empower youths in colleges and universities this is the only way at this juncture of time to accelerate entrepreneurship. It is found that students who learn innovation in young age,become far more enterprising and remain enterprising through out life. Universities have become key players in entrepreneurship systems. The ability of countries to grow and prosper now depends critically on the ability of universities and university system. This new role of universities is to be understood to keep pace with changing technology, avoid obsolescence, and keep work force competent by global standards. India is too slow to understand and adopt to this new role of innovation & entrepreneurship. Universities should not now be confined to national boundaries but they ought to go much beyond far and wide. This is the need in globalised world. Also how universities organize their linkages with industry and society, local as well as international has assumed great importance.

1.2 Entrepreneurship needs innovative persons. It is observed that innovative and enterprising persons with innovative skills always create jobs. Professors in India have high capacities to teach innovation & entrepreneurship but they need to be oriented and trained. Syllabii need to be revised to remove the deficoiency of innovativeness. Universities have to depart from traditional method and contents of teaching. This is not easy. Mindset of professors and mindset of university administration ought to be changed. Because of the fast obsolescence of technologies Job contents in vocations & professions are changing very fast. Enterprising persons are observed to be quick to adopt and lead in ever emerging new situations.

1.3 Jobs of today won't be the jobs of the future. **Jobless growth can happen**. The people need to be trained, again and again, life long so as to retain them on the job and avoid joblessness. People have to exert to shift from low productivity jobs to higher productivity jobs. Immidiate challenges under globalization pressures are therefore to make college education job oiented and enterprising, and offer continuing education courses lifelong for inservice personnel. Men become out of date like machines. Competency of men and women depends on their learning and relearning rate. The challenge before university is to make learning joyful, innovative and enterprising.

Government is giving slogans at the election time to provide jobs to all. This is welcome. But is this possible without enterprises and competent entrepreneurs, without cooperation from universities? The visions of university should include Entrepreneurship skill oriented education. The present methods adopted in becoming entrepreneurs are improper and divorced from what is the need of time. Higher education in India is expanding, is a good sign. But why innovation and entrepreneurship falling behind? Time demands more of entrepreneurship.

1.4 How to produce more entrepreneurs, and how to improve skill set of work force on continuing basis should be the main vision and mission of universities. A beginning is made in India by Modi government in this direction. Start-ups are coming up more in number. Hackathon meets are organised. National Innovation Board is set up. This is good. But, most of the start-ups today are in the area of well established or sunset technologies, and far too less in sun rise i.e. New Technology Based Firms [NTBF]. First Mover entrepreneurs are almost absent. This is because of the lack of adequate research & innovation in universities & colleges, which provides foundation to entrepreneurship and spinn-off i.e. NTBFs. India has to go a long way to properly address the entrepreneurship education. The problem is too big and reforms are far too inadequate. Research skills, Innovation skills and Entrepreneurship skills need to be taught in universities & colleges. It can undoubtedly provide a sustainable long lasting solution.

A question is often asked what is the cost of not adequately educating students in innovation & entrepreneurship? Who pays? The cost is far too big, so big that the whole country remains poor, developing catagory, with 20% people living below poverty line. There remains a shortage of hi-tech entrepreneurs, with many youths job less and under paid. Besides, increased crime rate, corruption, poverty, robbery and many other undesirable things.

1.5 Poverty of knowledge leads to economic poverty. Today, job contents are changing due to emergence of new technology. Jobs of yesterday are going outof date. Developing countries ought to focus on technology growth. Research & entrepreneurship is the only way to grow in technology. New culture of technology must be nursed. This demands increase in national budget. Universities & colleges ought to be provided much higher budget. Increase in state budget for research and innovation is strongly recommended, by many commissions and committees,in the past, but yet they remain on paper. Research funding is far too less, of the order of only 0.8% of GDP where as in developed countries it is around 5%. If colleges are not provided adequate budget for S & T it is a step towards obstructing the growth of enterprising culture. Shall India realise importance of research,which is the seed corn for benefits? The unemployment rate in developing countries like India is very high. At the same time many jobs in new technology are vacant. Colleges are not able to educate students in skills demanded by industry, hence many are going abroad by spending huge funds, a huge brain drain and money drain. Indian universities in the absence of innovation infrastructure have become mediocre, they are not counted in world. Cost to the nation is very heavy. it is the students, young generation who have to pay by foregoing opportunities in life. India should have to put conscious efforts to create a culture of entrepreneurship, for which universities ought to educate youths.

India Government ought to give top priority in national budget to universities in funding education for entrepreneurship development,. International Aid giving organizations like world bank, UNESCO, Asian Development Bank etc. ought now to provide much more aid to universities so as to develop new culture of entrepreneurship and innovativeness. Well known saying goes, if you want to feed a hungry man, donot give him fish, instead teach him how to catch fish.

1.6 What is Innovation? Innovation is about value addition in goods and services. But this in India is less attended. Universities are not teaching how to exploit technology in vocations & professions to make living toady comfortable. Thesis written are not related to problems of professions, they are too bookish. They give degrees to students, which does not bring them jobs. They do not make any value addition in economy. This reduces relevance & utility of research done so also financial return on investment. It is a good sign that higher education in India is increasing but innovation and acquisition of skills for commercial exploitation, which is the demand of time, is lagging.

1.7 New visions of new world needed. Indian universities & colleges do not have activities to generate new knowledge and new technology. They do not have a culture to produce new technologies. Thinking of key people in colleges is small, they have ample funds. Students & professors in Indian universities have high capabilities but they are not utilised instead wasted. It is observed that many CEOs of world famous companies like Microsoft, IBM are indians. Many indians went abroad for studies,did masters & doctorate there, served there for many years and then they rose to CEO position. India needs to think in bigger terms, global terms to acquire enterprising culture, like in foreign and then brain drain will be less.

2. Experience of Developed Countries

2.1 Stanford university gave birth to 3000 hi-tech, New Technology Based Firms [NTBF]. They employ millions of talented men and women, on high pay. These companies pay royability to University, millions of dollars each year, the same is ploughed back in research and innovation from which many more new companies are again born. Universities in other developed countries like Germany, France, etc are also following this model. Universities in developed countries actively also conduct high end research producing high tech entrepreneurs. University sells patents to companies all over the world and money earned is again put it in research.

The birth and perpetual success of Silicon valley is attributed to Technopreneurs, who draw continuous support, inspiration and technological ideas from research conducted in university. Silicon valley has progressed not because they are wealthy entrepreneurs but because they are technopreneurs. Industry today is more Technology driven. A new observation is that research based companies buy space in research Parks of the universities, so as to have quick exchange of knowledge and technology. This is to obtain virgin technologies coming out of research and innovation. Why developing countries yet do not have such programs? They have brilliant people to execute such projects. But they are exporting their talent, and developed countries are benefitted.

2.2 MIT Boston Experience MIT is an innovative & enterprising world ranking university. It has so far spinn - off thousands of entrepreneurs like in Stanford. I have personally visited this institute. It has a Entrepreneurship Department having six full professors teaching, promoting and researching entrepreneurship. It has a technology licencing office selling patents and IPR to industries. It has yet a centre donated by Dr Gururaj Deshpande. MIT every month organises a face to face meet for both innovators on one side and entrepreneurs on the other. I did attend one of the meetings. It is a very fruitful meeting. The discussions of MIT and similar discussions of other universities are broadcast on TV every day. Entrepreneurs suggest many of their view points, market needs to innovators. This dialogue leads to continuous upgradation of technology in NTBFs. MIT has its own Venture Capital Firm for giving financial support to its start-ups.When these start-ups become big and earn profit they pay royalty to MIT, which is further plouged back in research and innovation, giving boost to entrepreneurship & employment.

Chinese universities are now giving birth to 100 NTBFs every year. Australian universities are giving birth to 50 start-ups, NTBFs. India ought to adopt this model for their universities for developing entrepreneurship. They have to envision to make industry win.

2.3 Medical and Related Sciences Research Park in Torronto University, [Canada]

Unique feature of this Research Park is that it is housed in 17 big tall buildings in down town of Torronto. There are many research based companies in this park, employing more than 6000 PhD degree holders. MaRS was started by prof Evans 50 years back, in one building. It did good work and expanded itself in 17 buildings. For expansion, MaRS purchased near by properties in down town at market price and built buildings as per their own requirement. Researchers in this park give lectures to students in university, and they use research ideas and experiences in the university for furthering their work in the company. MaRS provides an innovative infrastructure for research and learning. It is providing extension services to institutions & universities in many foreign countries like in India. There are 17 Research Parks like this in seventeen universities of Canada. It is on account of such innovative structural reformations that Canada has enterprising culture in society and very small unemployment rate. India ought to emulate this model. It will undoubtedly win.

2.4 Innovative universities are epicenters for new technologies, and industry from world over come to them to buy. Research Park is a proven model in developed countries. For high tech industries, they have become a magnet. India must jump start and adopt this model forthwith. Evaluation reports by Association of University Related Research Parks done in USA clearly indicate that this is the only way to make a region innovative, and enterprising. Universities in India should not close their eyes towards such innovative infrastructure and adopt them without any delay. The expenditure on these centres is not unproductive but most productive. A beginning is made in IIT Mumbai, IIT Chennai etc but the progress is too slow

3. Characteristics of Innovative and enterprising persons

Students when they learn in young age, they do not forget entrepreneurship lifelong. They practice it throughout life. Passion is developed in them for innovation which is so critically important for entrepreneurship. Developed countries have more of innovators and so they are taking away jobs from less developed. Innovators are successful entrepreneurs and hence are indispensable

3.2 Importance of NTBF: Universities and colleges are the legitimate places where new knowledge and new technologies could best be generated and simultaneously released to young generation for their commercial exploitation. NTBFs are found to instill a culture of innovation, and play a key role in developing systems of innovation, and encourage investment needed for generation of necessary skill sets. They ought to spinn-off NTBFs so as to enable India to solve employment problem. Universities are vital contributors to R & D.. This long range vision in India is found wanting, consequently, R & D base is far too weak.World exoerience says that university research is the engine of job growth.Role of universities are changing fast in favour of research, innovation and entrepreneurship.

4.1 Infrastructure for innovation needed: Why India does not have such creative centres yet? So long as universities do not have innovation infrastructure they are bound to remain behind their counterparts in developed countries, and the culture of entrepreneurship may not be growing. The challlenge is how fast innovation infrastructure could be built.

5. Government of India Initiatives commendable: Government of India has recently started schemes like Atma Nirbhar Bharat, Start-ups, Skill India, Technology Incubation, Research Park, Make in India etc This is most welcome. They are in infant stages. Many jobs are being created. Many entrepreneurs are coming up. Innovation systems are being developed. Technology incubators in partnership with industry are being installed in universities and engineering colleges. Best of the foreign universities are invited to put up their campuses on Indian soil. Prime Minister Mr Modi has taken a drive to give fillip to innovation in universities & colleges. Industry is also responding to it and trying to compete on innovation in international market. Government has set up a national innovation board to provide funding to universities & colleges. The challenge is to implement this scheme effectively.

5.1 Revamping of universities in India is in process. *NEP -2020 is being implementated. Insufficient innovative activity in India is due to shortage of people possessing innovation skills because innovation was not taught in universities & colleges. This is cited as a key factor behind under performance, low productivity and unemployment. India has now recognised the full scope of Innovation phenomenon and Innovation board at centre and in states are set up.*

Initiatives are taken by government in various sectors to revamp the systems of working, for example in defence, agriculture, industry, construction, Roads, Railways etc.The challenge is how to implement the innovative schemes in colleges effectively?

5.2 World class universities and world class professors needed to promote entrepreneurship. India is aimimg at developing world class universities.It is because those universities which rank high are found to produce globally competent professional and political leaders, besides able human capital so badly needed to manage peoples affairs at national and international levels.Countries are developed only when they have world class universities, not other wise even if they have abundent natural resources. World experience tells us that in knowledge based economy of today, employment is driven by research, innovation and entrepreneurship, which thrives in only world class universities. if India wants to cpme in to the catagory of developed country it has no other way than to make universities world class. If India creates research based world class universities, it is more likely to become a develoed country, as dreamed in 2047.

5.3 How long Industry can be run on borrowed technology? Multifacetated units like, Innovation centre, Technology transfer centre, Venture capital, etc, which constitute infrastructure is found to lead creation of enterprising atmosphere enabling students to learn innovation skills is wanting. Installation of these centrees in universities costs but not installing is much more costly. This needs to be realised by Indian authorities. Nations become wealthy by commercialization of technology. In India this innovation teaching is far too less, hence unemployment is far more. In developed countries a wave is created in favour of entrepreneurship in the whole society, people are creative, they are tapping the market from developing countries, and the whole world. Unfortunately, the wave of entrepreneurship and innovation is not yet developed in India. People by tradition are inward looking and not outward looking.

Joblessness is a common phenomenon in India on accountof lack of innovation. A OECD study observed that *those nations which lead in innovation tend to be more enterprising to win jobs from those who lag.*

5.4 Effective licening of IPR needed to enable enterprises to succeed. Low end jobs depend on generation of high end jobs. *Strong relationship exists between effective licencing of Intellectual Property and innovative technology diffusion, entrepreneurship, generation and economic growth. So as to speedily diffuse innovative technology coming out of incubators, Research Parks, Centers of excellence effective licencing of IPR is essential. Then only much desired global level entrepreneurship with good quality jobs, of high tech, high income, will be generated, in the absense of which India is likely to be trapped in low growth, low income, low wage driven catagory economies of the world. National IPR policy holds the key to growth of innovative, creative industries, research based disruptive industries which are so essential to generate high end jobs. Low end jobs depend on generation of high end jobs. Strong IP standards can alone fuel the growth of domestic research based industries. They help to attract FDI and bolster India's prosperity. Hence effective licencing of IPR is strongly advocated for successful entrepreneurship, generation of employment and economic growth. Today licencing poicy is weak. It needs to be strengthened, so as to promote entrepreneurship & employment.*

Well known saying goes, ***low aim is a crime. Indian entrepreneurs*** must dream high, think great, one day they can hope to be on top of world.

6. Conclusion

- **Entrepreneurship development in India is at risk for want of due role of universities & colleges in entrepreneurship education.**
- **Universities in India are critical to Entrepreneurship education. Entrepreneurship development will grow by leaps and bounds only if UGC and universities give a fillip to it. If UGC & universities ignore India undoubtedly will remain a developing country. Brainy students will keep migrating to developed countries.**
- Universities & colleges constitute Key component responsible for innovation capacity of India
- What drives entrepreneurship? It is the Innovation and research in universities and colleges..
- Indian universities ought to produce NTBFs, and First Mover Entrepreneurs.
- There is no reform more urgent than reform of universities and colleges for entrepreneurship education, promotion and growth.They are supposed to produce leaders for industry [Intrapreneurs] and leaders for all other walks of life, so as to generate enterprises and in turn employment with growth.
- Should colleges not provide innovation infrastructure? If they do then entrepreneurship will grow faster.
- Funding for innovation should be done by government on priority basis. First priority should be given to create innovative universities.
- TV programs daily, like in USA will have to be started arranged for young budding entrepreneurs.
- Every university will have to arrange weekly discussions on innovation produced by it and to make it available to entrepreneurs in society.Research -Innovation-start-ups provide guarantee for future and also economic security to the nation.

Research, innovation and start-ups is today's Guru Mantra for entrepreneurship education.

References

- Naik B M, Book "Education & Leadership, Role of Indian universities & colleges in nurturing future leaders" Atlantic publication, second edition, 2018.
- National academy of sciences(2007) Rising above the gathering storm report published by National Academy of Sciences US.
- India, National Knowledge Commission (2007), Report New Delhi.
- Bowden Rob (2004) Globalization, Impact on our lives, Chicago, Rain Tree Publications.
- Rhodes H T, [2003], Role of American university, the creation of future, Cornell university press.
- University of Ontario Canada, Research & Development Park at Sarina Lambton campus and London campus, web site.
- The role of Science Parks in the promotion of innovation and transfer of technology, proceedings of Science Parks association, Annual conference 6-7 April 1989.
- Great Minds meet at MaRS centre-Taking Canadenian innovation to world-University of Research Park, "MaRS" in Torronto-Canada Research Park.
- Astudy entitled " Driving Regional Innovation and Growth"conducted by AURP and Battele in the year 2012in USA.
- Fang Zaho, Academic entrepreneurship, A case study of Australian Universities, published in International journal of entrepreneurship and Innovation, pp. 1-97IP Publishing Ltd Vol-5Number 22004.
- B M Naik Needed Innovation & Entrepreneurship in Higher Education published in the journal of Technical Education, January-March 2004, Vol. 27, No. 1, pp. 27-32
- Gap Analysis, between Indian Institutes and their counterparts abroad, published in University News, 2010.
- James Duderstadt, a university of 21 century, the university of Michigan Press.

Chapter - 14

Marketing Needed to Make Universities Globally Competitive

Abstract

The article aims at improving the quality of higher and technical education in India to world class standard. Institutions in knowledge economy are reckoned to be the drivers of development. Indian institutions are making efforts, investing money, appointing professors, students are studying hard but due to the lack of marketing strategy, their efforts do not bring the expected results. Industries do not get new knowledge, new technology from the institutes, and they remain uncompetitive in the global market. Thousands of students with degree in hand are jobless, 25% of people live below poverty line, India remains a low income economy, with Human Development Index as low as 135. Purpose of the article is to drive deep in the minds of key people, global the winds of change. The institutions are expected to be extrovert, benchmarking the world best institutions. Professors and students have high potential and it can be developed by adopting marketing strategies. The article recommends that we should adopt them without any delay and bring fruits of development to Indian people.

Keywords: Technology Research, Technology Transfer, Campus Culture, Outreach, Research Park, Incubation Centre, Commercial Exploitation, Intellectual and Technological Capital, Venture Capital, Globally Competitive.

INTRODUCTION

Many Technological Universities have five star infrastructure, brilliant faculty and scholarly students, who do possess lot of advanced scientific knowledge needed most by national and global economy. They continuously generate new knowledge through research at Ph.D,

P.G, U.G levels. Mechanism for transfer of knowledge from lab to land, in both the private and public universities in India, is however almost absent.[1] True image of universities is therefore not depicted in global market. Indian universities are found to be insensitive to market demands. Government has perfected systems for import of technology, but not perfected systems for technology transfer from universities within the country to industry.[2] Feedback loop today is incomplete. Marketing of Indian university expertise to industry, world over, is the need of the hour. In its absence feedback from Students, Alumni, and Industry to reform Education is not received, as a result what is wanted is not taught and what is taught is not wanted. Productivity of various professions and vocations on this account remain low. 25% people live in poverty; the rate of return on investment due to lack of outreach is far too low. Economic value of the investment in university, due to lack of commercial exploitation, is not fully obtained. Technological universities are expected to be industry oriented.[3] They are expected to be innovative providing ever emerging new technology to industry, to keep them globally competitive. But today their engagement with industry is far too low. So they are misdirected. Universities of today are like an irrigation project of dam built, without canal system. This has resulted in mismatch in skills provided and skills needed. This paper presents in brief, the need & importance of employing world proven strategies, including marketing like Western Schools to make Technology Universities competitive by world standards. What is the experience of western schools? If Indian universities follow the proven methods elsewhere in the world, industry in India will be greatly benefitted.

The article aims at reformation of Indian Technological Universities, Engineering colleges and polytechnics, that they do not remain outdated, teaching all that which they taught for previous generations. They should produce globally competent Graduate Leaders in Engineering, leaders in industry and leaders for various walks of life. Indian institutes should learn what to teach, how to teach and benchmark with the world best. They should give birth to new technologies and new technology based firms. They should give birth to sunrise technologies and become like "heart" to our body, continuously keep pumping brand new technology in industry, so as to make them globally competitive. They should enable Indian industry to become leader and not remain follower like in the past. Can they become a "Light House" for industry? This paper suggests and gives directions to institutions for reformation.

Scope of the Study

The study encompasses all engineering colleges, polytechnics and universities which are engaged in turning out technological manpower. It covers education, research and technology transfer to industry. The study addresses the educational planners in government, administrators' in private institutions, professors and all the key people who matter most. Most of the institutions in private sector are managed and maintained by politicians. It is observed that they do not have deeper sense of technical education. The article targets at them, to improve the governance of the institutions under their control. Academic culture in most of these institutions is far too weak. Their visions and missions need improvement. It is now not a matter of only appointing more men, or baying more equipment, or constructing more buildings. It is now a matter of adopting appropriate strategies, visions and missions. An institution with lesser resources may give better output than others with higher resource level, if it adopts proper strategies. No region, nation or society, howsoever well endowed with natural resources, can ever prosper on sustainable basis without good institutes of higher and technical education. Indian institutions can certainly turn out better educated, technologically more competent men and women if they adopt the guidelines given in this article. This will lead to better creation of better leaders for construction of roads, railways, water supply schemes and industries. It is to be realised that health of Indian economy depends on health of higher and technical education institutes. The subject of this paper is critical to well being of Indian people.

Universities, colleges are main players to create brave new India. Knowledge is power, but that knowledge which today is relevant and purposeful. Intellectual property is more important than any other property. India cannot progress leaving the institutions behind. In fact it is they who can best push India on the path of progress. They ought to be the engines of development and no bogies. They need to be modernised urgently to create leaders of world class standard, lest India is bound to get mediocre leaders to manage its professional affairs at national and international levels. Leaders matter most in creating future. They should dream big, think great and show commitment to implement dreams to create new knowledge, new theories and new technologies. In knowledge society of today they matter most.

Purpose of the Study

Purpose of the article is to transform Indian economy, industry, and its standing in the world. Purpose is to inform the key people in Higher and Technical Education about the policies and practices, visions and missions being pursued by the world class institutions elsewhere in the world. Indian institutions ought to learn from outside become extrovert and not remain introvert. The world is changing very fast, technological obsolescence rate in high, Indian industry and people must have to cope with. They cannot afford to be stationary or moving slowly in high velocity world technology environment. Indian economy ought to come out of low income and offer higher income and higher standard of living to its people. Dream of India to become a world power will be achieved only if technological institutions improve, not otherwise. If they do not improve, there is no hope to create bright future for India. Purpose is to bridge the gap between Indian institutes and foreign, bring out issues which when attended technical education will improve, and better standard of living will come to people.

Can we not do what world best institutions are doing?

The article traces Indian systems and procedures and makes an attempt to compare them with the world class, so as to improve the lot of people. What counts most now is the intellectual and technological capital of a nation, hence the paper.

Many western schools, on the other hand, are having well defined and perfected knowledge transfer systems and procedures. They are not only educating students to keep them competitive lifelong but practically generating and aggressively marketing, new technology/ new knowledge and transferring their full scientific capacities to the benefit of society in their vicinity and all over the world. The outreach of technical universities and feedback is far and wide. Thereby they are enriching themselves and augmenting new ideas for the conduct of courses besides providing budget support for future growth.[4] Technological Universities are large in number exist in US, Germany, Japan. By virtue of knowledge, they have moved from periphery to the centre of development and taken the nations to greater heights. They have become the drivers of economic and social prosperity. The visions & missions of Universities are dynamic, adaptive based on sharing experiences with people at large, and not only giving off the shelf irrelevant and outdated course prescriptions like in India.[5]

Marketing is Essential[6]

Marketing is a usual practice in profit making companies. Companies earn money by selling their goods and services. In non profit organizations like universities and colleges however, marketing is rare. They consider them to be in sellers market, like in the past. Universities from developed countries have of late, opened marketing departments and are adopting strategies to sell education and technology, in international market. They have been organizing campaigns in India, so also in many other countries, to lure students. They, on campus, have been vigorously conducting scientific research, obtaining patents & IPR and selling technology brands to the whole world. Through technology transfer, they are contributing to human civilization. Thereby they are earning money which is ploughed back to support institutional budget, and contributing to make education affordable. Technology transfer from knowledge organizations to industry to improve productivity has become a major phenomenon. It is considered as the key to industrial development and competitiveness. Technology generation, dissemination, patenting & IPR, are some of the current important issues before the nations. Universities need aggressive marketing to popularise new knowledge and new technology. Will the Indian universities depart from traditional practice and adopt new?

This paper is presented based on the experience in the world of new directions to the Indian universities especially technological so as to make them world class. They should not remain mere examination bodies, with outdated policies and practices, as they are today, producing soldiers fit to do lower end jobs at best in the army of multi nationals. Uniform standard of education all over as is often talked, will not serve any purpose, and rather is a hindrance in achieving excellence. Who wants uniformity? People want excellent education. They know creative and excellent things are never uniform. Students have to be educated in what they like. It is like, a fish should not be taught to fly, so also a bird should not be taught to swim. Freedom to learn as per liking is the need of the hour. India needs reformers, innovators, creators. India needs variety of engineers with capability of creating brand new ideas. Uniform standard should find no place in Technical Education, for it generates mediocrity.

Does India need Marketing of University knowledge and Courses? Universities must have Marketing Departments to know what the Market Needs are and accordingly design Courses and conduct needed Research.

Can India do without it? A nation needs not only soldiers to win a war, it needs Captains and Generals. Producing Graduate Engineers [Soldiers] is good, but not enough. Balanced output of M.Techs, Ph.Ds [Generals] is needed. It is they who give strength to technological advancement. Governments in the world have realised that no city, region or nation, can ever prosper fast and have sustained growth without having world class institutions essentially covering marketing of Higher & Technical Education. They are the main energy/ idea sources, brain power factories needed to bring India at par with developed world. Well educated citizenry in technology is an essential condition for faster growth and prosperity. People's development is national development. They need to be educated, on priority, to the level they are capable for, in a best possible manner. It is the well educated men and women with globalised imagination, capability and competency, who matter most for productive utilization of physical, financial and intellectual resources. Government is convinced that, to run its affairs ably at National and International levels it requires leaders, leaders in engineering, leaders in industry, and all other walks of life having professional competency nothing less than world standard.[7] Where are such professionals nurtured? Seeds are sown within the four walls of classrooms. Mediocre institutes produce mediocre leaders. They, in ultimate analysis are found to be more costly than the cost of their upgradation. So, it is advisable to spend with priority on modernization. Presence of world class institutions is reckoned to be a differentiating factor between developed and developing nations. Nations develop faster only when world class institutes are within the reach of citizens. If India does not envision building world class technological universities to generate as well as market new technologies, with priority, then India is destined to lose in world brain race. India will then trail behind. Having young population more in India is good; but, not enough. It must be trained to global needs, for which continuous assessment of market needs and sharing experiences with people at large in society is necessary.

World Experience in Technical Universities

Germany in 19th century with the help of its technical high schools is the first country to capitalize on technology. In German language they were then known as, “Technische Hoch Schule”. Now they are upgraded to the level of, “Technical Universities”. Today, there are more than 84 technical universities, such few names of them are: Berlin Technical University, Stuttgart Technical University, Karlsruhe Technical University, and Aachen Technical University. The author, under a UGC scheme, has personally visited them and studied the organization, technology transfer & management marketing style of them. The technological advancement of Germany is attributed greatly to the successful working of Technical Universities.

USA has more than 100 Technical & Research Universities for example, Massachusetts Institute of Technology, California Institute of Technology, Rochester Institute of Technology, etc. The model of technical universities is now adopted in almost all countries in the world. Japan, Canada, Korea, China has many technical universities. In the name of some universities the word technical may not be there, but essentially their character is technical.

On the campuses of these universities what we notice is that research companies are flocking round them. Technology Incubators, Research Parks, Innovation Centres, Patent & IPR bureaus are distinctly visible. Venture Capital companies have opened offices in campuses in search of new technological ideas for commercialization.[8] These universities are like magnets, which attract not only scholars; but, also Industry, Entrepreneurs, and VCF companies across the world. Taiwan has set up a science town at Hsinchu with some 13000 researchers, in two universities, 6 national laboratories and around 150 companies specializing in Electronics. Tsukuba Science city near Tokyo is another example of technical university-Science park collaboration. Another feature of Japan is that on the periphery of technical universities, there are several specialised research institutes/companies to absorb persons coming out of universities with new qualifications. Students get access in these research labs and researchers get access in teaching, which make teaching, learning, research supportive to each other. Teaching, research and extension thus become more powerful by coupling with each other. This is achieved in Japan by locating research labs on the periphery of universities. Spin off of companies from universities is a common phenomenon, so also spin off of technologies. A foundation is set in MIT with facility of venture capital fund enabling professors and students to start new ventures based on technologies they develop during the MTech/PhD research effort. Every year as many as 20 to 30 New Technology Based Firms [NTBF] are born in MIT. According to a study, around 3000 companies owe their origin to MIT. This is not unique with MIT. It is true of almost all research universities in US, Canada, Australia and China. Universities have become maternity homes for safe birth of hi-tech companies. Indian technological universities will have to follow this enterprising route.

On the basis of successful working of technical universities abroad, it is recommended that, establishing technical universities with marketing effort is the only way for India to build its Industry and Economy globally competitive. We envision to starting the Technical Universities, not only to award M.E and Ph.D degrees; but, also to become "light house" for industry. We have to get technical university model, with market orientation; otherwise, we will miss the bus or trail behind in Hi-Tech industrial development.

Universities & colleges without outreach, without efficient marketing in modern world are not effective, not productive not regenerative and are non viable in modern sense.

How to Set up Market Oriented Modern Institutes?

IITs were conceived as world class technological universities. From very beginning, world best professors in countries like Germany, UK, USA, Russia, were invited to shape them. They were mentored by foreign collaborators constantly for 20-30 years. Programs like exchange of faculty, research partnership, global visions & missions, systems & procedures, gave them international character and so they could shine in the world. Establishment of universities even in the developed Countries, today is normally done like this under close supervision, of worlds best professors, some of them from within the country and some from foreign. They are appointed as mentors, as many as 15 to 20, one for each discipline. It is the mentors who accelerate creation of world class academic culture. Universities right at birth must be groomed to be fit for tomorrow. They should not be outdated or handicapped right at birth. Currently, with a view to increase gross enrolment ratio, many new universities and colleges in public and private sector are being set up in India. Should they not adopt such innovative proven approaches? They must, otherwise they are likely to be born handicapped, and removing handicap afterwards is so difficult.

There is a thinking in some circles why collaborate with foreign universities, when IITs within the country are available? Are IITs not good enough to guide? Many new things like patenting and outreach have come up elsewhere in the world after IIT were set up. Good policies and practices for industrial development from elsewhere in the world will have to be incorporated in the newly coming technological universities. It is good to involve existing IITs, but wiser to involve worlds best professors in technical universities wherever they are and remain all along in global network. They will bring to India close interaction with world market.

Envision First Creating Imaginative Technology Leaders

Importance of Technological Academic Institutions in today's knowledge driven society is very high [9]. It is they who are furthering human civilization to greater heights. It is the academicians who provide new knowledge, new theories, new technology and competent manpower to business and industry. They are supposed to provide not only knowledgeable; but, also ethical leaders to government, to the total economy and the world. Industry, society and government in return ought to provide adequate funds to academics to make it grow. India can be richer only by the use of advanced technological knowledge. There is no other way. What kinds of graduate institutions produce and decide the future? If institutes produce mediocre irrelevant to market needs engineers, future of India will be mediocre. If they produce world class relevant leaders, future of India will be world class. Are Indian institutes aiming at producing leaders of global standard? Do we have a mechanism for building leadership in academic institutions like principals, vice chancellors? The well known saying goes, "First we shape institutions, and then they shape us for generations". Do the key people in Government attach proper value for upbringing of youths and provide adequate budget for marketing matching with market pull?

Want to be Globally Competitive?

Then India ought to have many technological universities, of world class standard. Students now demand world class education. They are ready to pay for in terms of time, effort and money. But where do you find such institutions? IITs are very few. Thousands of students to obtain quality education are forced by circumstances to go abroad by spending huge sums of money. Some of them suffer bad treatment in foreign, like in England and Australia in the year 2011. Yet, the number of students going abroad is increasing. Technological Universities and Colleges in India now will have to be competitive by nothing less than world standard. Education has become a global subject.

Foreign universities are marketing their services in India, many have come and many more are coming. They are attracting best of our talent and may soon dominate the Indian scene. Where do the Indian institutions stand in comparison? Let us humbly admit that, Indian institutes are far too behind the world. Have we made a gap analysis between Indian institutes and their counterparts abroad? Why are our universities woefully unsuited to the quality demands of globalization? Why they are far too behind their counterparts in the developed world? It is a national failure that they are not globally competitive. They remain away from market needs. Indian men and women intellectual potential is far too good. They have contributed immensely in American universities and made them forerunner. In India, similar people fail to perform, because they are under poor governance, poor systems and procedures, without market studies. Professors and institutions need to be responsive to market fluctuations.

We need to make introspection, especially in the light of world proven policies and practices and improve governance of technological universities. Do our institutions lack new visions of new world? The present method of governance which is under the "grip of government" although at one time served well; but today, it falls too short of requirement. It needs to be reformed, made flexible enough without any delay and made competitive in global context. How can the technological universities become autonomous in true sense? How can they become knowledge generators? How can they have effective and imaginative governing boards? This is a challenge before Indian academicians. How to face these challenges effectively? It essentially demands the willingness to embrace change. The world under the forces of globalization is changing fast. Only those professors and institutions who change to innovate and again innovate to market ends can educate the students on correct lines. Innovation for social and market needs is almost absent from curriculum.

Technology level of a nation is the key determinant of its economic and social wellbeing. Therefore, efficient organization and management of technology generation and its effective transfer to community in any nation more so in India, is the need of the hour. Will the present technological universities pay adequate attention to these aspects? They create the future of India. Will India remain a technology follower or become technology leader, matters for future of children and grand children.

Performance of institutions in isolation from market forces ought to be discouraged. Fresh initiatives to integrate the working of universities, colleges, industrial estates, chamber of commerce need to be introduced forthwith. Gone are the days when universities enjoyed sellers market. Then they did not need marketing. Now transnational migration of students and high mobility in search of quality has become common. Indian technological universities now have to deserve the rank on National and Global planes on their own merit. They face now competition with Domestic and International at their own door steps. Foreign universities are posing a threat to Indian Higher Education System. Indian universities will stand to gain from globalization only if they learn lessons from their counterparts, and quickly adapt to changing times. Otherwise they may trail behind.

Universities, world over, are getting less and fewer budgets from Government, but are expected to produce more and more. Expectations of students are soaring high. They aspire to make career on global plane. Universities are expected to perform far better than in the past, for which they are pressurised to increase outreach for the welfare of community and generate revenue to support their own activities. Self finance universities and colleges are allowed by law. Universities and colleges are assuming key role in global economic systems, where new technological knowledge and highly skilled people are perceived as critical inputs for economic and social development.

Following observations are pertinent in this regard. They give a hint as to what our universities should be doing now and how they can stay fit and competitive in global market.

Participation in Exhibition

A few years back, the author visited the Hannover Industrial Exhibition in Germany. There was a pavilion meant for universities and colleges. It was most crowded by visitors. Students and Professors were explaining the new researches, emerging technologies, like patents and IPR to visitors. Universities had come from all over the world to display and sell their research and innovation output to the global industrial community. Visitors came to this pavilion to know which of the new technologies are on horizon and would dominate their business operations tomorrow. Japanese companies in particular were far too ahead, remaining in touch from research stage till completion with the universities not only in Japan but also those in USA, UK, and Europe. It is this strategy which has enabled Japan to become an industrial leader. Good universities are aggressive in tapping the industrial clientele world over. Participation in exhibition presenting new knowledge, new technology, and new theories to create new society is demanded of a modern Indian technological university. If they start doing they will improve and compete ably in the world market.

What is the Use of that Research Which inspite of Potential is not Exploited Commercially?

There are many researches done in universities and which could add value in industry. But, there is no vision and mechanism to market them. Students do research for Ph.D, Masters and Under Graduation. In the absence of marketing mechanism, those remain in library on cupboards. Commercial exploitation is not done, and hence quality of research remains mediocre, less useful and irrelevant, and in turn the quality of education suffers. Full gains from research are not achieved. Many times these type of similar papers are published in National and International Journals; but, patents on them are earned by the foreigners. We need to make most of our capacities and outputs for which a well designed; well connected marketing and technology transfer department in a university is a must. Without that we are losing benefits, under utilising capacities of universities and shall continue importing technology from foreign.

Do our universities participate in industrial exhibitions? Do they have patents & IPR to sell like their counterparts abroad? Can we do this? We can, but we need to have a vision. In India, how many universities have so far obtained patents and marketed them. American universities obtain as many as 1000 patents each year, whereas Indian universities obtain less than 10, and they have no mechanism to market. Their use and application is left to chance.

Technology Transfer from University to Industrial Estate

Can an Indian university propel industrial development? So far it has not, but now time has come. A major reason for the success of the US computer industry has been the development of a host of small firms in Silicon Valley and in Boston. These firms grew directly out of research in the neighbouring universities. Professors have acted as consultants to these firms, new grads have provided the workforce, and research projects funded by government have provided ideas. The companies benefitted, so also the nation with new products, new jobs and new market strength. Chinese universities are not behind, so also Australian. Can the Indian technological universities not do this? They can certainly do. But we need a technology transfer department and marketing to learn and practice entrepreneurship.

Marketing Gives Feedback to Produce Technologies that Can be Sold

A friend of mine, 25 years back went from Pune to USA. He studied masters and PhD and then started a company in Silicon Valley. He returned to India after a gap of 25 years. We received him on Mumbai airport. He was curious to see the progress made by India. We were driving by car to Pune. He was happy to see the new express way, which is as good as in USA. When we came to Pune the author was telling him that they have entered Pune. He was not able to see any signs of his time on roads. He would not believe that this is Pune. He said how Pune can change beyond recognition. We came to Deccan Gymkhana, and he did not see the shops and restaurants of his time, but saw a new flyover. He was not ready to believe that this is Pune. Then we brought him on Laxmi road. He did not see a single bicycle, which at his time used to be crowded. Then we came to a railway station. He did not see a single horse cart. He refused to accept that this is Pune. Then we brought him to the university where he studied. Immediately, he exclaimed, now I cannot refuse. He said the whole city has changed but the university has not. The same old buildings and roads, labs & classrooms, same old procedures and systems in university he could notice.

He said in USA, the Universities are changed faster than the cities. Universities change first, and then they show the way to cities and industry to change. In India, unfortunately, it is the other way round; universities have become bogies instead of engines. They do not drive; but, follow the change. It is mainly because they are not in touch with industrial and technological market. They have no knowledge/ technology transfer and marketing departments. They have no eyes and ears to sense what the society wants and which way the world is moving. The situation can be changed if marketing departments, marketing studies and surveys are introduced. Marketing department will enable a university to be in navigator's seat having binoculars in hand for distant vision to navigate university activities in needed direction. Lack of marketing strategy is a serious deficiency in our universities.

Creativity, Discovery, Innovativeness Enable Nations to Win in Global Competition

The author was reading an article written by an American author, in the magazine" Fortune". The author of that article, from US was addressing the question, "Can India ever compete with US in software business?" To answer the question, he made an analysis of higher education in both countries and recorded that Indian system is rote learning that is to say it is mechanical, stereotype based on memorization and not creative thinking. Students are taught sunset knowledge, presuming that knowledge is finite. Institutes in India produce too less of sunrise knowledge, new theories. Students are not learning innovation, and hence they do not learn how to discover unknown. They are reflexion centres teaching that knowledge which comes to them from developed countries. It does not focus on creativity, discovery and innovation. He came to the conclusion that, Indian institutions can produce at best followers in technology; but not leaders. On the other hand, thrust of US universities is on producing leaders, discoverers, and creators who obtain patents and intellectual property. It is US which are pumping new technology most in the world market. 85% of world IPR is held by Americans. He said students of today are leaders of tomorrow. Their education is an enabler in competitiveness of the software industry.

He came to conclusions that, a nation creating follower's can never compete with a nation creating leaders, unless in future it changes its strategies and improves. Universities in India need to incorporate creativity, discovery and innovativeness in syllabi and aim to produce leaders, which require market study to increase outreach on continuous basis. Technology generation, its marketing and technology transfer department is now a must, is on critical path, if India has to make a mark in world.

What can be the new Agenda for Technological Universities?

A university by definition is a place where knowledge is generated. They should be technology generators, obtaining patents & IPR, and transferring them to industry. To make this happen, the technological universities should have to set up on Campus Research Parks, Incubation Centres, Patent & IPR Centre, Innovation Centres, Technology Transfer Centres, and Marketing Departments. This is what universities in foreign are doing. Why our technological universities cannot do?

Research Parks and Incubation Centres

It is the success of projects like Cornell's Centre for Advanced Technology that has led many universities all over the world to establish research parks and incubation centres on their campuses. In these parks, space is rented to small, developing companies-often headed by recent graduates- and the university provides facilities as well as scientific and business advice and support. The model is now adopted the world over. Research Parks are providing spring boards for students to swim ahead of all in creative activity. Incubation centres and Research Parks take universities nearer to the market.

Success in the international marketplace in the coming years will depend chiefly on the successful and swift application of new S & T to manufacturing and processes and products. And that in turn will depend on close and effective partnership between university, government and industry. Are these models worth adaption for Indian universities? Yes, so as to be globally competitive.

Is the apex bodies like UGC/ AICTE which have to show the way?

There is a story of two armies which were fighting a battle with each other. One army had a lion as its captain, but the soldiers were sheep. The second army had a sheep as its captain but the soldiers were lions. The lion captain employs bold strategies, while the sheep captain employs strategies like a coward sheep and looses battle although the soldiers are lions, because the soldiers have to follow the strategies drawn by captain.

It is the strategies drawn by apex bodies like UGC/ AICTE which can enable India to win. They have to make bold decisions like a lion captain. They have not yet drawn knowledge transfer & marketing strategies, nor conducted any studies and surveys. In India, it is only agriculture universities, which have research department with research staff with an extension department, and so productivity is increasing. Knowledge transfer from universities is solving India's food problem, although population has increased three times. Marketing will lead to the improvement in quality of education; make it relevant and purposeful, besides cost competitive. Will UGC/AICTE benchmark with world best technological universities and adopt appropriate strategies? Indian universities do not see beyond UGC and AICTE, who by themselves are behind the world. Our situation today is like the army of lions led by sheep captain.

Foreign collaborators thus far have propelled Indian industrial growth. Can Indian Universities not go nearer to the Industry and contribute?

Most of the companies have foreign collaborations. Truly India is late starter in that industry. Now, enlightened industries are coming forward to join hands with universities to jointly conduct research and innovation. Department of Science and Industrial Research Government of India have started many schemes. It is good that they are recognizing their role and responsibility. They have to play a leading role in innovation and entrepreneurship. Foreign collaborators have so far been transferring technology to industry at high cost and with time lag, besides making us too dependent on them. Industry will be flocking round the technological universities if and only if they generate technologies.

National Knowledge Commission [2006] and Yeshpal Committee Report [2009] have Prescribed Universities to be Enterprising

Both the reports have suggested reforms in governance and increasing outreach of universities. They said creation of new knowledge, discoveries and creative endeavours should be the integral components of higher & technical education. Technology innovation, patent & IPR, technology incubation, entrepreneurship, privatization, Public Private Participation [PPP] are strongly advocated. They further said some institutes are planning to be in top 20 of the world list. They certainly have the potential. But now it is not just a matter of putting more money or appointing more men on the job. It is more a matter of using current and appropriate strategies, including marketing and knowledge transfer. They should work with internal ideas but supplement them with the external ideas from industry and alumni. Winning institutes are those which are flexible, constantly changing with time. Indian universities must have to learn from case examples in foreign countries. How Japan with the help of universities has moved the nation forward? How Germany has maintained leadership by marketing technological knowledge through relay centres? How USA has created technopreneurs in Silicon Valley? All this demands universities to be not introvert but extrovert. National Knowledge Commission has recommended universities to be enterprising. How do they become enterprising? They have to resort to strategies like marketing, outreach, technology transfer through patenting, etc. US academy of sciences in its report said that, "Rising above the Gathering Storm" said

"Civilization is on the brink of new industrial order. The big winners in the increasingly fierce scramble for supremacy will not be those who simply make commodities faster and cheaper than competition. They will be those who develop talent, technologies, techniques and tools so advanced that there is no competition."

These observations are useful to our universities also. Universities can be enterprising only if they have effective knowledge transfer & Marketing Department.

Conclusions

From discussions above following conclusions emerge.

- Marketing is the first and foremost thing for universities to do.

Marketing is not only for profit making companies, but also for profit organizations. If they adopt marketing they will undoubtedly be more purposeful and qualitative. But for marketing technology level in India is low, productivity is low. Unless universities adapt to marketing, it is less likely that they will be world class, in spite of potential.

Technological universities at this juncture of time must focus on Marketing of Intellectual, technological capability in to saleable goods and services. Public service, carried out chiefly through teaching, was the motive for the creation of the earliest universities and colleges. Even today teaching remains the core of the university's public service. But now in the globalized world, trend of public service extends far beyond, to entrepreneurial activities like technology transfer, Research Park, Technology Innovation, and Patent & IPR etc., which needs marketing. Only this will lead to the improvement of quality of education.

- Technology Universities should show lead in industrial development.

Only classroom teaching is not enough, although essential. Technology clusters, innovation centres, research parks must be started in and around them. This will fire the imagination of young. Technical Education Quality Improvement Program [TEQIP] Government of India through World Bank is aiming at this. Universities must have to think out of box and enable industry to win. This will increase imagination of young generation.

- Technological universities must be responsive to world dynamics

World experience tells us that but for effective "technology push matching with market pull"; universities remain out of tune and isolated, as "Ivory Towers".

- Restructuring and repositioning of Indian technological universities with respect to society and the world market is needed.

True image of universities needs to be depicted in the market for which more effort in marketing is needed.

- Technological universities can accelerate Brain Gain. Thousands of students are going abroad every year. They have been going from Gandhi, Nehru period. This is happening mainly because our universities are highly deficient in knowledge generation & knowledge transfer to the industry and society.

If India creates research based, world class technological universities, and market new technologies, to industry the universities will be providing world class graduates to run India's professional affairs nationally and internationally. India will then tend to become a technology leader.

References

1. **Government of India, (2006).** *National Knowledge Commission Report, 2006.* Retrieved from http:// knowledgecommissionarchive.nic.in/reports/default.asp
2. **Government of India, (2009).** *Yeshpal Committee Report, 2009.* Retrieved from http://www.academics- india.com/yashpal-committee-report.pdf
3. **B.M Naik & W.S Kandlikar, (2010).** *Higher & Technical Education: Book of knowledge.* Gyan Publications.
4. **Frank H.T. Rhodes, (2001).** *The Role of American University, the Creation of the Future.* Cornell University Press.
5. *Green Paper of European Union on Innovation and Technological Transfer Enterprise,* Unit DG, EUFO, pp. 2295- 2920, Luxemburg.
6. **Fang Zaho, (2004).** "Academic Entrepreneurship: Case study of Australian universities". *International Journal of Entrepreneurship and Innovation,* pp. 91-97, IP Publishing Ltd, Vol. 5, No. 2.
7. **B.M Naik, (2015).** "Role of Universities and Colleges in Nurturing Future Leaders". *Education & Leadership,* Atlantic publishers, New Delhi, 2015.
8. **James Duderstadt, (2005).** *An University of 21st Century,* The university of Michigan Press, 2005.
9. **US Academy of Sciences Report, (2007).** *Rising Above the Gathering Storm.*

Chapter - 15

Universities ought to be innovative, creative, and enterprising to play vital role in generation of hi-tech employment in emerging skills in changing world

"Universities and colleges are crucibles to produce innovators."

Synopsis

National Education Policy [NEP-2020] has emphasised the need and importance of research, innovation, and entrepreneurship in university education. It prescribes that Indian Professors in universities and colleges need to be oriented and trained now in teaching emerging skills of innovation and skills for entrepreneurship. Professors are qualified and competent in their respective fields of specialization but now in rapidly changing world they need to change their mind set in favour of skills for research, skills for innovation & entrepreneurship. They ought to acquire theoretical knowledge and practical experience and teach the needed emerging skills ably to their students so that they become creative and innovative in 21st century for lifelong use. On line education, the world over, due to Covid-19 has become necessary. Training programs for professional growth being run in staff colleges must now be redesigned to include these emerging skills in changing world. Governing bodies of universities and colleges have now to give high priority, to giving skill training to all employees for overall capability building and organizational success. Universities are now expected to prepare youths as competent leaders, particularly in innovation and entrepreneurship. Government ought to give boost to staff training institutions, to improve their, outlook, so also make them oriented to global needs and provide necessary funds for the purpose. The paper invites attention of government to improving service conditions of professors enabling them to grow to the level they are capable of. Universities ought essentially to groom professors in innovation, patenting & entrepreneurship to world class standard, for without them universities cannot play vital role in generation of hi-tech employment in emerging skills in changing world. Innovation is the foundation of start-ups, and start-ups are necessary to bring new ideas to market. Experience of Japan, USA, UNESCO, and European Union in support of the theme of paper is given in brief. Interaction of Indian professors with their counterparts in world best universities is advocated. Innovative universities will undoubtedly give good momentum to the mission of government of Amenabar Abhiyan.

Introduction

Universities & colleges in developed countries, have now been playing new Innovative Roles namely, Creating Hi-Tech startups, generation of New Knowledge, New Technology, Patents & IPR, New Technology Based start-ups etc. This is with a view to enable people to be more competitive to make most of global opportunities. Strong higher education system is however, a pre-requisite for development, without which India despite potential cannot hope to become a 5 trillion economy and provide jobs to youths. NEP-2020 has recommended urgent steps for strategic changes in creating entrepreneurs, start-ups. Conventional wisdom, of universities as "teaching shops" in present stormy weather of globalization falls too short of the purpose, and does not suffice. Teaching without research base and without innovation is found to be ineffective, outdated, irrelevant and obsolete. From experience in the world, it is recommended that India should harvest its untapped research, innovation, patenting, and entrepreneurship potential lying idle in universities. Brilliant students and faculty are eagerly waiting to participate. Colleges and universities in India after independence in 1947 have made a laudable progress, yet they are observed to be poorly equipped and woefully unsuited to the demands of globalization. They are far too behind their counterparts in developed world. Thousands of students every year are going abroad for higher education. Universities today emphasize memorization that is "rote learning," and do not offer innovation, entrepreneurship and leadership skills needed in world market. In globalization they must play a key role in developing knowledge society. They need to be repositioned, and restructured in terms of their relationship with people, government, industry, private sector, and the world. Our true wealth resides in educated citizenry. NEP-2020 has recommended substantial increase in budget for education. This is a welcome sign. More so because people without skill education tend to become a liability and threat to the national as well as world peace. It is being realized that lack of skill-based education is closely linked with unemployment and in turn to crime. It is time for Indian universities to be innovative to produce Leaders for various professions and globally competent captains for industry. Development to take place fast and remain sustainable requires educated people and visionary leaders in various walks of life. Universities ought to produce world class leaders for which essentially, they would have to be world class by themselves, which is so essential to win in world economy. We know that today's leaders in economy, politics, industry etc were students yesterday. We must look at today's students as tomorrow's leaders, and institutes as generators of visionary and creative leaders. World class universities are always generating new ideas and producing graduates as idea men. They produce innovators who have extra energy and high passion for the purpose. They are never satisfied with existing; they create new and again new. They are never jobless instead they create jobs for others. They are wealth creators, enriching the nations. India desires to have world class universities standing high in global list. In view of the growing importance of innovation in higher education in dynamic world Government has brought out a worthy National Education Policy-2020, with focus on innovation. Systematic meaningful implementation of the NEP-2020 remains now a bounden duty and responsibility of the universities & colleges.

What does National Education Policy-2020 recommend?

Government of India rightly so has now in National Education Policy [NEP]- 2020 laid great emphasis on research, innovation, and entrepreneurship [1]. It recommends close relationship of higher education to the world of work, which includes industry, service Secor, self-employment and entrepreneurship. NEP has recommended establishment of National Research Foundation to provide increased funding for research and innovation. Government in the recent past has set up an Innovation Board and started Atal Innovation Mission. India is organizing HACKATHON competitions every year. This will undoubtedly transform the culture in favour of innovation & entrepreneurship. How can this be accelerated and made more successful is the theme this chapter. NEP recommends that companies and universities collaborate forthwith with each other to develop technologies to lead in world and not only to follow. NEP recommends strong relationship between university and industry, and synergies with each other for mutual growth and prospects. NEP has now recommended to set up a National Higher Education and Research Council [NHERC], in place of UGC and AICTE. This council along with universities will have to redesign schemes and projects for promoting innovation and entrepreneurship. Colleges will have to be autonomous. Professors will have to be geared up with these new schemes and innovative projects. There are key challenges before the universities in implementation of NEP-2020. The key factor behind unemployment is insufficient innovation and insufficient entrepreneurship. Innovation is a strong stimulant. Persons with innovation skills in India are in short supply. This is the major barrier in job generation & development. NEP-2020 aims at removal of these barriers. The interaction between industry and institute for technological research and innovation in India is far too weak and holding back teaching of emerging skills of innovation and entrepreneurship and in turn competitiveness and growth of both the industry and university. Government of India recently has done right in starting rewarding innovators and arranging innovation meets like Hackathon. India must now accelerate and take a massive drive to float its own companies on national and global plane., which universities in USA, China, Japan etc are doing. It should take advantage of cheap and yet competent graduates. Eight graduates can be employed in India against one in USA. India ought to double up in this direction. World class universities are turning out not only managers but "First Mover

Entrepreneurs," that is those who are the first to encash brand new technology like Bill Gates, Mark Zuckerburg, Elon Musk etc. There are however, as usual a few difficulties. Some students want to start Research, Innovation & Entrepreneurship enterprises based on their research in colleges. But they lack finance. Their family situations demand immediate earning. Colleges do not have provision of venture funds. Professors want to support students and students want to take their backing for starting enterprises. But professors are not allowed to take leave for one or two years for the purpose. Such difficulties need to be suitably answered. It is high time for Indian universities and colleges to dream high and think great and inspire students for entrepreneurship, remove hold ups and create a ATMA NIRBHAR BHARAT. There are many new things in NEP, complex in nature and advanced in technology. Meaningful implementation of the NEP-2020 policy requires understanding in proper perspective of various recommendations. This poses many challenges, some important are given below.

Time ahead is challenging. Challenges are:

(a) How to give a turn to mind set of university governing bodies and professors, to make them Innovative? How to generate jobs in emerging skills? Why Indian universities should now teach research skills, innovation skills and entrepreneurship skills to students? Should universities have schemes to build world class professors? Should universities have a vision & ambition to build professors to world class standard? Can a nation in competitive world come to people's expectations without world class professors? World over, it is believed that if a university or college does not have innovative, creative, and enterprising professors in modern time the university is not worth the name [2]. Research innovation & entrepreneurship is assuming a greater role around the world due to its positive correlation with economic growth and job generation. USA and many developed countries have already followed and relied upon the promotion of a university-based entrepreneurship and innovation development model and have successfully established low-, medium-, and high-technology accelerators for industry creation, start-ups and their growth and sustenance. India has been slower to understand the need and importance of innovation & entrepreneurship but is now slowly waking up to the important role that universities and incubators can play in promoting growth through entrepreneurship. NEP-2020 has prescribed innovation & entrepreneurship in university education. It is hoped that the authorities concerned will change their mindset and do its implementation in its letter and spirit.

(b) How to make education relevant to jobs is another challenge before universities & colleges? Professors need reorientation to change their mind set. Today, universities in India do not stand high in the world ranking [3]. They are far too behind. As a result, skill set of graduates coming out of universities is not compatible to the job opportunities available in national and in international market. Students are dissatisfied, what is taught is not wanted and what is wanted is not taught. There is a huge mismatch. Many Indian university graduates are unemployed. Some of the students who can afford are leaving the shores and going by paying huge fees to foreign universities for better advanced education. This is mainly because the professors in universities in India lack in training in professional cutting-edge knowledge and skills of changing world. Professors themselves are outdated in professional knowledge and skills, and so teaching is irrelevant. How can they become better knowledgeable and skilful is a moot question? New technologies like Artificial Intelligence, machine learning, digital technology, Cloud computing, people management, analytical reasoning, animation etc are emerging at a fast rate, rapid obsolescence of old technologies is frequent. Professional, behavioural and communication skills of high standard are acutely needed. Students are ambitious to learn the latest. Professors are brilliant, they want to teach latest, but for want of proper opportunities of professional growth education, research, and training they cannot do so and they fail to satisfy the students. They are sincere, and honest in teaching to the best of their abilities.

They by themselves are not satisfied with what they teach because what they teach is not compatible to the world of work. It is irrelevant due to lack of innovation content, hence it is not useful to graduates either to get a job or be self-employed [4]. According to MacKinsey report only 17 % of graduates get jobs. Import of foreign goods from east and west countries in India is rampant. Opportunities for entrepreneurship are far more but takers are too few. Companies from developed countries take away the huge chunk of market. The students due to noninnovative universities lack in capabilities, skills of entrepreneurship and knowledge. They are hungry for latest and relevant knowledge and skills. The article outlines need & Importance of upgradation and providing proper training in emerging skills to university & college professors in India to enable them to teach latest.

(c) How to design Skill based Curriculums? Besides, curriculum design and examination system in India is not proper. Without which universities and colleges remain ineffective, dysfunctional incompetent to produce competent graduates needed for job market. Students learn passively by memorization and not actively through practical's, experimentation, and innovation. Their level of achievement at graduation level is less by international standard to become leaders to do ably their jobs in India on local and international planes for various professions & vocations, including in politics. University graduates expect to get jobs soon after graduation, or be self-employed on local, national, and international planes. India is rich in natural resources but far too poor in skills of advanced knowledge and technologies. Gross Enrolment Ratio in university education is of the order of 22 % which is far too low as compared to world average of 60%. As a result, poverty is wide scale, almost 25 % of people are living below poverty line. living standard of rest of the people is too low.

(d) How to reorient Professors in Emerging skills in changing world? How to harness professors' creative energy for developing a culture of innovation & entrepreneurship? University and college professor is understood to be a king pin in university education. He is very important to Indian people and to human civilization. He is the architect and a sculptor of the future of young generation. He is expected to provide leaders with advanced knowledge & skills for various professions including politics. Although teaching profession is important in nation building it is neglected in budgeting. Budget allocation to education is too low of the order of 3% of GDP, when developed countries are providing in the range of 10 percent. So, India remained a lowly educated, and less developed country. Creation of Innovation & entrepreneurship culture both in industry and in universities in India is the need of the hour. Are Indian professors' innovation minded? Unfortunately, not. They are intelligent but their mind set need to be changed in favour of research, innovation & entrepreneurship. Can professor's creative energy not be harnessed for this cause? Certainly yes. Professors have immense potential. Today it is untapped, going waste. It is a strategic organizational failure on the part of governing bodies. India has first class creative professors. The real challenge before colleges today is how to harness professors' creative energy for developing a culture of innovation & entrepreneurship. They should have debates & discussions on again & again on this subject. You need to have world class professors and world class service conditions to sustain them to lead in innovation & entrepreneurship. There are schemes in India at national and state levels to ensure faculty training and their professional growth. They fall too short of requirement. Professors are dissatisfied with them. Service conditions are not satisfactory encourage them to devote to profession of teaching, like their fraternity in developed countries. Teachers are treated like government servants. who retire at the age of 58/60, when they are about to get a tooth of wisdom they are retired and sent out of profession, their capacities are wasted, and expertise is not available to younger generation. Service conditions do not permit them to take leave of one or two years to support start-ups of graduates. An institution is said to be as good as its professors. Service conditions of professors in India are old and outdated, and not fit to create an enterprising society. Opportunities for reaching to excellence and to become enterprising are not available. Colleges have no ambition, no scheme to build faculty to world class level. So also, the professors themselves do not have ambition, although they have potential. They have no autonomy, they are treated like any other government servants, when they are working for a noble cause of making people capable for future. Students and professors in innovation & entrepreneurship by their own imagination can do a lot, but freedom and flexibility to do that is not permitted by service conditions. Today, bright students are being taught by lowly qualified professors.

(e) Building Synergy between Industry & University holds the key to innovation & entrepreneurship is another challenge? Both the industry and universities in India are far too behind their counterparts in the world. It is mainly because the synergy between the two, which is a must for mutual growth and prosperity is missing. The well-known saying goes, "together you stand, divided you fall". The partnership between industry and institute is almost absent. They both are working hard but in isolation, in "Stand Alone "style. A bird can fly with two wings operating in harmony with each other. Industry and university are like two wings of Indian economy. They must be mutually supportive to each other. But the synchronization between industry and institutes is missing. To illustrate, Delhi- Mumbai Industrial Corridor [DMIC] project is spending thousands of crores on roads, bridges, land acquisition, electricity etc. but not spending a single rupee on research, innovation and entrepreneurship in local universities and colleges. Yet DMIC is expecting local people to actively come forward and establish industries, but they are not having any investment strategies to promote locals. Government is not maintaining compatibility in investment between industry and institutes at local level. On the other hand, government is complaining that local entrepreneurs are not forth coming to take benefit of DMIC. How will they come? Their own policies are a hindrance. Will the government take steps to synergies the industry and institute working? Industry requires latest technology to be competitive globally. Universities must be able to provide "Technology Push" matching with "Market Pull" and turn out graduates as leaders, entrepreneurs who are in short supply. Realising the need & importance of their partnership Government have passed the law namely Corporate Social Responsibility [CSR]. This is good but not enough. Compatibility between industry and institute now is not an option but compulsion. Make education compatible to industrial development: In India it is observed, on one hand many graduates are unemployed and on the other hand many posts in industry are vacant for want of suitable competent graduates with required skillset. There are many industrial estates built with huge investment in water, electricity, roads etc. But then plots in them for want of entrepreneurs are vacant. Many of the enterprises are sick and performing far below the optimum level. They are using old outdated technology and professional practices hence remain less competitive. Academicians have become sterile for want of appropriate service rules and regulations, providing them an access to influence industry. Bill Gates in his book, Business at the Speed of Thought has highlighted that in India and many developing countries because there is almost a complete lack of coordination between universities and industry, the installed capacity of most of the industries is not fully utilized. Organizations like C.I.I., chambers of commerce, and FICCI have been complaining about the irrelevance of education. They have reported to government that Indian industry is missing opportunities due to the incompatibility in government policies of higher education and industry

(f) Are colleges & Universities in deep Crisis? Yes, they are in deep crisis, due to lack of innovation. That is why thousands of students are going abroad for higher education. Conventional teaching in class rooms which is diverted from industrial needs falls too short of the purpose. Higher education institutions, without centres on campus for technological innovation, entrepreneurship development, patent and technology transfer, venture capital, hi-tech start-ups, spin-off of companies and spin-off of technologies are incomplete, irrelevant, and nonviable in modern sense. If India dreams to be a developed nation by the year 2047 the present higher education system as per NEP- 2020, needs to be strengthened urgently in respect of above stated centres. They must redesign their systems to generate new knowledge and new technologies ahead of others. The present departmental store approach, teaching knowledge generated elsewhere in the world only is unfit for the purpose. They will have to install systems in colleges as WELL SPRINGS of new knowledge. How can the institutions remain ahead of time? Institutions must establish above stated centres afresh in their campuses, essentially in partnership or in association with industry. Restructuring in the context of global winds of change is a great challenge in implementation of NEP, without which the intellectual resource will continue to be wasted and opportunities missed. Now after NEP-2020 Higher education & Research Council should have to do bench marking with the world best and make gap analysis. This is urgent because, our institutions should have to produce innovative graduates competent by global standards. They are facing a crisis in able leadership at state and national levels. Academics elsewhere in the world are playing a vital role in economic development. They generate new theories, new knowledge, and new technology for the welfare of public at large. They do not hold the wheel of development in hands but they navigate, show the way to politicians and administrators. Colleges and universities can play a vital role in economic development of India, provided they use innovative and creative talent with imagination.

(g) Can Indian universities spin-off Hi-Tech start-ups? Yes, they can provide if they follow proper visions and missions. In the present time of dynamic economy and fast changing technology the biggest factor contributing to progress and prosperity of a nation is continuous spinning off hi-tech start-ups in sun rise technologies. How to produce more entrepreneurs and how to encourage more firms to grow are the main missions, and visions of world best institutions. This is the way to generate jobs in emerging skills. India becoming increasingly important globally, it needs to adopt world proven policies and practices, for developing people's entrepreneurial and innovation capability. From experience in the world India needs to focus its attention on creating globally competent entrepreneurs and enterprises. Today young university graduates leave campuses with their minds set on becoming well paid employees. Far too few dream to become entrepreneurs, First Mover Entrepreneurs, because that is not what we are teaching them to become. Their role models in globalization ought to change to becoming Bill Gates, Mark Zuckerburg, and Narayan Murthy, Elon Musk. They need education for risk taking. Will universities adopt this vision? In Knowledge-based economy competition between nations is fierce. To win in world competition India essentially requires men and woman with innovation skills for which enterprising universities & colleges are necessary. But such people are in short supply. This is the main reason for educated unemployment. Its need is critical now than ever before. As per the declared dream to become a developed nation by the year 2047, India can fulfil its ambition only if it has innovative technically trained work force, not otherwise even if they have many bookish degrees. How India can chart its road to become a dream destination in innovation & entrepreneurship? It must consciously develop a culture of innovation & entrepreneurship. The university atmosphere, syllabi, teaching methods, laboratory working ought to be charged with a spirit of innovation & entrepreneurship. Is this a challenge for university authorities?

(h) Can existing Governance systems manage this change [5]? No, existing governance systems are old out dated. They do not fit to modern purpose. It should be borne in mind that education, innovation & entrepreneurship do not grow where governance is ineffective. Governing bodies need to understand NEP-2020 and innovation philosophy in proper perspective. Many changes in state and national levels are necessary. Principals, vice-Chancellors mind set need to be changed, they need to be exposed trained to implement such systems of innovation and entrepreneurship. Government should orient governing members to world standards. Professors essentially need to be involved in governance. Governor of the state, who is a politician should not be the chancellor of universities. Experience says, he is the bottleneck in meaningful implementation of NEP-2020. There could be many problems in adoption & implementation of innovative schemes. The efforts made by the Department of Science and Technology Govt. of India through programs like entrepreneurship and Science & Technology Entrepreneurship Park [6] are too good but they are insignificantly small for the size of the country. They suffer from inadequate finance. The strengths of Indian economy like availability of technical manpower, raw materials, and huge market with buying potential, but for innovation are underutilized, and wasted. Innovation remained neglected so far not because of shortage of resources but because of lack of global vision. Now is the time to show our wisdom, to make up the lost ground. Initiating a mass movement to stimulate innovation with adequate finance should therefore be a high priority item on national agenda. Lessons of Experience from following organizations in developed countries can show us the way. Will India derive benefit from them?

World Experience

(i) Experience of USA deserves consideration: Innovative universities like Stanford in USA are giving birth to hundreds of new technology-based start-ups every year, employing thousands of graduates, in hi-tech on high pay with first class job conditions. Many "First Mover Entrepreneurs" every year come out to make USA and human civilization richer. Stanford University has developed an in- built mechanism and established a culture of innovation and entrepreneurship, in intimate contact with Silicon Valley [7]. Mother-child like sweet relationship between university and entrepreneurs is distinctly visible. A mother feeds milk to the child, similarly the Stanford university is feeding new technology to its start-ups, and so the enterprise lifelong is in love with university. The university receives royalty from these companies every year which is ploughed back in research, to spin-off further more firms. This university is known world over as a magnet for innovators and entrepreneurs. It is reported that thousands of Stanford graduates are running active companies, all over the world. Stanford is doing research, obtaining patents, and giving state of the art knowledge and skills to students. Professors have flexible service conditions. They can take leave for one or two years to support startups of their graduates. Can our universities and colleges not do this? Why not? Now is time in ATMA NIRBHAR ABHIYAN in India to tighten belts, become enterprising and come fast in front. Landscape of higher education in the world is changing at rapid rate. Are Indian universities coping with the winds of change in world? Do Indian universities have Innovation centres, Incubation centres, Research Parks, Intellectual Property Right centres, Venture Funds for students? Foreign universities have adopted innovation strategy long back, and because of it they are preferred by students and industry and ranking high in the world list. By virtue of innovation skills possessed by men and women common man's income and living standard has gone up. Brilliant students from anywhere and everywhere in the world are aspiring to study in Stanford. Thousands of Indian students are leaving shores and migrating to such world class universities by paying huge tuition fees. A huge brain drains and money drain from India is taking place. In the absence of innovative & enterprising culture in Indian universities youthful time of students is spent unproductively. Students must study in India for four years to get B Tech degree and two years in to get MS in USA to get the same job which US students get after three years. That means our students spend six years to reach the level attained by USA students in three years. It is because innovation &

entrepreneurship skills content in our courses is in too short, and this is the major barrier in employment generation. Innovation skills possessed by students have a great influence on nation's capacity for research innovation and in turn on national prosperity. To cope with world dynamics, research, innovation, and entrepreneurship is now not an option but compulsion. Government of India in the wake of Coved=19 Pandemic has announced, "Atma Nirbhay Bharat Abhiyan "which aims at increasing domestic production and becoming self-reliant reducing dependence on foreign. This provides a lasting solution and great opportunity especially in sectors like electronics, coal, defence etc. Defence minister has announced priority for import substitution of hundreds of products. This is a most welcome step. However, the road to ATMA NIRBHAR Bharat goes essentially through innovative and enterprising universities & colleges. For without adequate research & innovation in them production is most likely to be in old, outdated technologies which is less likely to be qualitative and globally competitive. This cannot be acceptable. Therefore, setting a tone of innovation & entrepreneurship to university education is desperately needed. Government of India in NEP-2020 has rightly announced to set up a National Research Foundation to give boost to research & innovation. This is good. Young students and mid-career professionals ought to learn innovative knowledge & skills not only once but again and again lifelong, to remain competitive to cope with the rapidly changing needs in the world of work. University Related Research Parks Model from USA needed in India [8]. It is a world proven model in use in USA, Canada, Japan, China, European countries, etc. The author has personally visited many of them in these countries. Those universities which have research Parks are qualitatively far superior in education than those who do not have. A university Related Research Park [URRP] is an industrial complex adjacent to a knowledge centre like university, college, or research lab. Research based companies from anywhere in world come to park in university campus or around it. They rent space or own for self to conduct their activities. They draw the benefit by employing university students and faculty in companies besides using college infrastructure like labs and library. Executives deliver lectures in university to students and actively participate in university research. They interact swiftly with each other. This is found to benefit each company so also students and accelerate the industrial development. No industry can do all the research it needs for becoming globally competitive all alone by itself. It must depend on academics and others. It is observed that industry needs access to first class research in universities to be globally competitive, so also professors need access to industry to test findings of their research. A study entitled "Driving Regional Innovation & Growth" conducted by AURP and Battelle in the year 2012 in USA reported that university related Research Parks have accelerated industrial development and generated hi-tech, high pay employment. On park enterprises are found to be more successful, making more profit than those off park. But it is not yet popular in India. Can India ignore such a wonderful scheme? Association of University research Parks [AURP]conducts courses of 2–3-week duration for those who wish to start Research Parks. It is strongly recommended for universities and professors to attend. Recently, IIT Chennai, IIT Mumbai and a few more have started Research Parks, but universities do not.

(ii) Japan is well known for its innovative universities & colleges [9]. They are most innovation friendly in the world. The people are educated more for innovation and less for PhD degree. Innovation is the key to university education in Japan. Most of the robots, 90 % in world are designed, developed, and used, in Japan. Japanese people see robots as equal partners in production. Government of Japan has been providing adequate funds for innovation. Innovation is the nucleus of growth strategy of Japan. Japan's strengths have always been in innovation, product innovation, process innovation, organizational innovation, finance innovation etc. India Government, its universities and colleges must learn a lot from their counterparts in Japan. Japan's growth is attributed to Innovation & entrepreneurship. Indian universities will also benefit if they adopt innovation & entrepreneurship. Their potential is high but untapped. It is for the National Education & Research Council which is expected to replace UGC/AICTE to frame rules and provide opportunities for growth to faculty such that they become enterprising. Key concepts behind innovation are diversity and excellent higher education.

(iii) UNESCO observed that compatibility between higher education policy and industrial development policy is crucial for techno economic and social wellbeing of a nation [10]. It has recognised the need and importance of partnership between industry and university and so it has started a program called as University Industry Science Partnership UNISPAR. It is being implemented with its financial support in many countries, especially developing. Many international conferences have taken place. The program aims firstly to match university education with industry needs, secondly transfer research findings from university to industry, thirdly to retrain it's mid-career personnel and maintain them competent lifelong, and finally to continuously reorient university curriculum to cater to every developmental sector. This way university on continuing basis is expected to supply and maintain enough qualified and competent manpower in business, trade, and industry, and provide newer knowledge to enable economy to remain competitive. UNESCO further observed that most of the universities, especially in developing countries, are divorced from local needs. Courses offered by them and research conducted, are suffering badly from insularity to ground realities. The book lays emphasis on partnership between industry and university.

(iv) European Union [EU] has launched a scheme known as "Innovation Relay centres [IRC] [11]". Now hundreds of them are spanning in 30 EU countries. They are in a network with each other and in partnership with universities or research labs. Each IRC maintains a huge data base of relevant industrial products and processes from across the world and makes it available to all enterprises These IRCs in partnership with universities have succeeded in giving a technology push to the economy. EU has granted huge budget for the mission. Short term and long-term loans are extended to organizations to carry out innovation. It has granted insurance to enterprises against failures. Training schemes like Leonardo-do-Vinci are started to educate industry personnel to absorb new technology. Grants are given liberally for industrial research. This scheme has provided a spring board to enterprises to jump up in international market. As many as 42% of MSMEs have in-house innovation centres; and 10% of

MSMEs join the collaborative schemes. They all have close links with higher education institutes or research institutes. It is believed that the companies which are not involved are likely to go out of business. They fully realize that future prosperity of Europe depends on what they invest today in hi-tech education, research, and innovation. Patent & IPR help centres are established in all the universities. They provide a common platform for meetings for both innovators from industry and innovators in academic institutions. Innovation meets are arranged frequently, winners identified and awards given, Enterprises in partnership with institutes need to innovate constantly if they are to remain competitive. The same is true of countries which need to transform new ideas rapidly into technical and commercial successes, if they are to achieve higher growth rate. Innovation is an essential precondition for growth and for generating employment and improving competitiveness. Those nations which lead in innovation tend to lead. European Union identified that innovation and technological transfer infrastructure in competitive world matters. Educationists, policy makers, administrators, as well as research professors, would have now to expand their thinking, introduce to new possibilities and global opportunities arising out of ever emerging new technologies. They would have to think great, go beyond class rooms, and contribute to improve public systems and public life on national as well as global plane. The article will help them to set new agendas for the thought and action and contribute in fast changing world. Innovators discoverers and creators, Governing body members of colleges & universities who would like to reform higher & technical education, make it competitive globally would have to act.

Conclusion

Indian youths are desperately seeking jobs in emerging skills. Can they be generated in India? Yes, why not? For that we need to have Innovative, creative, and enterprising Universities. They alone can play a vital role to create an eco-system fit for the purpose. Making youths fit for knowledge-based society, depends upon how well systematically NEP - 2020 recommendations are implemented. Realization of declared dream of ATMANIRBHAR BHARAT ABHIYAN depends largely on innovative, imaginative, and enterprising universities. This paper has provided guidelines for their smooth implementation. Experience of USA, UNESCO, Japan, and European countries in support of theme is illustrated. To make education qualitative professor should be oriented to innovation & entrepreneurship and enabled to rise to the level he is capable of. Following recommendations deserve attention. The real challenge before colleges today is how to build overall capability of the university, and necessary leadership qualities at every level, besides harnessing professors' creative energy for developing a culture of innovation & entrepreneurship. India ought to grant adequate professional growth opportunities comparable to the international fraternity to professors. Talent with professors and students is not less. They need to be trained, reoriented, and enabled to upgrade their expertise in innovation & entrepreneurship with emerging skills in changing world, without which employment will not grow at expected rate. Research, innovation and entrepreneurship have to be at the heart of every university. India needs to have world class universities, for which world class professors is a prerequisite. A culture of patents ought to be created. Faculty training institutes need to be restructured on priority for training professors in innovation & entrepreneurship. They are critical to progress and prosperity of India. They must be reformed forthwith. Interaction of Indian professors with their counterparts in world best universities is advocated. Courses, seminars, and conferences for promoting innovation and entrepreneurship need to be organised to increase acceptance and accelerate the arrival of innovative culture in universities and colleges. Research & Innovation leads to creation of jobs in sunrise technologies. It avoids stagnation and explores the flow to newer horizons. Indian universities must constantly attempt to catch up with winds of change in world. Synergy between university and industry from ministry level to college level need to be achieved. This will happen only if Policy changes in both the ministries take place. This is very critical to the success of NEP-2020 Governing bodies must have to give priority to building culture of innovation and entrepreneurship. Service conditions of professors ought to be revised and made flexible to accommodate innovation and entrepreneurship. Governance of universities should be modernised and oriented to innovation. Traditional bureaucratic approach should be abandoned. There must be a paradigm shift from traditional memorization approach in colleges to creativity and experimentation. Examination should be based on creativity, rather than memorization. Technology transfer offices, to transfer knowledge from university to industry should be started. Corporate education centres should be opened in each university. High tech industries are observed to be flocking around the innovative universities. To attract industries to knowledge centres, infrastructure facilities should be enlarged. Industry should be encouraged to take a long-range view of the interaction with institute. It cannot do all the research it needs to be competitive, so it must join hands with universities for research and innovation. Service conditions of faculty should be revised on lines of world ranking universities. They should be allowed to take leave for one or two years to go with graduates to promote start-ups. "Innovation and entrepreneurship, the world over, are today's Guru Mantra.

References

1. Government of India, National Education Policy-2020, web site
2. Frank H T Rhodes, Role of American university The Creation of the Future- Cornell University Press USA, 2001 214
3. News item, Economic Times 20 September 2019, of Times Higher Education UK,
4. Chris Johnson, Innovation is the key, Times of India, 26.11.1997
5. Naik B M, Book "Education & Leadership, Role of Indian universities & colleges in nurturing future leaders" Atlantic publication, second edition, 2018
6. B M Naik, Needed Innovation & Entrepreneurship in higher education institutes, published in the journal of Technical Education, January- March 2004, Vol. 27 No. 1, pp. 27-32
7. Stanford University USA web site, and observations during personal visit last year, 2019.
8. National academy of sciences (2007) Rising above the gathering storm report published by National Academy of Sciences US
9. Higher Education in Japan, Web site
10. Science Policy of UNESCO, Website
11. Geen paper of European Union, on Innovation & Technology Transfer, Enterprise Unit, DG, EUFO, 2295-2920 Luxemburg. 215

Chapter - 16

India Desperately Needs Alumni Support for Making universities & colleges globally competitive

Alumni are. Found to work as catalytic agents to enhance culture of innovation and start-ups in alma mater, nurturing youths to the level they are capable of.

India is at risk, if universities & colleges do not mobilise and share their visions & missions with their alumni. No institution in the world has ever grown well to its dream without the support of alumni. Alumni are important stakeholders of university/college. They are termed as ambassadors. They are lifelong family members of university/college. They work in diverse fields and at various geographical locations in India and abroad. They are a great force by virtue of their ideas, wisdom, innovative minds, and experience. However, this valuable alumni force, in most of the Indian colleges and universities today are disconnected; lying scattered, unutilised and stands wasted. It needs to be urgently tapped. Innovative alumni entrepreneurs when they meet with innovative young enthusiastic students and faculty a catalytic action is found to take place, resulting in much desired synergistic out of box creative thinking. But to make this happen requires imagination and able leadership at various levels. It is a strategic failure on the part of institutes if they do not bring alumni in a network and do not engage them to contribute for the development of the alma mater and in turn Indian society. This has left the Indian higher education by world comparison behind. Institutes abroad use alumni force extensively, and so they are way ahead. Should we in India not harness this valuable resource available at hand, free of cost? Can we afford to ignore? India in 21st century aspires to be a knowledge hub with innovative and creative minds laying emphasis on generation of knowledge in Science &Technology. Indian institutes today do not stand high in the world list mainly because they have not yet fully harnessed the creativity of alumni for uplifting institutional performance. It is hoped that institutions after NEP-2020 will harness the strength of alumni in full.

Alumni Contribute to Make Education innovative, Quality and Cost Competitive

So much is demanded from college by students and society today that a college/ university how so ever well-endowed in terms men, money resources, and technology, it cannot do justice and provide all services demanded all alone by it. Internal faculty, staff, principal contribute well, to teaching to ensure educational quality. This is good but not enough. External support from alumni to build reputation, need truthful feedback on design and scope of courses. This is necessary to promote start-ups, entrepreneurship, technological innovation, training for students, placement, fund raising etc. Alumni having spent valuable part of life in alma mater and acquired useful knowledge coupled with practical experience within the industry in India and abroad are a great source of virgin ideas to increase effectiveness of courses to societal needs. Indian colleges must take support. They can contribute to avoid an institute from stagnating and keep it ahead of time.

Alumni Bring Latest Professional Advancement to College

The alumni and their associations may when engaged bring to college from their firsthand experience latest developments in professional fields. They may like to back the alma mater in respect of effective upbringing of younger brothers & sisters studying. Colleges must utilize the strength of alumni to upgrade and navigate the institutional advancement to excellence. It is needless, to say that the alumni have great love and affection for alma mater, like children have for parents. They lifelong remember college premises, canteen, sports, good great professors, and staff. Those who are not so good are also not forgotten. Many alumni in their professional life become great and they can contribute to make the alma mater greater. There is no substitute, no match or alternative to what the alumni can do for the alma mater. Alumni although are scattered all over, their minds are always clinging with college where they spent golden period of life and acquired Insights in to Research, Innovation & Entrepreneurship and acquired intellectual capital. They are a flowing stream of bubbling energy and breakthrough ideas, who with their greatness can best energise the college with new ideas, funds, and research activities? Who can make the alma mater relevant, imaginative and keep college focussed on societal needs? It is the alumni who are most suited to energise the college activities. What the alumni can do no one can. Should the colleges then not keep institution doors open for their contribution? Imagination of college BOG, faculty & staff to utilise imaginative contribution of enthusiastic alumni play a vital role.

Alumni Build Bridges Between Industry and Institutes

What does an ambassador do in a foreign land? He represents his country to build programs of cultural exchange; he builds bridges of human relationship between the people of two countries. He facilitates exchange of ideas, facilitates commerce and trade, and develops proper understanding between the two. Similarly, alumni who know the alma mater on one hand and the industry on the other can shape both in a competitive manner to meet each. others professional needs. Giving feedback on college teaching, research, innovation, and technology transfer to meet market needs can best be understood and done by none other than alumni. In return Technology and knowledge push from institute matching with Market Pull, can best be provided by college. Not taking readily available support from alumni in this respect to update courses is a strategic failure on the part of alma mater. It is found to result in mismatch between the demand and supply. The present mismatch in education like what is taught is not wanted and what is wanted is not taught is an outcome of lack of alumni feedback. No institution has ever grown to excellence without alumni support. All world class institutes have effective engagement with alumni and their associations.

Alumni Engagement is Effective to Bring Out Best Within Students

An alumnus having received education in alma mater is interested in bringing out best in each of his younger brother and sister studying in college. The success of a college is measured not only in terms of passing of students, but in terms of what is the character and reputation of alumni in society. Does the college enable the alumni to rise further in professional life? Should there be a lifelong bond between the college and the alumni? How the college maintains relationship with them matters? This indicates the college culture; when it is matured it is mutually beneficial to both the alumni and the college. College should also contribute and add value to make the alumni big in their professional life. The organizations for which the alumni work have needs of upgrading skills of employees, sponsored research, and innovation. The college can attempt to satisfy. They both together can function as one family lifelong to reach to excellence.

Alumni Give Market Orientation to Make Education Joyful

Students of today want to have world class education, and are ready to pay for in terms of time, effort, and money. But where it is available? Not many colleges and universities in India can give. They are going abroad by spending huge sums of money. Foreign universities are increasingly coming in India. It is urgently necessary to strengthen Indian higher education, so as as to become a developed nation in 2047. Otherwise students will keep going abroad and foreign universities will spread tentacles within the country. Now Indian national budget from 2020 has allowed foreign direct investment [FDI]. It is expected that some good universities from abroad may set up their campuses on Indian soil. This is welcome. Why are foreign universities coming? Is it not because more is expected of Indian institutes, but they are not able to give? A study by NASSCOM observed that only 30% graduates are employable. Finishing schools at extra cost and time are being run to make up the deficiencies. Coming of foreign universities is more a threat as well as an opportunity. Will they bring professors from abroad? They will bring at the most only leaders. But they will certainly bring proven systems and procedures, policies, and practices.

They will bring new visions of new world to universities. They will make use of contacts of alumni, expertise, and financial support from alumni. These are the good proven policies and practices followed by world best institutions. Can and should we not emulate them on our own without waiting for foreign universities to come? Does India need them to come and teach? This is a challenge for academics in colleges to be equal to best in world. Do we have a crisis in institutional leadership? Who contributes to bring world class professional visions and missions to colleges? It is none other than the alumni.

How to Mobilise Alumni Support?

By Involving Alumni for Crystallising Dreams

Alumni can bring technological problems of research and innovation from industry to laboratories. They are the most qualified to synergise with students and professors. They can harness alma mater strengths for solving industry problems and keep them globally competitive. Should the colleges keep institution doors open for their contribution? How? Imagination of college faculty & staff to utilise imaginative contribution of enthusiastic alumni plays a vital role in inculcating professional competency and excellence. They create a brand name of their own personality, character, and professionalism to earn positions of importance. This creates an impact on growth and prosperity of human civilization. Mid-career changes in the professional life of alumni and their mobility by the association is made easy by activating Alumni Association.

Alumni association is required to be a registered society

It is an independent body, but attached to college having separate rules of conduct and discipline. It must be financially independent of college having separate bank account, separate office bearers with chairman preferably from amongst alumni. To begin with at many colleges principal is the chairman. The association can undertake activities independently and jointly with college. The head of the institution sits as a member on the governing body of the association to maintain bond between the two. Usually college gives land/ space to association. To be able to become a world class institute alumni and college must be working in synergy, putting each other's strength together. In India awareness is now developed and a wave is set in motion to activate alumni associations, for contributing to elevate the performance of institutions. Indian institutes today do not stand in world list mainly because so far alumni force was not involved in institution development. Now alumni and colleges have woken up. Practically every college is keen on using alumni strength and alumni are keen on contributing.

By Arranging Alumni Meet

Alumni meet are joyful brain storming events. They usually include cultural activities. The culture of college is reflected from the activities they conduct, especially caring for the young students. Alumni can help college to conduct any statistical surveys in industry, for employability, technology transfer etc. Possibility of sponsored research and participation in innovation may be explored.

By bringing out e-News Letter

The newsletter could be electronic with a frequency monthly or six monthly. The newsletter should have an editor and an advisory committee. It could include the significant events taken place in recent past and events planned in future. Events like admission, gathering, examination results, and lectures delivered; MOU signed with industry may be covered. Emphasis may be given on technological research and innovation achievements. Students who have attended long or short-term courses in college ought to receive e-newsletter.

By Setting up centres of excellence like patent & IPR

Incubator, Research Park, Venture Fund etc under Public private partnership [PPP] mode, may be set up. Now a days only teaching in class rooms although essential is not enough to improve quality of education. Creativity, innovation, enlarging imagination, global perspectives is necessary. These demands setting up of centres as stated above jointly under PPP mode. Stanford University did research in its labs based on which companies like Yahoo, Google, and CISCO are born. 3000 companies owe their origin to research in MIT Boston.

These companies are tied with MIT on retainer basis lifelong. They created lot of employment and income. These examples and many more amply explain the point. Chinese universities so also Australian and Japanese are moving fast in this direction. Where are Indian institutes in this respect? A small beginning is reported to have been made in IIT Mumbai, IISc Bangalore. This is certainly good but not enough. Many institutes should must start research collaboration with industry, for which alumni entrepreneurs can be instrumental. They should have to move fast and work as start-ups.

What have the Alumni Done so Far in India and Abroad for their Alma Mater?

Alumni association of Government College of Engineering, Aurangabad have been organising meets regularly stimulating young students for entrepreneurship, creativity, and innovation. Many distinguished alumni entrepreneurs have come out of this endeavour. Alumni have generously donated for constructing a big building in college premises to devote to activities for the purpose. How prideful the alumni of this college are?

SGGS Institute of Engineering and Technology Nanded is also conducting alumni meets every year in various cities in India and in USA. It has installed the facility of a good canteen for which an alumnus has given donation of Rs 30 lakhs and preferred to remain unidentified. The college is proud of him.

IIM Ahmedabad has outsourced a part of its management curriculum teaching to alumni association. This is to mitigate the faculty crunch. President of association has taken this responsibility. Instead of reducing the courses and overburdening the faculty, it is better to outsource. In engineering and other professional colleges there is an acute shortage of faculty, besides jobs like teaching in finishing schools; courses for weaker sections of society in TEQIP scheme is increasing. Budget is provided but it remains many times, unspent. Colleges must not try to do everything by themselves, but outsource to alumni. This is a smart move, in a way like our good old Gurukul system where alumni were used extensively.

ISB Hyderabad has started an entrepreneurship development centre, initiative by alumni entrepreneurs. Alumni of IITs have contributed immensely in terms donations, technology development and raising the reputation. IIT Mumbai has set up a Technology Incubation Centre in partnership with NRI alumni Dr Kanwal Rekhi Management Education Centre. College of Engineering Pune has set up Entrepreneurship Development Centre with an estimated cost of millions. University Institute of Chemical Technology, Mumbai has modernised its infrastructure made it ultramodern with the help of alumni in the year 2011-12. What the alumni can do for Alma mater can be seen in UICT Mumbai.

Wisconsin Alumni Research Foundation [WARF] is a leading agency of USA, established and running a Research Park from 1925. It is obtaining patents, commercialising them, earning money to plough back for research in university. It employs more than one hundred people. WARF is giving scholarships to PhD students. WARF from the year 1925 has contributed billions of dollars to university. The mission of this private, nonprofit organization like WARF is to support scientific research of the university. This is achieved by patenting, licensing the technologies to companies for commercialization, and returning the licensing income to university to support further scientific endeavour. The income is utilised by university to fund research, build facility, and purchase land, equipment, and student fellowships each year. Once an invention is proposed by researcher WARF staff evaluates the discovery patentability and commercial value. Then it provides patent attorney to researcher. WARF keeps contacts with companies for sale of technologies. 20% income is given to the inventor, and 80% to university. Every year as many as 100 technology transfer agreements with companies are signed. There are branch wise specialists appointed to make a sale of patents. WARF is a separate entity but attached to university.

Many Alumni Associations in US maintain close contact with alumni, so much so that when any one is sick in the family of alumni or dies the association reaches to the bereaved family to share grief. When any one expires usually in the name of person departed, father, mother, brother, and sister they donate things like money, property, books, equipment, furniture etc to the university in his/her memory and create award of prizes, create endowments etc. The amount raised through such endowments in the universities is sizable, so much so that many research projects out of endowments are funded. There are staffs appointed by association whose job round the year is to meet bereaved families and maintain liaison with them. American universities have become world class, how? Initially they were behind German, Italian, and UK universities. They made best utilization of Alumni scattered the world over for university development. They made collective ambition and devotion for the cause of education. National Knowledge Commission reports of 2006- 7 and now NEP-2020 have strongly recommended activating and creating alumni associations in our colleges and universities. Technical Education Quality Improvement Program [TEQIP] being implemented in the country has included this as a key performance indicator.

What are the Benefits to Alumni from Alma Mater?

Main benefit is in terms of mental satisfaction, giving Guru Dakshina. Research and innovation findings are valuable benefits to alumni in their industries. They enhance them professional standing so also gives technology push to industry to make it globally competitive. Alma mater enables them to update in emerging skills.

Alumni Draw Benefit from Research and Innovation output Industries cannot do all the research they need to be globally competitive, all alone by them, even if they have their own R & D centres. They must depend on academics in public institutions for fundamental research. Colleges have bright students and learned faculty with research infrastructure like library, laboratory. Research in college is found to be cost effective and purposeful. Research subsidises cost of education, and education subsidises cost of research, increasing the rate of return from investment in institutions. Research being done today in Indian universities and colleges for PhD, degree in the absence of interaction usually is not much industry oriented. Besides, whatever is research output small or big even if usable is not fully utilized by industry? There are no channels existing, in most of the universities, to carry the research findings from lab to land.

Outreach of university is almost absent. The research remains in the form of thesis on library cupboard. The researchers based on thesis may get promotion or some such benefit. Papers may be published in Indian and foreign journals. But commercial exploitation of the findings of research through patenting, licensing technologies to industry is far too weak. Industry has a tradition to import technology from abroad, often penultimate at high cost and with time lag. Industry with penultimate technology is then less likely to make Indian industry globally competitive. Dialogue between Indian industry and Indian academia in research is urgently needed. Research in universities is expected to be fundamental, with an eye on industry application. What use is of research if not used in professions? Earlier it is used, faster is advancement of human civilization. College should circulate research findings through newsletter to its one and all alumni especially those who did post-graduation and doctorate. This is a substantial possible gain to alumni and their companies. Research output from college updates alumni and alumni provide inputs for research.

Draw Benefits from Cross Fertilization of Ideas with Academics

Modern industry is knowledge intensive and research driven. Industry and academics both cannot reach peak performance without the support of each other. This can best be facilitated through joint research and joint innovation projects. Professors in colleges are not only teachers but termed as research scientists. When professors make a mix of research with teaching, both teaching and research become effective. They are like the two ends of a bow tied by the string, neither has force without the support of other. They ought to get continuous feedback to reorient research to industry needs. and use research findings to improve industrial competitiveness. Rate of return on investment in research then increases. This creates favourable climate for investment in research and makes research more viable. Industry and institutes for mutual growth & prosperity essentially are required to be interdependent. They cannot be standalone entities. Collaboration begins with joint research activity. History tells us that technical schools in Germany initially gave technology to industry. They jointly built newer products, processes. Industry and institutes in India should not mutually be exclusive, but remain mutually supportive. Industry cannot stand high without the support of academia and vice versa. They both strengthen each other. They cannot achieve peak performance in isolation. Alumni Can acquire Business Technology today from Research in Alma Mater Success of a nation lies in its ability to commercialise new technology. This is what the world best universities today are doing, giving economic security and confidence to its people. Research in those countries is propelling the industrial and economic advancement in their countries. Obtaining synergy between industry and academia now in competitive world is not optional but compulsory, especially so for India to fulfil peoples aspirations. Disconnect between industry and academia is far too costly for any nation. In most of the Indian institutions they do not have a common platform, a meeting place like technology incubator, business incubator, innovation centre, Research Park etc which are the known proven models for the purpose. Dialogue between the two is beneficial and absence of it is harmful to both yet why this separation? If the alumni come to know research and innovation being done in college, they may get inspired to keep continuous contact and even sponsor their problems to India Desperately Needs Alumni Support for Making universities & colleges globally competitive Alumni are found to work as catalytic agents to enhance culture of innovation and start-ups in alma mater, nurturing youths to the level they are capable of.

Conclusions

Mobilising alumni support does not cost money, but it generates. Besides, it gives joy to both alumni and students. It also gives economic security to a nation. Productive contact between alumni and college energises both, makes them supportive to each other. If the colleges do not do this, India is at great loss. It may become easy to attain developed nation status by 2047. Will it then be a good thing? Colleges must mobilise alumni support in national interest and grow fast to world class level. College and Alumni Should Synergies with each other. First and foremost, thing college should do is to make a collective ambition with alumni, define a shared vision and possess a collective passion to contribute to the public cause of education. Where there is a will, there is a way. Passion internally by faculty alone, by director alone, staff and students is good but not enough. External backing and inputs of collective wisdom from alumni is essential. There is a tremendous strength, energy in collective wisdom and collective ambition. This energy exists in all colleges & alumni and their associations. We do not have to import. Institutions have simply to make doors open to alumni. The college and the alumni should dream big, think great, and come together for a nobler mission. They can and should dream to build institution of world class level. Low aim is a crime. If there was no collective ambition and vision, would the man have ever reached moon and Mars? Initially this ambition of president of USA was thought to be impossible, but it became possible only through imagination of many scientists, world over and their systematic working. Likewise, making an Indian institution world class although sounds difficult it can be made a reality with creative participation of alumni. The strength of collective ambition is far greater than the arithmetic sum of ambitions of individuals. It is the best way for rapid progress to ensure bright future for children and grandchildren. Alumni and their associations can play a crucial role in making India a developed nation. Synergy between alumni and college provides economic security to India. Creativity and imagination of both the alumni and students through joint efforts gets enlarged. The author is sure that alumni in India although late in starting will not lag. They will contribute with their full might and play their role effectively to make their Alma mater innovative and enterprising. It is hoped that in every college/ university alumni will work together to expand the horizons, go beyond teaching in class rooms, to achieve creativity, imagination and innovation so badly needed. This raises the name and fame of India in world market. Life of common man will then be enriched. Brave new India of tomorrow is being created today in Indian universities & colleges. If alumni and alma mater synergies they will be producing graduates far too superior, by international standards, to lead India's affairs ably at national and international levels.

References

1. NEP-2020 Government of India.
2. National Knowledge Commission, (2007), Report, New Delhi.
3. US Academy of Sciences (2007), Rising Above the Gathering Storm, Energising the Us Economy, Report.
4. Government of India, NP1U, PIP 2009.
5. Economic Times, (2012), Editorial Where do Indian Universities Stand in World List 22 October.
6. World Bank, Governance of Technical Education in India, edited by Blomkamp; Cheong.
7. Web site MIT Boston.
8. Web site of Wisconsin Alumni Research Foundation USA
9. Web site of Stanford University.
10. Naik, B M (2010). Higher & Technical Education- Book of Knowledge, New Delhi, Gyan Publication.
11. Naik, B M (2012). Universities & Colleges Should Do More Research, Indian Journal of Technical Education, Jan-March.
12. AICTE Guidelines for Starting New Institutions 2012.

Conclusions

Research Innovation and start-ups are today's Guru Mantra. It is high time for India, to reengineer higher & technical education and make it globally competitive.

Following global visions & missions along with strategies for leaders in higher & technical education emerge from discussions in various chapters.

Leaders in politics ought to provide far more funds to higher & technical education

Modernization program on massive scale for upgradation of higher & technical education is the crying need of the hour. Upgradation requires money. Due priority in national budget and state budget for higher & technical education today is not accorded. Today, many faculty posts in many universities are not filled up due to non-availability of budget, research activity is almost nil. Innovation infrastructure is absent. Priority must be increased. Government in 1991 thought of increasing budget to 6% of GDP but till today it is not done, it is only around 3%. Developed countries consider higher education as a driver of development. It is more because superior higher education that the developed countries got developed. Does India consider education as driver of development?

Universities & colleges ought to adopt best global practices, to become globally competitive

Adoption of best global practices derived from world ranking institutions undoubtedly will make Indian higher & Technical education globally competitive. Foreign collaborations and partnerships are the only way to succeed in transformation to higher status. It is also the cheap and best mode. Universities & colleges in India today undoubtedly lag not because they are short of resources but because they are short of usage of best global practices. Mindset of leaders in universities is old, outdated, and primitive teaching oriented and not research, innovation, and creativity oriented. The leaders are inward looking and not outward looking, to winds of change in world. Unless they adopt the best global practices, India is less likely to be globally competitive in education

Initiate Reforms in organization structure in the light of Triple Helix model. Triple Helix model of organization structure is needed to ensure success to bring organizational efficiency. We are following an old outdated organization structure. India to become a hub of education must focus its attention on triple helix structure which is far more efficient. This will also help to attain higher productivity in industry and whole economy.

Create synergy between higher education & industry. Leaders in academia and leaders in industry should form a forum to meet frequently and create synergy. The forum should be at national, state, and institutional levels. The government should give rewards and incentives to those who achieve synergy. India can become a five-tri lion economy and a hub of education, as envisaged in NEP-2020, only if synergy with industry is developed. Joblessness, a serious problem in India, will be alleviated only if institutes synergize with industry. Projects like ATMA NIRBHAR BHARAT ABHIYAN, Smart Cities, make in India, Digital India, startups, and incubation canters initiated by the government need synergy between industry and institutes to succeed. Without synergy, these projects will be less effective. Both industry and universities must change their traditional mindset of remaining in isolated cocoons in Favor of cooperation, especially for research and innovation. Leaders in politics & in Government would have to take bold steps in this regard.

Universities & colleges ought to Spinn-off start-ups. All Universities & colleges should have to adopt new vector direction to giving birth to start-ups, like in Stanford rather than merely teaching bookish. This is the way to generate jobs at high as well as at low ends. In knowledge-based economy of today, universities & colleges being knowledge organizations are meant to create new knowledge, new technology innovation and research and assume driver's role and give birth to hi-tech start-ups. Indian institutes should make a beginning to play this role effectively. Labs in college must always be innovating, doing experiments to discover new knowledge, new theory, and establish ever more efficient practice rather than merely testing old theories and technologies. Universities without innovation and entrepreneurship, so also without the mission of giving birth to Bew Technology Based Firms are incomplete, irrelevant, and dysfunctional in modern world.

Research & innovation infrastructure need to be built on priority A University/college without innovation infrastructure is not worth the name. Universities in India, should have forthwith to install innovation infrastructure, to solve the problem of unemployment. It is the bounden duty of universities & colleges to provide innovation infrastructure, which leads to quality education and enhancement in student's competency, in turn job generation. Universities have a major influence on nation's capacity for innovation. The role played by them in India is not satisfactory. Can Indian universities produce new technology Based Firms, and how many is a pertinent question to be asked to universities? Do the Indian universities have innovative character? Education charged with the spirit of innovation, entrepreneurship, and discovery, is not a luxury, it is the basic need to make education competitive, and to increase employability

Mobilise Alumni support. Colleges and universities must mobilise alumni support available almost free of cost and grow fast to world class level. College and Alumni Should Synergies with each other. First and foremost, thing college should do is to make a collective ambition with alumni, define a shared vision and possess a collective passion to contribute to the public cause of education. Passion internally by faculty alone, by director alone, staff and students is good but not enough. External backing and inputs of collective wisdom from alumni is essential. There is a tremendous strength, in collective wisdom and collective ambition. This energy exists in all colleges & alumni and their associations. We do not have to import. Institution leaders have simply to make doors open to alumni. The college and the alumni should dream big, think great, and come together for a nobler mission. They can and should dream to build institution of world class level. Low aim is a crime. Alumni can play a crucial role in making India a developed nation. Synergy between alumni and college provides economic security to India. If alumni and alma mater synergies they will be producing graduates far too superior, by international standards.

Faculty upgradation schemes in universities and colleges needed. World class universities and colleges are necessary to make India a developed country. Institutes become world class only if India has world class faculty. Schemes must be designed for faculty upgradation. Service conditions of professors must be designed on the lines in world ranking institutions. Exchange of faculty with their counterparts in developed countries are needed. Many more international seminars and conferences should be arranged.

Demand for higher education in decades ahead will grow exponentially. Advanced education will become even more pressing both for individuals and society. Education will change in profound ways; much of the change will be driven by market forces. We must develop capacity in institutions to change with time. This is a big challenge before the nation. Universities must remove constraints. We cannot afford to waste talent.

Universities ought to contribute corporate development. Universities must produce research output and innovations for product development, process development, organizational and finance development. Also, they must produce able captains to create world class global level industry. New technology is driving business to greater heights, requiring more skilled and flexible graduates. Universities and corporate presidents should work hand in hand to achieve this and establish a new forum of partnership

Special drive for advanced education. It is becoming ever more pressing both for individuals and society. Much of the change in higher education is being driven by research in technology and market forces. Institutes must take a new look at it, and on mass scale must improve quality of masters and doctoral courses.

Indian Industry can no longer do all the research; it needs to survive by itself. Engineering colleges/ polytechnics, universities in partnership with industry may have to conduct research more vigorously. Leaders in education and leaders in industry must have to walk hand in hand together for promoting advanced education..

Traditional regulations by universities and government in today's stormy weather of globalization do not suffice. Higher and Technical education must remove constraints, and introduce flexibility, and autonomy. Virtual and for-profit universities from across the world are on the horizon, and posing a serious threat. If higher and technical education is not revitalized in the light of above, opportunities will slip out of our hands and economic stagnation may result. If you charge education with the spirit of innovation, creativity, discovery then you do not have to do anything else, but if you do not do this and do everything else that is not going to matter much

Having world-class universities is a prerequisite in a knowledge-based economy to qualify for the status of a developed nation. What makes a university great? It is undoubtedly the professors, their research, and innovation output. The Government of India should urgently reengineer the service conditions of professors and make them comparable to the best universities in the world. Professors ought to be autonomous, having the freedom to think and the freedom to act, to create a worthy future for coming generations. Mediocre universities produce mediocre leaders who cannot efficiently manage the affairs of companies at local, national, and international levels. India is a poor country, a low-income economy because universities are producing mediocre graduates in the global context, who in turn become mediocre leaders in their respective chosen fields of specialization. Education should be reformed to world standards; until then, India will remain behind. Mediocre universities are far more costly than the cost involved in making universities world-class. National or State planners should allocate more funds for modernization. Roads, railways, electricity, water supply, etc., are all important, but for budget provisions, education should be of paramount importance. Policy for industrial development and policy for higher technical education should be made compatible.

Research Park, start-up centre, incubation centre, entrepreneurship centre, IPR etc. If the centres are developed then much desired high quality, high tech, high-income, high-end jobs in India will be generated, which is the need of the hour. In the absence of which India will be trapped in low tech- low income - low wage driven category of economies of the world, instead of innovative. To make India a education hub as per National Education Policy-2020 and a developed country by 2022 as declared by government, it is essential to reform higher and technical education to world class standard, without which our human work force will not have skills and knowledge to be able to face world competition. Mediocre institutes cannot make India a power in the world and a developed country, as is eagerly desired. Suggestions, like professors need to be deputed to world best institutions to study their policies and practices, visions and missions and adapt them in India, as early as possible, are made. Do we enable professors to teach emerging skills for a changing world of 21st century?

Institutions ought to work on advanced technology research projects. Research, Innovation & entrepreneurship in curriculum is seriously lacking. The institutions are inadequately funded by government and inadequately supported by self-finance students. The institutions do not explore the Possibility to conduct research & innovation and obtaining funds from industry by way of doing innovation & research for them. Industry has yet no confidence in capability of institutions to give innovative technologies to industry, and helping industry to win and hence they do not financially support the institutions.

UGC and AICTE honestly are behind time, and in fact so India is failing in creating vibrant educational ecosystem that supports cutting edge research and in turn high end jobs. Service conditions of professors are primitive. Consequently, professors are behind in the state of the art in knowledge and do not grow to world standard. Professors are not having research fund. They have become teaching professors, mostly teaching stale outdated yesterday's knowledge coming from abroad. Consequently, graduates have degrees in hand but no jobs. Educated unemployed is a major problem. They work hard, acquire knowledge, mostly irrelevant. Research, innovation and creativity are our weaknesses.

A paradigm shift in universities and colleges in respect of research and innovation is the need of the hour. Can youths make bright future without transforming universities to world class level? Are technical education institutes behind time? Honestly, they are far too behind. Lack of Research and innovative culture so far led to brain drain and money drain.

It is observed that innovative nations take away jobs from less innovative. Small countries like New Zealand, Singapore, Switzerland have world class innovative universities, and by virtue of them they could become developed. Why India a big country cannot? Money is not in short supply, global visions and missions, policies, and practices. Our rules and regulations, in respect of research and innovation are backward and outdated. For example, Professors retire at the age of sixty, they are then disconnected from students for PhD. In foreign they guide up to the time they wish. So many Nobel Laurates are in age of 70-75 years.

Insufficient research and insufficient innovation are the key factors on account of which unemployment exists. Shortage of people with research and innovation skills is a major barrier in professional development. Universities and colleges have a major influence on India's capacity for innovation. Colleges therefore should have to resort to these new strategies to induct research and innovation skills in economy. They should provide new ideas and new technology to keep industry competitive in world market.

Governance ought to improve. Governor of state should not be the chancellor of universities. In public interest, in the interest of young boys & girls government should not fear for taking hard decisions. Benchmarking with governance systems of world best institutions followed by strategic planning is the need of the hour. This is the only way to build world class Institutions.

There is no reform more urgent in India than the reform in higher and technical education. Future depends on knowledge and technological capability of men and women, rather than availability of natural resources. A realization that universities and colleges are the main drivers of development and not driven, is lacking in the minds of planners. Education is an engine of development and not a bogey. Will the Indian planners attach due importance to higher education and introduce research and innovation in universities and colleges? Future of India in knowledge society depends on how seriously reforms in NEP-2020 are implemented.